For my father
who made all of this possible

Contents

CONTENTS

CONTENTS

CONTENTS

Foreword

Professor Robert D. Mayo of Northwestern University, Illinois, was the first to voice the present need for a full-length bibliography of scholarship devoted to the eighteenth-century Gothic novel. The necessity for such a bibliographical compilation had long been felt among Gothic scholars. Dr. McNutt's publication comes at the right moment to fill this important gap in literary criticism and provide a manual for future research scholars.

As early as 1940, Montague Summers, the pioneer of Gothic studies in the twentieth century, while presenting his *Gothic Bibliography*, had thus stated: "Here I do not claim to have done more than point the direction to other scholars, who as time goes on will be led to investigate in ampler detail." He further added that "I am very well aware that full-dress bibliographies of Lewis, of Maturin, and (above all) of Mrs. Radcliffe are badly needed." Summers had accomplished many tasks of extraordinary difficulty and perplexity, and his overwhelming enthusiasm and interest in the subject opened new avenues for succeeding scholars. Dr. McNutt's large, scholarly and discriminating study now provides a more complete and wholesome bibliography of the Gothic romance than has yet been offered.

Dr. McNutt displays remarkable qualities of thorough investigation and critical acumen; by his rational arrangement of considerably vast materials he has produced a sound and balanced, well-researched study of the bibliographical aspects of the Gothic novel. It covers an astonishingly extensive field on aspects of Gothic criticism; it presents items dealing with the aesthetic and literary backgrounds and explains those viewpoints that are indispensable to the understanding of the

FOREWORD

Gothic movement at large. Particularly, the sections dealing with the psychological and social *mise-en-scène* are strikingly informative. The fact that Dr. McNutt has traced and included a large number of unpublished theses further adds to the comprehension and breadth of his study. Some of the contemporary reviews quoted, and discussed here for the first time, certainly widen the field of Gothic criticism even further.

This bibliography will save a considerable amount of time for future explorers of the Gothic realm. Dr. McNutt has completely revitalized the current state of research in Gothic scholarship. It is quite obvious that this work is going to be *the* indispensable tool for all specialists of the Gothic, or, for that matter, of Eighteenth-century studies at large.

The publisher deserves the gratitude and thanks of all Gothic scholars for the timely publication of this bibliography which has been in great demand and deserves wide circulation. It is gratifying to note that a second volume by Dr. McNutt (covering Charles Brockden Brown, Mary and Percy Shelley, John Polidori, C.R. Maturin and a number of other less known Gothic writers of the time) is in preparation. The world of scholarship will await the second volume with excited anticipation.

Devendra P. Varma

(Author of *The Gothic Flame*)
Professor of English
Dalhousie University
Nova Scotia, Canada

Maurice Lévy

(Author of *Le Roman* '*Gothique' Anglais*)
Professor of English
University of Toulouse
Toulouse, France

The British Museum
August, 1974

Preface

The work which follows is the only full-length bibliography of scholarship devoted to the eighteenth-century Gothic novel. Cast into thirteen chapters, it offers an investigation into the aesthetic, literary, psychological, social and scientific backgrounds which made conditions favorable for this "renaissance of wonder", then moves on to look at the six most eminent practitioners of the eighteenth-century Gothic novel — Horace Walpole, Clara Reeve, Charlotte Smith, Ann Radcliffe, Matthew G. Lewis and William Beckford. The more than one thousand entries range from early reviews to modern scholarship, and, in addition, the opening chapter provides bibliographical sources for further study. Selected foreign language items are to be found in the appendix.

Since this bibliography is intended for the specialist already familiar with literary research, little needs be explained as to format. Entries, whenever possible, follow the style laid down by Roy McKeen Wiles in his *Scholarly Reporting in the Humanities* (4th ed., Toronto: Univ. of Toronto Press, 1970), but since such a variety of material is included, certain liberties are taken, both in the bibliographical entries and in the annotations. At all times, my utmost concern has been for clarity; therefore, when deemed essential, consistency has been sacrificed to this end. Thus, information appears on a "need to know" basis. For example, the appellation *Necromancer* is used rather than the full title *The Necromancer; or, The Tale of the Black Forest*, but when a reviewer regards Lathom's *Midnight Bell* as a tale translated from the German, then the use of the full title, *The Midnight Bell, a German Story*, becomes necessary for clarification. Similarly, whenever brevity is desirable in an annotation, abbreviations are used. Thus, Horace Walpole becomes HW; Mrs. Radcliffe, Mrs. R or AR; William Beckford, WB, etc. Titles of the novels are abbreviated, but since this is done only in context, no confusion should result. Abbreviations of titles of journals are taken directly from the 1971 *MLA International Bibliography*, Vol. I, and are reproduced in a table which follows this preface. Thus, since no abbreviations originate in this bibliography, the researcher should encounter no confusion over titles. In the same vein, *Festschriften, op. cit., ibid.*, and other such forms are not used. A briefer form for a subsequent citation is employed only when one follows immediately upon the other. Hopefully, the reader may thus utilize this bibliography in bits and pieces, and individual sections may be isolated and copied. Cross-references are held to an absolute minimum, and a single work, the *Dictionary of National Biography*, for example, may appear several times, but always with complete publishing information.

A typical entry might be:

Frye, Northrop. *Anatomy of Criticism: Four Essays* [1957]. New York: Atheneum, 1969.

The date 1957 in square brackets indicates the original date of publication. The specific edition listed here (New York: Atheneum, 1969) represents the actual copy which the compiler has used. This is not necessarily the most recent issue nor is it to be viewed as the "recommended" one. In a few instances a note in parentheses gives publishing details of a more recent edition, usually from a reprint house, which represents a revision or updating of the bibliography for the information of the reader.

At this point, perhaps it should be noted that all items — books, articles, dissertations, introductions, editions — listed in the thirteen chapters have been examined for this study. No entry has been drawn from a previous bibliography, from

PREFACE

Dissertation Abstracts, from the *National Union Catalog*, or from any other such source and incorporated without verification or examination. Thus, any mistakes which appear are my own.

In some very few cases, editorial changes silently appear within quoted material. In early reviews, titles of novels are underlined, and in all works, when space is at a premium, ordinal numbers are changed to cardinal and names of authors and titles become abbreviated. No editorial touches are used to change, suppress, or distort meaning, and inconsistencies in capitalization (*gothic* vs. *Gothic*) and in spelling (*favor* vs. *favour*) remain as in the sources. Similarly, some modern sources, for example, use "Ancient Mariner", others *Ancient Mariner*, but since no confusion should result, no standardization has been imposed. Ellipses are used as recommended by Wiles[1], and when a sentence or sentences are dropped, as occurs frequently in transcriptions of early reviews, no ellipses or asterisks mark the omission. Instead, one sentence is terminated with quotation marks and the subsequent one opens with similar marks. Thus: "Yankee Doodle went to town." "Stuck a feather in his hat. . . ."

Traditionally, bibliographies are arranged in alphabetical order and, again, some small adjustments are necessary for the sake of clarity. When a critic has written more than one work on a specific problem, and the subsequent article or articles represent a continuation of the initial piece, then the works are arranged chronologically as if they were numbered volumes. Also, when articles by two or more critics are so interwoven as to be meaningless when seen separately — as in a point and rebuttal or question and answer — then strict alphabetical order is set aside. Hopefully, this progression should aid anyone who sets out to read the bibliography

---

[1] Roy McKeen Wiles, *Scholarly Reporting in the Humanities* (4th ed.; Toronto: Univ. of Toronto Press, 1970), pp. 9, 21.

xv

book-style. Those who use the work as a research tool should therefore consult the index to check for the inclusion of any specific critic.

Each chapter devoted to an author (VIII-XIII) begins with subcategory (a) "selected texts". Two purposes are here intended. The editions chosen are recent, twentieth century or very late nineteenth century, and if a wide selection exists (as for *Otranto*), then those with textual authority or noteworthy introductions or illustrations are recommended. The second purpose is simply to show the availability of these novels. Thus, we see that modern reprints of all of Mrs. Radcliffe's works are available, but titles by Charlotte Smith and the bulk of "Monk" Lewis's canon remains practically inaccessible. Again, the list is selective, not comprehensive. The interested researcher should consult the *National Union Catalog* for additional recent issues.

The second subcategory of the author chapters, "bibliographies", is necessary because this work is a *Gothic* bibliography. It is not a bibliography of scholarship on Walpole, Reeve, Smith, Radcliffe, Lewis and Beckford, but rather a bibliography devoted to specific aspects of these writers. Thus, we look at all of Ann Radcliffe's literary output while restricting ourselves to a small part of Horace Walpole's. Not all of Charlotte Smith's novels are "Gothic", but in order to investigate her interest in poetry and landscape, and to establish both her popular and critical success, certain non-Gothic items are covered. Thus, in this fashion, the compiler omits certain works which might be of interest to students pursuing a different approach, but the bibliographies listed in these sections may help those persons. In a similar manner, the first five chapters evince a certain selectiveness. No attempt is made at completeness, but the remaining eight chapters contain a complete itemization of all scholarship.

Perhaps, in retrospect, it might be said that the most

PREFACE

difficult problem encountered in this study was the obligation to maintain distance. Who has the answer to the tangle of *The/Apology for/Tales of/Terror/Wonder*? When was the *Monk* published? Which came first, the Lausanne or the Paris edition of *Vathek*? Surely these problems merit study but a bibliography cannot, indeed should not, attempt to be itself a work of criticism. In honesty rather than humility it must be said that as a research tool for Gothic studies this bibliography remains incomplete. Traditionally, the era of the Gothic novel is regarded as that period extending from *Otranto* (1764) to *Melmoth* (1820); therefore, a bibliography of the eighteenth-century Gothic novel covers but part of the movement. A second volume including work on Charles Brockden Brown, Mary Shelley, Percy Bysshe Shelley, John Polidori, Charles R. Maturin, and the lesser-known writers of that period, already in progress, will complete this study. Also, this present work, like others of its kind, requires periodic updating; it can be considered *complete* only up to 1971. Yet, rather than discard items appearing after 1971 which have come to his attention, the compiler presents this work with a ragged edge, sacrificing a neat termination date for utilitarian purposes. Thus, there are works from 1972, 1973, and 1974, although this same completeness is not claimed for these years.

D.J.M.

Acknowledgements

I stand indebted to many people who have aided me during the preparation of this bibliography. The Inter-Library Loan Department of the Killam Memorial Library, Dalhousie University, has been most helpful and I wish to express my sincere thanks to Patricia Grant, Susan Publicover, and Chris Lewell for their services on my behalf.

My thanks go also to those libraries that co-operated in the inter-library loan effort: Memorial, Cape Breton Regional, Eastern Counties Regional, Cumberland Regional, St. Francis Xavier, Acadia, Mount Allison, University of New Brunswick (Fredericton), University of New Brunswick (St. John), City of Montreal, Montreal Museum of Fine Arts, University of Montreal, McGill, Sir George Williams, Quebec Legislative, St. Suplice, Laval, Ottawa Public, National Library, National Science Library, Parliamentary Library, Carleton, Queen's, Toronto Public, Metro Toronto Central Library, University of Toronto, Victoria University, York, McMaster, Waterloo, University of Western Ontario, University of Windsor, University of Manitoba, University of Saskatchewan, University of Alberta, Edmonton Public, Vancouver Public, Simon Fraser, University of British Columbia, University of Victoria, Provincial Library, Victoria, Cornell, Fordham, Harvard, Rutgers, Stanford, Yale, Florida State, Kent State, Northern Illinois University, Northwestern University, University of Alabama, University of Connecticut, University of New Mexico, University of North Carolina, and the New York Metropolitan Museum of Art.

Gracious assistance has been rendered when I worked in the reading rooms of the Killam Library and the MacDonald Science Library of Dalhousie, and at King's College, St.

ACKNOWLEDGEMENTS

Mary's, Mount St. Vincent, Nova Scotia Technical, Halifax Public, Acadia, Metro Toronto Central Library, the Toronto Public (Osborne Collection), the Robarts Research Library and the Thomas Fisher Rare Book Library of the University of Toronto, Victoria University, the Royal Ontario Museum, Waterloo University, the National Library, Ottawa Public, and Carleton University. Special thanks are offered to Ruth Hafter, Librarian of St. Mary's University for placing her staff and facilities at my disposal. Bob Atkinson has aided in the inter-library effort and Doug Vaisey, Head of Reference, has given much help and advice.

The Research Development Fund grants awarded me by Dalhousie University have made possible the travel and photocopying necessary for this project. To Dean G.F.O. Langstroth, Dean K.T. Leffek, Professor D.H. Elliott, and those members of the Faculty of Graduate Studies who advanced my requests, I offer my thanks.

This work was compiled as a doctoral dissertation at Dalhousie University. Deepest thanks are owed to Dr. Devendra P. Varma who supervised this effort, and to my committee members, Dr. Allan Bevan and Dr. Ronald Hafter and to Professor Richard Raymond. Their aid and suggestions have proven invaluable.

Finally, my greatest debt is to my wife Elaine who has encouraged me through these six years of graduate school, aiding me in all possible ways, and typing more papers and drafts of papers than we care to remember.

Halifax, Nova Scotia   Dan J. McNutt

TABLE OF ABBREVIATIONS

ABC -   American Book Collector

AN&Q -   American Notes and Queries (New Haven, Conn.)

AQ -   American Quarterly

Archiv -   Archiv für das Studium der Neueren Sprachen und
             Literaturen

BB -   Bulletin of Bibliography

BC -   Book Collector

BRMMLA -   Bulletin of the Rocky Mountain Mod. Lang. Assn.

CE -   College English

CL -   Comparative Literature

DUJ -   Durham University Journal

EA -   Etudes Anglaises

EJ -   English Journal

ELH -   Journal of English Literary History

ELN -   English Language Notes (U. of Colo.)

EM -   English Miscellany

ErasmusR -   Erasmus Review: A Journal of the Humanities

ES -   English Studies

FS -   French Studies

HLQ -   Huntington Library Quarterly

HSL -   Hartford Studies in Literature

ISLL -   Illinois Studies in Language and Literature

JAAC -   Journal of Aesthetics and Art Criticism

JBS -   Journal of British Studies (Trinity Coll., Hart-
            ford, Conn.)

JEGP -   Journal of English and Germanic Philology

JWCI -   Journal of the Warburg and Courtauld Institute

KSJ -   Keats-Shelley Journal

LC -   Library Chronicle (U. of Penn.)

Library -   The Library

M&L -   Music and Letters (London)

MLN -   Modern Language Notes

MLQ -   Modern Language Quarterly

MLR -   Modern Language Review

MP -   Modern Philology

N&Q -   Notes and Queries

NCF -   Nineteenth-Century Fiction

Neophil -   Neophilologus (Groningen)

NEQ -   New England Quarterly

NLWJ -   National Library of Wales Journal

PAPS -   Proceedings of the American Philosophical Society

PBSA -   Papers of the Bibliographical Society of America

Person -   The Personalist

PLL -   Papers on Language and Literature

PMLA -   Publications of the Mod. Lang. Assn. of America

PQ -   Philological Quarterly (Iowa City)

PR -   Partisan Review

RES -   Review of English Studies

SAQ -   South Atlantic Quarterly

SB -   Studies in Bibliography: Papers of the Biblio-
            graphical Society of the University of Virginia

SFQ -   Southern Folklore Quarterly

SIR -   Studies in Romanticism (Boston U.)

SP -   Studies in Philology

SR -   Sewanee Review

SSF -   Studies in Short Fiction (Newberry Coll., S.C.)

SVEC -   Studies on Voltaire and the Eighteenth Century

TLS -   [London] Times Literary Supplement

TSL -   Tennessee Studies in Literature

TSLL -   Texas Studies in Literature and Language

UTQ -   University of Toronto Quarterly

VN -   Victorian Newsletter

VQR -   Virginia Quarterly Review

WC -   Wordsworth Circle

YR -   Yale Review

YULG -   Yale University Library Gazette

xxii

I

BIBLIOGRAPHIES AND RESEARCH GUIDES

a.

Annual Bibliographies of Scholarship

Annual Bibliography of English Language and Literature. Mod-   1/1
ern Humanities Research Association. Cambridge: Bowes
& Bowes, 1920 --.

Covers language and both British and American literature.
Arrangement is by periods, and entries include books, articles, dissertations, and new editions. Without annotations, but reviews are noted.

Philological Quarterly: A Journal Devoted to Scholarly In-   1/2
vestigation in the Classical and Modern Languages and
Literatures. Iowa City: State Univ. of Iowa Press,
1922 --.

Traditionally, literary research begins with the bibliographies in PQ and PMLA (1/3). Although there exists
overlapping, works sometimes appear in one bibliography
and not the other. Thus, both journals must be consulted.
The PQ bibliography of English literature, 1660-1800, appeared first in 1926 and features annotated entries listing articles in journals, newspapers and magazines, critical books, reviews, new editions, anthologies, etc. PQ
is interdisciplinary, not confined solely to literature.
The 1660-1800 annual bibliography appears in the July issue, and since 1950, a Romantic bibliography comes in the
April issue.
    Cumulative bibliographies, reprints of the annual bib-
liographies, are also available. (English Literature,
1660-1800: A Bibliography of Modern Studies. Compiled
for Philological Quarterly. 6 vols. Princeton: Princeton Univ. Press, 1950 --.)

1

Publications of the Modern Language Association of America. 1/3
Baltimore, 1884 --.

Unlike the PQ bibliographies (1/2), those in the PMLA
deal exclusively with literature and are not restricted
to a single period. Also, the PMLA differs in that it
does not include reviews and it has dispensed with annotation "unless a title requires elucidation". The
first annual bibliography appeared in 1922, and since
1969 a four-volume bibliography exists as a separate publication. Previously, annual bibliographies were located
in either the May or June issues. Before 1957 only articles and books written by American scholars were listed;
since that date international scholarship appears.
MLA annual bibliographies for 1921-1962 have been reprinted separately by the Kraus Reprint Corp., N.Y., in
1964, and subsequent issues by the New York Univ. Press,
1963 --.

The Year's Work in English Studies. Edited for the English 1/4
Association. London: Oxford Univ. Press, 1921 --.

An essay-type annotated bibliography of critical works
and new editions. In 1958 a separate subsection, "the
novel from 1740", was established. Previous to this, a
search through the entire chapter treating the 18th century was necessary. YWES excludes American literature.

b.

Bibliographies of Scholarship

Altick, Richard D., and Andrew Wright. Selective Biblio- 1/5
graphy for the Study of English and American Literature
[1960]. 4th ed. New York: Macmillan, 1971.

A highly selective guide to research materials. Chapter
titles include: "The Scope, Aims, and Methods of Literary Scholarship", "Bibliographical Handbooks", "The Techniques of Research", "Scholarly Style", "Guides to Libraries", "Aids for Tracing Particular Copies of Books",
"Book-Trade History", "Paleography". Contains also "A
Glossary of Useful Terms".

Bateson, F[rederick] W., ed. The Cambridge Bibliography of   1/6
English Literature. 4 vols. New York: Macmillan, 1941.

Supplement: A.D. 600-1900 [CBEL, Vol. V]. Edited by George   1/7
Watson. New York: Cambridge Univ. Press, 1957.

For years, the standard bibliography of English literature. Vol. V, Supplement, updates to 1954. Both now replaced by NCBEL (1/16).

Bell, Inglis F. and Donald Baird. The English Novel 1578-   1/8
1956. A Checklist of Twentieth-Century Criticisms. Denver: Alan Swallow, 1958.

A brief work, arranged alphabetically without an index or
table of contents. Unannotated listing of both books and
articles. Of no use for the Gothic novel.

Bond, Donald F. A Reference Guide to English Studies [1919]. 1/9
Chicago: Univ. of Chicago Press, 1962.

Covers "Treatises on Methods of Research", "Dissertations",
"Biography", "Genealogy and Heraldry", "Library Catalogues
and Guides", etc. Some entries feature brief annotations.

Cordasco, Francesco. Eighteenth Century Bibliographies.   1/10
Handlists of Critical Studies Relating to Smollett,
Richardson, Sterne, Fielding, Dibdin, 18th Century Medicine, the 18th Century Novel, Godwin, Gibbins, Young,
and Burke. To Which is added John P. Anderson's "Bibliography of Smollett". Metuchen: Scarecrow, 1970.

A gathering together of the twelve Eighteenth Century Bibliographical Pamphlets issued by Long Island Univ. Press
from 1947 to 1950.

--------. A Register of 18th Century Bibliographies and Re-   1/11
ferences. A Chronological Quarter-Century Survey Relating
to English Literature, Booksellers, Newspapers, Periodicals,
Printing and Publishing; Aesthetics, Art & Music; Economics,
History & Science [1950]. Detroit: Gale Research, 1968.

Tables, from 1926 to 1948, "bibliographies and bibliographical aids for the student of 18th century English literature and history". Sometimes has brief annotations; sometimes cites reviews.

3

Draper, John W. Eighteenth Century English Aesthetics. A   1/12
Bibliography [1931]. New York: Octagon, 1968.

Lists works on aesthetics written during the 18th century. Has five divisions: "General Works on Aesthetics", "Architecture and Gardening", "Pictorial and Plas-
tic Arts", "Literature and Drama", "Music, including Opera".
An appendix indexes "some recent comments on 18th century aesthetics".

Kennedy, Arthur G., and Donald B. Sands. A Concise Biblio-   1/13
graphy for Students of English [1940]. 4th ed. Stanford: Stanford Univ. Press, 1960.

Covers both English and American literature and includes
works on travel, description, psychological studies,
witchcraft and demonology, etc.

Tobin, James E. Eighteenth Century English Literature and   1/14
its Cultural Background: A Bibliography. New York:
Fordham Univ. Press, 1939.

Offers brief treatment of 169 writers and covers history,
economics, travel, culture, philosophy, religion, society,
education, social problems, memoirs, diaries, anecdotes,
works on literary criticism, poetry, prose, drama.

Watson, George. The Concise Cambridge Bibliography of Eng-   1/15
lish Literature 600-1950 [1958]. 2nd ed. Cambridge:
Univ. Press, 1965.

"Apart from its final section (1900-1950), it is a com-
pression by rigorous selection of the only comprehensive
work in this field, the CBEL (Cambridge, 1940 [1/6]) and
of its Supplement (Cambridge, 1957 [1/7])."

--------. The New Cambridge Bibliography of English Litera-   1/16
ture. 3 vols. Cambridge: Univ. Press, 1969 --.

A revision of the 1941 CBEL (1/6) and its 1957 supplement
(1/7). The NCBEL follows the form of the CBEL, a chronological arrangement, subdivided by topics. Now the standard bibliography and may be supplemented with the annual
bibliographies of MHRA (1/1), MLA (1/3), and PQ (1/2).

c.

Critical and Biographical Dictionaries

Allibone, S[amuel] Austin. A Critical Dictionary of English   1/17
Literature and British and American Authors Living and
Deceased.From the Earliest Accounts to the Latter Half of
the Nineteenth Century. 3 vols. Philadelphia: Lippincott, 1871. (Reprinted, Detroit: Gale Research, 1965.)

Contains over 46,000 articles arranged in alphabetical
order. Entries provide biography and feature in addition,
extracts from other books and journals.

Browning, D[avid] C. Everyman's Dictionary of Literary Biog-   1/18
raphy. English and American. London: Dent, 1958.

Entries are brief and strictly biographical. Supersedes
the Biographical Dictionary of English Literature compiled by John W. Cousin in 1908.

Kunitz, Stanley J., and Howard Haycraft. British Authors Be-   1/19
fore 1800. A Biographical Dictionary. New York: Wilson,
1952.

--------. British Authors of the Nineteenth Century. New   1/20
York: Wilson, 1936.

"Biographies are arranged alphabetically, with cross-references from variant name forms. The sketches range in
length from approximately 300 to 1500 words, roughly pro-
portionate to the importance of the subjects. Following
each sketch is a list of the principal works of the author in question, with dates of original publication as
generally accepted. Selected source material about each
author is also listed as a suggestion for further study."

Moulton, Charles Wells, ed. The Library of Literary Criti-   1/21
cism of English and American Authors. 8 vols. Buffalo:
Moulton, 1901-1905. (Reprinted, New York: P. Smith, 1935.)

A valuable guide to 18th and 19th-century criticism. Author entries include biography and give extracts from
biographical and critical books and articles. For ex-

ample, 74 extracts of criticism are provided for Walpole, with opinions taken from the great and the obscure, including Byron, Wordsworth, Scott, Gray, Macaulay, Beers, Bulwer-Lytton, Eastlake, and Agnes Repplier.

Moulton's Library of Literary Criticism of English and American Authors Through the Beginning of the Twentieth Century. Abridged, revised, and with additions by Martin Tucker. 4 vols. New York: Ungar, 1966.   1/22

Adds some new materials, drops some old. Includes eleven additional writers and inserts lists of current standard editions for each author.

Myers, Robin. A Dictionary of Literature in the English Language: From Chaucer to 1940. Compiled for the National Book League. Oxford: Pergamon, 1970.   1/23

"Each entry consists of full name and title, dates, biographical note and a list of bibliographical sources used in compilation or suggested for further study, arranged alphabetically under the author of the bibliography. Then follows a list of the first editions of separately published literary works in chronological order."

Patrick, David, and J. Liddell. Chamber's Cyclopaedia of English Literature. A History Critical and Biographical of Authors in the English Tongue from the Earliest Times till the Present Day, with Specimens of their Writings. 3 vols. London: Chamber's, [1922-1938].   1/24

Embodies articles on authors, subjects, forms, etc. Author entries contain, when possible, biography, critical comment, bibliography, specimens of writing, and a portrait.

Stephen, Leslie, and Sidney Lee, eds. Dictionary of National Biography. 63 vols. London: Smith, Elder, 1885 --.   1/25

First published in 63 volumes; reissued in 1908-1909 in 22 volumes, the last being a supplement. At present, seven supplements update to 1960. Indexes to later supplements go back to the initial addition thus eliminating the need for a volume by volume search. The DNB, including its supplements, contains signed articles covering practically all Britons of note deceased at the time of writing.

The Concise Dictionary of National Biography. Edited by   1/26
Sidney Lee. London: Oxford Univ. Press, 1903.

Includes all persons in the DNB and supplements, but entries are greatly reduced to "one-fourteenth of the number of words that appear in the text of the original
memoir".

Corrections and Additions to the Dictionary of National Bio-   1/27
graphy. Cumulated from the Bulletin of the Institute of
Historical Research, University of London. Boston: Hall,
1966.

Watt, Robert. Bibliotheca Britannica, or a General Index to   1/28
British and Foreign Literature [1824]. Reprinted as
Burt Franklyn Bibliography and Reference Series, No. 75.
4 vols. New York: Burt Franklyn, [1965].

The first two volumes contain "upwards of 40,000 authors",
with entries in alphabetic order. Sometimes contains
biography, list of works, notes on various editions,
sizes, and prices, but frequently lists only works. Predates DNB (1/25); incomplete and unreliable.

d.

Indexes of Early Reviews

Nangle, Benjamin Christie. The Monthly Review: First Series, 1/29
1749-1789. Oxford: Clarendon, 1934.

--------. Second Series, 1790-1815. Indexes of Contributors
and Articles. Oxford: Clarendon, 1955.

These two volumes index the MR and are indispensable for
those interested in early reviews.

Ward, William S. Literary Reviews in British Periodicals   1/30
1798-1820: A Bibliography. 2 vols. New York: Garland,
1972.

Lists 16,000 reviews and 1,000 non-review articles. Many
18th/early 19th-century Gothic novelists are treated, including Barrett, Beckford, Brown, Horsley Curties, Dacre,

7

Godwin, Helme, Ireland, Kelly, Lathom, the Lee sisters,
Lewis, Maturin, Opie, Parsons, Polidori, Ann Radcliffe,
Mary Ann Radcliffe, Roche, Mary Shelley, P.B. Shelley,
Sleath, Smith, Walpole.

e.

Indexes of Theses

Habicht, Werner, ed. English and American Studies in Ger-   1/31
man: Summaries of Theses and Monographs. A Supplement
to Anglia. Tübingen: Max Niemeyer, 1969 --.

This work "is intended to cover doctoral dissertations,
Habilitationsschiriften, and independent monographs".
Each author has prepared a 2-3 page summary of his work,
and the editor gives details of how to procure copies of
these books.

McNamee, Lawrence F. Dissertations in English and American   1/32
Literature. Theses Accepted by American, British and
German Universities, 1865-1964. New York: Bowker, 1968.

--------. Supplement I, 1964-1968. New York: Bowker, 1969.

The initial volume lists 14,521 dissertations for the
first 95 years. The supplement covers five years, cata--
logues 4,382 dissertations, and is expanded to include
Canadian and Australian universities. There is a section,
"Monk Lewis and the Gothic Novel", devoted to theses on
the Gothic novel, but a check should also be made of
other divisions, including "Minor Writers of the 19th Century", "Motifs in the 18th Century", "Minor Writers of
the 18th Century", etc.

f.

Indexes of Fiction

Baker, Ernest A. A Guide to the Best Fiction in English.   1/33
London: Routledge & Kegan Paul, 1913.

An extensive rewriting of his 1903, A Descriptive Guide
to the Best Fiction, British and American. Extends from
the Anglo-Saxon version of Apollonius' tale to the date of
writing (1913). Includes English, American, Belgian,
Dutch, Flemish, Celtic, French, German, Ancient and Modern Greek, Hungarian, Italian, Latin, Slavonic, Scandin-
avian, Spanish, Yiddish, Indian, Arabic, Persian, Chinese,
and Japanese fiction. Lists title, author, gives plot
summary and critical comments. Includes many Gothic
novels.

--------, and James Packman. A Guide to the Best Fiction   1/34
English and American Including Translations From Foreign
Languages [1932]. New and enlarged edition. London:
Routledge & Kegan Paul, 1967.

The third edition of his Guide, expanded and in a different format. The national divisions have been abandoned
in favor of an alphabetical order. The index, however,
provides groupings by nationality.

Bleiler, Everett F. The Checklist of Fantastic Literature: 1/35
A Bibliography of Fantasy, Weird, and Science Fiction
Books Published in the English Language. Preface by Mel-
vin Korshak. Chicago: Shasta, 1948.

Lists "fantastic elements in fiction from the romances of
chivalry and the Gothic novel to its present day development". Korshak calls Summers' Gothic Bibliography (1/39)
"useless, by itself, for the purposes of the fantasy-spe-
cialist" since it includes "all known Gothic novels, many
without the elements of fear and terror". This bibliography catalogues first by author, then by title, and features a listing of critical works. The familiar names of
the late 18th / early 19th-century Gothic appear, and included also are "fantastic" pieces of such writers as
Dickens, Conrad and Shaw. The count often seems incomplete; for example, only three of Radcliffe's novels are
listed: Sicilian Romance, Mysteries of Udolpho, and

9

Gaston de Blondeville. The lists are not segregated, so, other than by guessing from the titles, there is no way to separate Gothic from other varieties of fantasy.

Block, Andrew. The English Novel 1740-1850. A Catalogue In- 1/36
cluding Prose Romances, Short Stories, and Translations
of Foreign Fiction [1939]. London: Dawson's, 1961.

A dictionary-like listing of novels printed between 1740
and 1850. Mentions publisher, date, place, illustrations.
Compiled from secondary sources.

Shipton, Clifford K., and James E. Mooney. National Index of 1/37
American Imprints Through 1800. The Short-Title Evans.
American Antiquarian Society. 2 vols. [Barre]: Barre
Publishers, 1969.

"A short-title list of both Evans and additional items,
in one alphabetical order, incorporating all of the tens
of thousands of bibliographical corrections of the Evans
entries turned up by the staff of the Society in the
course of fifty years of work."
     The American Antiquarian Society offers, in microprint,
"the complete text of every existent book, pamphlet, and
broadside printed in the United States in the years 1639
through 1800". Among the 42,000 titles (Early American
Imprints. First Series [Evans] 1639-1800. Readex Microprint Corp., N.Y.) are included American editions of the
works of Lewis, Reeve, Smith, Radcliffe.

Siemon, Fred. Ghost Story Index: An Author-Title Index to 1/38
More than 2,200 Stories of Ghosts, Horrors, and the Ma-
cabre Appearing in 190 Books and Anthologies. San José:
Library Research Associates, 1967.

A cross-reference system enables the reader-researcher to
locate specific short stories by citing the modern anthologies in which they appear. Includes 18th, 19th,
and 20th-century tales.

Summers, Montague. A Gothic Bibliography [1941]. New York: 1/39
Russell & Russell, 1964.

Consists of a listing of original works extending from
1728 to 1916, with the bulk falling in the first part of
the 19th century. Treatment seems uneven and erratic.
C.B. Brown is the only American of note to receive at-

tention; there exists nothing on Poe or Hawthorne. Summers does not single out Gothic, or near-Gothic, from the
works of a non-Gothic writer; i.e., Bleak House and Barnaby Rudge are absent. Also, there is nothing on Le Fanu,
Collins, Sir Walter Scott, or the 20th-century men, Lovecraft, Blackwood, and M.R. James. Treatment varies from
a simple list, either full or selected (two items for Walpole), to a coverage with comments on publishing history,
spurious works, stage adaptations, translations, abridgements, unauthorized redactions, etc.
    An essential book, yet one to be used with caution.
See Bleiler (1/35), Tarr (6/30), Henderson (6/42).

g.

Guides to Special Collections

Ash, Lee, and Denis Lorenz. Subject Collections. A Guide to   1/40
Special Book Collections and Subject Emphases as Reported
by University, College, Public, and Special Libraries in
the United States and Canada [1958]. 3rd ed. New York:
Bowker, 1967.

An unindexed listing, in alphabetical order, of "an esti-
mated 35 to 40,000 references to special collections or
libraries' emphases on special subject interests". Under
"Fiction, Gothic", lists two special collections, the
UCLA Gothic Novel Collection of 300 volumes, and Virginia's
Sadleir-Black Collection of 2,000 volumes. Other collec-
tions of interest include "Crime and Criminals", "Alchemy",
"Occult and Sciences", "Demonology", "Psychical Research",
"Spiritualism", and "Superstition".

Becker, Sidney. English Fiction to 1820 in the University of   1/41
Pennsylvania Library. Based on the Collections of God-
frey F. Singer and John C. Mendenhall. Philadelphia:
Univ. of Pennsylvania Library, 1954.

A checklist designed by U. Penn., "in an effort to make
its holdings more widely known and to provide those working in special fields with a comprehensive view of the materials available at the University". Indicates holdings
by Dacre, Helme, the Lees, Meeke, Opie, Parsons, Porter,
Roche, and Smith.

11

McBurney, William H. **English Prose Fiction 1700-1800 in the**   1/42
University of Illinois Library. Urbana: Univ. of Illinois Press, 1965.

Illinois has extensive holdings in the 18th-century novel,
primarily Secord's work on Defoe, but also many Gothic
works. McBurney lists books by Beckford, Helme, the Lees,
Lewis, Parsons, Prévost, Radcliffe, Reeve, Roche, and Smith.

h.

Miscellaneous Works

Abstracts of English Studies. An Official Publication of the   1/43
National Council of Teachers of English. Boulder, Colo-
rado, 1958 --.

Issued ten times a year with an index in each issue and
an annual cumulative index. Screens "approximately 1,500
journals and numerous monographs", and provides brief summaries of articles without critical comment. Entries
arranged in four major sections: "General", "English",
"American", and "World Literature in English and Related
Languages".

Annals of English Literature 1475-1950. The Principal Publi-   1/44
cation of Each Year Together with an Alphabetical Index
of Authors with Their Works [1935]. 2nd ed. Oxford:
Clarendon, 1961.

Intended "to give the student, at a glance, the main literary output of any year or series of years; to show
what books people were likely to be reading at any time,
and with what rivals a candidate for literary fame had to
reckon". Under the year, lists authors alphabetically,
gives date of birth, name of book, genre. Inside column
lists national and international events, translations,
births, deaths, etc.

Halkett, Samuel and John Laing. Dictionary of Anonymous and   1/45
Pseudonymous English Literature. Edited by James Ken-
nedy, W.A. Smith, and A.F. Johnson. 7 vols. London:
Oliver & Boyd, 1926-1934.

This work appeared first in four volumes in 1822-1888,
was revised, enlarged and reissued in six volumes, with
the last containing a supplement. In 1934 a final volume appeared containing an index and a second supplement.

Dictionary of Anonymous and Pseudonymous English Literature.   1/46
Edited by Dennis E. Rhodes and Anna E.C. Simoni. 2 vols.
London: Oliver & Boyd, 1956-1962.

A continuation of the above, (1/45), Vol. VIII, contains
"additions from 1900 as far as 1949", and Vol. IX covers
the same period and pre-1900 as well.

Harvey, Paul. The Oxford Companion to English Literature   1/47
[1942]. 4th ed. Revised by Dorothy Eagle. Oxford:
Clarendon, 1967.

A dictionary/handbook/reference guide, with entries on
authors, titles, fictional characters, terms, etc. The
best of its type.

II

AESTHETIC BACKGROUND

a.

Aesthetic Theories

Addison, Agnes. Romanticism and the Gothic Revival [1938].   2/1
New York: Gordian, 1967.

Deals primarily with the revival of Gothic architecture
after 1820 and assesses the contributions of Pugin, Ruskin, Scott, and Eastlake. Points out that throughout the
18th century, classical and romantic were not necessarily
antithetical, and notes the views of Pope, Addison, Gray,
Walpole, and others. The interest in Spenser, Shakespeare,
Ossian, and Chatterton is discussed, and although the
Gothic novelists receive mention, the author seems here
to tread upon unfamiliar grounds. Includes a very extensive annotated bibliography.

Allen, B[everly] Sprague. Tides in English Taste (1619-1800): 2/2
A Background for the Study of Literature [1937]. 2 vols.
New York: Pageant, 1958.

Conceived as a history of art to enlighten the history of
literature, this work covers the sublime, picturesque,
Italian painters, sham ruins, Shaftesbury, Kames, Dennis,
the garden controversy, Pope's garden, Defoe's Tour, Reynolds' Discourses, Hogarth's line, and the development of
wallpaper. Maintains that Walpole did not revive Gothic
architecture; it survived with "no real interruption".
Contends that Milton's Paradise was not a unique garden.

Carrit, E[dgar] F. A Calendar of British Taste from 1600 to   2/3
1800, Being a Museum of Specimens and Landmarks Chronologically Arranged. London: Routledge & Kegan Paul,
[1949].

A collection of short extracts on such topics as architecture, nature, gardening, painting, poetry, music, manners
and tastes, listed together with assorted historical landmarks. Drawn from a wide range of persons and frequently
offers comments on Gothic.

14

Fehr, Bernard. "The Antagonism of Forms in the Eighteenth   2/4
Century", ES, XVIII (1936), 115-121, 193-205; XIX (1937),
1-3, 49-57.

Attempts to correct the one-sided view derived from a
study confined exclusively to literature. Examines architecture, gardening, painting, and music, and points
out that an antagonism exists. Thus, for example, architecture might be classical at a time when painting and
literature were baroque. In fact, Fehr stresses that architecture was classical from 1652 to 1840. Similarly,
Pope's poetry represents "an exact counterpart of the formal garden" written at a time when the poet was moving
away from formal gardens.

Hipple, Walter John, Jr. The Beautiful, the Sublime, and the   2/5
Picturesque in Eighteenth-Century British Aesthetic Theory. Carbondale: Southern Illinois Univ. Press, 1957.

Hipple describes his work as "a philosophical survey of
a series of aestheticians, a survey in which the writers
are arranged chronologically chiefly for the reason that
the later ones had read the earlier, and argue with them".

Hussey, Christopher. The Picturesque: Studies in a Point of   2/6
View [1927]. Hamden: Archon, 1967.

Dates the picturesque period as 1730-1830 and calls it an
era in which "each art passed through a phase of imitating
painting before developing into the romantic phase that
came after, when the eye and the imagination had learnt
to work for themselves." The picturesque period began
when Thomson and Dyer described landscape in terms of pictures. Following this beginning, picturesque formed the
basis for the Grand Tour, then became manifest in gardening, architecture, and finally in the novels of Mrs. Smith
and Mrs. Radcliffe.

Monk, Samuel H. The Sublime: A Study of Critical Theories   2/7
in XVIII-Century England [1935]. Ann Arbor: Univ. of
Michigan Press, 1962.

Sets out "to trace the history of one idea, the sublime,
as it developed in England". Traces and summarizes the
various theories and relates them to literature, painting,
and scenery. Discusses the sublime, pathetic, picturesque,
Burke, Radcliffe, Longinus, Addison, Dennis, the Graveyard school, the Gothic novelists, the disintegration of

neo-classical taste, Ossian, Nathan Drake, Archibald
Alison, Gilpin, Michelangelo, George Barrett, and many
more persons and topics.

Staver, Frederick. "'Sublime' as Applied to Nature", MLN,   2/8
LXX (1955), 484-487.

Question -- "When did an English writer first apply the
adjective 'sublime', commonly used by literary critics,
to the objects and forces of nature?"
    Answers -- Well, Hildebrand Jacob's essay "How the
Mind is rais'd to the Sublime" (1735) is in this vein,
and a letter of 1742 from Elizabeth Montagu marks the
first recorded use of the term "outside formal literature". In 1745, Addison's "Great, Uncommon, or Beautiful" became Akenside's "the sublime, the wonderful, the
fair".

b.

Painting

Barbier, Carl Paul. William Gilpin: His Drawings, Teaching,   2/9
and Theory of the Picturesque. Oxford: Univ. Press,
1963.

The study of a specific aspect and neither a general
treatment of Gilpin, nor a history of the picturesque.
Illustrated with plates from the Gilpins, Salvator Rosa,
and others.

Blunt, Anthony. The Paintings of Nicholas Poussin: A Criti-   2/10
cal Catalogue. London: Phaidon, 1966.

Contains over 200 reproductions; catalogues all known
paintings by Nicholas Poussin, and in addition, offers
both a "lost" list and a list of erroneous attributions.
Notes to each illustration give dimensions and present location of the painting, include a thumbnail history, an
individual bibliography of criticism, and list copies,
engravings, etc. A general bibliography, arranged chronologically from 1627 to 1966 is appended.

16

Boetzkes, Ottilie G. Salvator Rosa: Seventeenth-Century   2/11
Italian Painter, Poet, and Patriot. New York: Vantage,
1960.

A semi-novelized account of the life of Salvator Rosa
complete with abundance of dialogue, but with total absence of footnotes. Includes fifteen black and white reproductions and lists the 1957 location of 219 of Rosa's
paintings.

Clark, David Ridgley. "Landscape Painting Effects in Pope's   2/12
Homer", JAAC, XXII (1963), 25-28.

Contests Hussey's view (2/6) that Pope had little appreciation of picturesque landscape and argues that there is
much of Claude Lorrain in Pope's Homer. This influence is
evident in Pope's "use of color" and in his technique of
"freezing actions into momentarily static pictures, by
framing scattered landscape items with single views, and
by continually emphasizing perspective where the original
has neglected to do so".

Clark, Kenneth. Landscape Into Art [1949]. London: John   2/13
Murray, 1966.

Traces "how in spite of classical traditions and the unan-
imous opposition of theorists, landscape painting became
an independent art". Argues that "the landscape of fact,
like all portraiture, is a bourgeois form of art", and
during the 18th century, "that winter of the imagination,
the landscape of fact degenerated into topography" and
"the landscape of fantasy degenerated into the picturesque, more particularly into that branch of the picturesque which derived from Salvator Rosa." Mentions the
fantastic and horrid landscapes of Altdorfer and Grüne-
wald.

Davies, Cicely. "Ut Pictura Poesis", MLR, XXX (1935), 159-   2/14
169.

Points out that during the 18th century, literature and
painting were regarded as closely linked together, and
so, theory and criticism overlap from one field to the
other. Emphasis of the article falls upon landscape
poets.

Gaunt, W[illiam]. Bandits in a Landscape: A Study of Ro-   2/15
mantic Painting from Caravaggio to Delacroix. New York:
Studio, 1937.

Offers studies of Salvator Rosa, Claude Lorrain, Richard
Wilson, Hubert Robert, Géricault, Delacroix, and others.
Includes brief and general comments on interest in romantic landscape, ruins, and the classical vs. romantic
struggle.

Manwaring, Elizabeth Wheeler. Italian Landscape in Eighteenth 2/16
Century England: A Study Chiefly of the Influence of
Claude Lorrain and Salvator Rosa on English Taste, 1700-
1800. New York: Oxford Univ. Press, 1925. (Reprinted,
New York: Russell & Russell, 1965.)

Predates and influences many of the standard works on 18th-
century aesthetics. Investigates the influence of Salvator, the onetime bandito, and Claude, the runaway appren-
tice to a pastry cook. Sees traces in English landscape
painting, in gardening and landscape art, in poetry, and
finally, in the novel. Looks at the works of Richardson,
Fielding, Smollett, Amory Mackenzie, Smith, Radcliffe,
Lewis, and others. Contends that Charlotte Smith influenced Ann Radcliffe, but says no other novelist followed
painted scenery as closely as did Mrs. Radcliffe.

Quennell, Peter. Romantic England: Writing and Painting   2/17
1717-1851. New York: Macmillan, 1970.

A profusely and beautifully illustrated outline of English Romanticism from "the Gothic Background" of Pope,
Walpole, Beckford, Radcliffe, Lewis, and Maturin to Pugin's dream of a Gothic revival. Of an elementary and
introductory scope but contains a noteworthy collection
of 18th and 19th-century paintings of romantic landscapes, crumbling castles, and pensive devotees of nature.

Templeman, William D. "The Life and Work of William Gilpin   2/18
(1724-1804). Master of the Picturesque and Vicar of Bol-
dre", ISLL, XXIV (1939), Nos. 3-4.

This "new and more comprehensive biography" represents a
long, scholarly investigation of the many sides of William
Gilpin. In addition to his work on the picturesque, we
are shown the man -- biographer, schoolmaster, and re-
former of curriculum. His work as critic of prints and as
pioneer in the picturesque is fully covered, but these as-

pects are not emphasized to the exclusion of his other
achievements.

Tinker, Chauncey Brewster. Painter and Poet: Studies in the   2/19
Literary Relations of English Painting. The Charles
Eliot Norton Lectures for 1937-1938. Cambridge: Harvard
Univ. Press, 1938.

Covers the major British artists; looks at their interests
in literature and their affinities with literary movements.
Notes Hogarth's interest in humanity, Reynolds' fondness
for children and primitives, Gainsborough's cottages and
his return to Nature, Wilson's depiction of solitude and
ruins, his Italian predecessors; Turner's highly imaginative, often supernatural scenes, his "ruined Paradise";
Constable's love of nature and ruins.

c.

Architecture

Bradbury, Ronald. The Romantic Theories of Architecture of   2/20
the Nineteenth Century, in Germany, England and France.
Columbia University Theses. New York: Dorothy Press,
1934.

Spans and neglects the late 18th century in Britain. Says
the 19th-century Gothic architectural revival has roots
in literature, and credits this movement in France to Cha-
teaubriand, in Germany to Goethe, and in Great Britain to
Sir Walter Scott. Discusses the architectural theories
of Kant, Hegel, Schopehhauer, Vischer, Pugin, Morris,
Gilbert Scott, and Ruskin.

Clark, Kenneth. The Gothic Revival: An Essay in the History   2/21
of Taste [1928]. Harmondsworth: Penguin, 1964.

Asserts that literary taste influenced architecture.
Spenser invented the Gothic properties; Gray and the
Graveyard school united poetry and archaeology, and "the
Gothic novelists were the natural successors of the graveyard poets". Literature and architecture combine in Walpole, Beckford, Gray, and Thomas Warton. Although Pope
in his 1725 edition of Shakespeare, and Hughes in his 1715
edition of Spenser note analogies "between non-classical

19

periods of literature and Gothic architecture", Clark
concludes that "it is impossible to show a smooth inter-
action, or even a close parallel, between 18th-century
Gothic novels and buildings." Discusses also sublimity,
emotional appeal, the Gothic = Catholic view, and treats
Pugin's theory of an organic connection between society
and architectural design.

Coleridge, Samuel Taylor. "General Character of the Gothic   2/22
Literature and Art"[1818], in Thomas Middleton Raysor,
ed., Coleridge's Miscellaneous Criticism. Cambridge:
Harvard Univ. Press, 1936.

"The Greek art is beautiful. When I enter a Greek church,
my eye is charmed, and my mind elated; I feel exalted,
and proud that I am a man. But the Gothic art is sublime.
On entering a cathedral, I am filled with devotion and
with awe; I am lost to the actualities that surround me,
and my whole being expands into the infinite; earth and
air, nature and art, all swell up into eternity, and the
only sensible impression left is 'that I am nothing'."

Colvin, H.M. "Aubrey's Chronologia Architectonica", in John   2/23
Summerson, ed., Concerning Architecture: Essays on Ar-
chitectural Writers and Writing Presented to Nikolaus
Pevsner. London: Allen Lane, 1968.

Called "a belated tribute to one who deserves recognition,
not only as our first archaeologist, but also as our earliest architectural historian", this essay deals with John
Aubrey's unpublished fifty-page manuscript, "Chronologia
Architectonica", the fourth part of his Monumenta. Written
in the 1670's, Aubrey's treatise contains the usual remarks on barbarism, but is the first attempt to establish
the chronology of English medieval architecture. A few of
the original sketches are reproduced.

De Beer, E.S. "Gothic: Origin and Diffusion of the Term;   2/24
the Idea of Style in Architecture", JWCI, XI (1948), 143-
162.

Begins by tracing Gothic from tribe, to synonym for bar-
barian, to term of abuse, to synonym for tastelessness.
Vasari, writing in 1550, was the first to call Gothic architecture "Gothic". He viewed this handiwork of the Ger-
mans as monstrous and barbarous, and presented his attitude in a book on art history, a work which was without
rivals until the 18th century. In England, John Evelyn

seems to have been the first to use the term, labeling as "Gothic", buildings which he saw in 1641.

Eastlake, Charles L. A History of the Gothic Revival: An   2/25
Attempt to Show How the Taste for Mediaeval Architecture
Which Lingered in England During the Two Last Centuries
Has Since Been Encouraged and Developed [1872]. Edited,
and with an introduction by J. Mordaunt Crook. The Vic-
torian Library. New York: Humanities, 1970.

More than a reissue, this facsimile reproduction of the
1872 edition has been updated and corrected. New illustrations, a bibliography, and an index have been added,
and Crook's lengthy introduction includes biography of
Eastlake and summaries of "recent research into the origins of the Gothic Revival in this country". Crook points
out merits and shortcomings of Eastlake, traces the Gothic
revival/survival from the Elizabethan to the Victorian
era, and offers his own comments on the Gothic novelists.
He sees in the 18th century two phases of architecture --
Rococo and Picturesque. "The origins of Picturesque Gothic were pictorial" and the popularity of the Rococo
came from "the cult of wild scenery and the craze for
'horrid' novels".

Frankl, Paul. Gothic Architecture. Translated by Dieter   2/26
Pevsner. Pelican History of Art Series. Baltimore: Penguin, 1962.

This lavishly illustrated work treats "the meaning and
the development of the Gothic style in medieval church architecture". Frankl concedes that Panofsky (2/34) seems
correct in establishing an "analogy between the form of
scholasticism and the form of the Gothic style", but is
not quite satisfied that the parallelism has been fully
explained. He calls for "fresh thought on the new and
firmer basis which Panofsky has given us".

--------. The Gothic: Literary Sources and Interpretations   2/27
through Eight Centuries. Translated by Priscilla Silz.
Princeton: Princeton Univ. Press, 1960.

A highly technical book for the specialist in architecture.

21

Girouard, Mark. "Attitudes to Elizabethan Architecture. 2/28
1600-1900", in John Summerson, ed., Concerning Architecture: Essays on Architectural Writers and Writing Presented to Nikolaus Pevsner. London: Allen Lane, 1968.

Traces the changing views on Elizabethan architecture.
Calls Horace Walpole "the father of Elizabethan architectural history" because, unfriendly as he was to the
style, he publicized the names and discovered John Thorpe's
book of architecture which he published with his own Anecdotes. Says the rise of Elizabethan architecture in the
second half of the 18th century was due to a "growing antiquarian and archaeological sense" and the "growth of
the cult of the Picturesque". Notes that sympathy came,
not from architects, but from "topographers, antiquarians,
novelists, and landscape theorists".

Heilman, Robert B. "Fielding and 'The First Gothic Revival'", 2/29
MLN, LVII (1942), 671-673.

Lovejoy (2/32) dates the first Gothic revival in the
1740's when Batty Langley was influential,but asserts that
this fad soon declined. Heilman here shows that Fielding
in his 1741-42, Journal from this World to the Next was
not adverse to Gothic, and in Tom Jones (1746-48), "was
more unmistakably well disposed toward Gothic", but this
attitude seems to have cooled in the 1754, Journal of a
Voyage to Lisbon.

Henderson, George. Gothic. Style and Civilization Series. 2/30
Baltimore: Penguin, 1967.

This profusely illustrated paperback covers the principles of Gothic but deals neither with the Gothic revival
nor with the Gothic novel.

Hussey, Christopher. English Country Houses Open to the Pub- 2/31
lic [1951]. 2nd ed., revised. New York: Scribner's,
1953.

Hussey comments on picturesqueness, equates architecture
with literary movements, presents remarkable examples of
various types of gardens and buildings, and offers examples of the work of famous architects. Includes 318 pho-
tographs.

Lovejoy, Arthur O. "The First Gothic Revival and the Return   2/32
to Nature", MLN, XLVII (1932), 419-446. (Reprinted in
his Essays in the History of Ideas. Baltimore: Johns
Hopkins Univ. Press, 1948.)

Gothic was disliked for its lack of simplicity and sym-
metry, its gloominess, its ornamentation without use or
structural necessity, and above all, its unnaturalness --
it didn't follow Nature. The Gothic revival, Lovejoy argues, was due to the "discovery" that Gothic was more "natural" than the classical edifices. Critics now saw Gothic
as forest-like, and the Gothic irregularity and variety was
analogous to the new Nature manifest in the English garden. Admiration for English or Chinese gardens, Gothic
architecture, and Shakespeare were all part of the same
taste.

Mâle, Emile. The Gothic Image: Religious Art in France of   2/33
the Thirteenth Century [1913]. Translated by Dora Nussey.
New York: Harper & Row, 1958.

Looks at mediaeval iconography and its sources of inspiration. Months, animals, numbers, positions, grotesques --
all are discussed in terms of their symbolic values; and
thus, Gothic architecture becomes viewed in a new light.
Profusely illustrated.

Panofsky, Erwin. Gothic Architecture and Scholasticism   2/34
[1951]. Cleveland: World, 1967.

Panofsky works on the interrelations of art, philosophy,
and literature. The writings of the Scholastics, he contends, share structural affinities with Gothic architecture. These similarities are studied in an investigation
of the two controlling principles of Early and High Scholasticism, manifestatio and concordantia. With sixty illustrations.

Pope, Alexander. "Preface to the Works of Shakespeare"   2/35
[1725], in Louis I. Bredvold, Alan D. McKillop, and Lois
Whitney, eds., Eighteenth Century Poetry and Prose [1939].
New York: Ronald Press, 1956.

Pope makes a comparison between Shakespeare's plays and
Gothic architecture. Both are "irregular" but "more
strong and more solemn" than modern finished and regular
taste requires. The poet praises "variety", but criticizes what he sees as inorganic structure.

23

Richardson, A.E. "The Gothic Revival in the Early Eighteenth   2/36
Century", Journal of the Royal Institute of British Architects, XVL (1937), 140-141.

Points out that Browne Willis (1682-1760), author of Survey of Cathedrals (1727-1730), was an important influence
on the design of Fenny Stratford Church, "a moving spirit
in the early Gothic revival", but yet "no architectural
critic has thought fit to mention his literary contributions as part of the sequence from the republication of
the Monasticon."

Sitwell, Sacheverell. British Architects and Craftsmen: A   2/37
Survey of Taste, Design, and Style during Three Centuries,
1600 to 1830 [1945]. 4th ed. London: Batsford, 1948.

Coverage of Restoration and early 18th century is excellent, but Gothic receives scant treatment.

Summerson, John. "Heavenly Mansions: An Interpretation of   2/38
Gothic", in his Heavenly Mansions and Other Essays on Architecture [1948]. New York: Norton, 1963.

Contends that Gothic is not opposed to classic, but is
"truly a continuation and development of the classical
line, a metamorphosis of classicism, temporary and unsta-
ble". The pointed arch was borrowed from the Arabs because "it had an air of fantasy -- perhaps, dare one
guess, of Oriental fantasy -- which went along with the
realization of the 'Pompeian idea'", or aedicular architecture.

                              d.

                 Scenery, Landscape, Gardens

Aubin, Robert A. "Grottoes, Geology, and the Gothic Revi-   2/39
val", SP, XXXI (1934), 408-416.

To the Augustans, ruins "suggested not merely tumble down
buildings, but also rocks, hills, mountains, wild nature
in general, 'rubbish' of all sorts",since after the flood
the world was itself a ruin. Thus, "it appears that grottoes and geological theory were intimately linked with
each other and with Gothic architecture, ruinous or other-

                             24

wise, and that interest in them may well have accelerated
the 'Gothic revival' of the 1740's."

Aubin, Robert A.   Topographical Poetry in XVIII-Century   2/40
England. The Modern Language Association of America
Revolving Fund, Series VI. Menasha: Collegiate, 1936.

"Until roads were improved and Italian landscape paintings
disseminated, until the science-conscious orthodox and
the deists had sought to prove mountains the handiwork of
a well-meaning Creator, and until the old critical ukase
about following nature had profoundly changed its meaning, the natural temples of the earth were (more or less
officially) so many evidences of divine wrath." Aubin
traces the changes,discusses classical roots, hill-poems,
the Claudian prospect, Salvatorian sublimity, Burkean
vastness, the influence of Milton, Denham, Dyer, and Thomson, and in Chapter IV, "Cloud-Capped Towers", deals with
the Gothic or ruin-sentiment which he dates from John
Dart's Westminster-Abbey (1721).

Baker, Carlos.   "The Cham on Horseback", VQR, XXVI (1950),   2/41
76-90.

Contrary to what is generally believed, Dr. Johnson was
not insensitive to natural scenery and enjoyed mountains,
turbulent waters, the roar of cascades, and various horrible, awful, sublime, striking, and terrific scenes.

Chase, Isabel Wakelin Urban.   Horace Walpole: Gardenist.   2/42
An Edition of Walpole's "The History of the Modern Taste
in Gardening" with an "Estimate of Walpole's Contribution
to Landscape Architecture". Princeton: Princeton Univ.
Press, 1943.

Consists of four parts. A richly footnoted reproduction
of the 1782 edition of Walpole's "Essay on Gardening"
forms the first section; "Background" discusses the changing concept of nature, the theory of the sister arts,
draws illustrations from aestheticians and writers, and
differs somewhat from the conclusions of Manwaring (2/16).
Section III analyses Walpole's "Essay" and supplements
where necessary with his letters. The final section
deals with famous gardens of Walpole's day and offers a
full account of the Strawberry Hill grounds.

Clark, H.F. The English Landscape Garden. London: 2/43
Pleiades, 1948.

Highly concentrated, yet clear, this very brief study
deals with gardens, architects, philosophers, poets, the
Italian painters, the associational theorists, and also
looks in detail at nine famous gardens.

Corder, Jim. "Spenser and the Eighteenth Century Informal 2/44
Garden", N&Q, NS, VI (1959), 19-21.

Advances Spenser along with Milton, Thomson, and Pope as
an influence on the "new" style of gardening. Says that
in the FQ, in three well-known passages, the poet praises
"a nature beautified only by the rules of nature and of
God. It is just here that we can see some reason for notice of Spenser in the 18th century as an authority, for
this adherence of the rules of nature, this destruction
of artificiality -- in theory, if not in practice -- was
the aim of English gardeners of the informal inclination
in the 18th century."

Hadfield, Miles. Gardening in Britain. London: Hutchinson, 2/45
1960.

A general history of gardening in Britain from the very
beginnings to the modern era which notes affinities in
architecture, landscape gardening, painting, and literature. Coverage of the 18th century is necessarily brief,
but especially interesting is the treatment of the taste
for exotic fruits and plants discovered on voyages of ex-
ploration.

Hibbert, Christopher. The Grand Tour. New York: Putnam's, 2/46
1969.

A richly illustrated work which draws heavily on Beckford's
journals and quotes from or refers to -- Dr. Johnson, Boswell, Smollett, Sterne, and Mrs. Radcliffe. This is not
a study of the sublime or the picturesque, but instead
deals with the more earthy aspects: prices, services,
food, prostitutes, bandits, diseases, routes, etc. Covers
France, Switzerland, Italy, Germany and Austria, and the
Low Countries. For the generalist, the undergraduate, or
the student of travel literature.

Hussey, Christopher. English Gardens and Landscapes 1700-   2/47
1750. London: Country Life, 1967.

A companion piece to his earlier English Country Houses
(2/31). Consists of two sections, the first dealing in
theory and background, the second describing thirteen
famous gardens. Emphasis falls upon the gardens, not
the aesthetics. Contains 245 plates.

Lovejoy, Arthur O. "The Chinese Origin of a Romanticism",   2/48
JEGP, XXXII (1933), 1-20. (Reprinted in his Essays in
the History of Ideas. Baltimore: Johns Hopkins Univ.
Press, 1948.)

Contends that "a turning-point in the history of modern
taste was reached when the ideas of regularity, simplicity, uniformity and easy logical intellegibility were
first openly impugned", and argues that the influence and
example of Chinese art was largely responsible for this
shift in opinion.

Macaulay, Rose. Pleasure of Ruins. London: Weidenfeld &   2/49
Nicolson, 1953.

"To explore the various kinds of pleasure given to various
people at various epochs by the spectacle of ruined buildings" is the intention of this study, and the author
sweeps from earliest times to the present era, noting
ruins in Europe, Mexico, Indochina, North Africa, and
many other places. "The human race is, and has always
been, ruin minded", contends the author. "The literature
of all ages has found beauty in the dark and violent forces, physical and spiritual, of which ruin is one symbol."

Malins, Edward. English Landscaping and Literature 1660-   2/50
1840. London: Oxford Univ. Press, 1966.

Sets out to trace the direct influence of contemporary
writers and artists on the formation of English landscapes.
Chronicles the struggle of art vs. nature, of French for-
malism vs. English romanticism; sees Shaftesbury's love
of freedom reflected in the English garden; regards the
French formal garden as autocratic and antithetical to
the Whig virtues of benevolence and moderation. Covers
the aestheticians and devotes special attention to Lance-
lot Brown, "the greatest of the professional landscapers",
a man who "thought of landscape in literary and intellectual terms".

Nicolson, Marjorie Hope. Mountain Gloom and Mountain Glory: 2/51
The Development of the Aesthetics of the Infinite [1959].
New York: Norton, 1963.

The 17th century saw gloom in mountains and believed that
God in anger formed these aberrations, but the Romantics
saw glory in mountains and derived a religious ecstasy
from them. How this change in attitude came about forms
the subject of this work, and Professor Nicolson pursues
her investigation by delving into theology, geology, and
astronomy, and rejects the common notion that the redis-
covery of Longinus brought about this shift. The sublime
in nature, she argues, exists independent of the sublime
in literature.

Pevsner, Nikolaus. "The Genesis of the Picturesque", Archi-   2/52
tectural Review, XCVI (Nov., 1944), 139-146.

Pevsner presents and answers three questions on the origin
of the landscape garden. (1)Why was it created by the
English? (2)Why at that time -- 1710-30? (3)Why by the
same men who advocated rigidly formal architectural style?
Answers: (1)"It was conceived by philosophers, writers,
and virtuosi -- not by architects and gardeners. It was
conceived in England, because it is the garden of liber-
alism, and (2)England just at that moment turned liberal,
that is Whig." (3)Palladianism was simple as Nature; i.e.,
built to follow nature and, "to be natural in a garden evidently was to recreate nature untouched by man".

Reynolds, Myra. The Treatment of Nature in English Poetry   2/53
Between Pope and Wordsworth [1909]. New York: Gordian,
1966.

An older work, but one which still has value, this study
traces in poetry, fiction, painting, travel, and gardening, the move from classic to romantic. Chapter III,
"Fiction", presents a chronological catalogue of nature
treatment. Thus, as examples: "In Roderick Random . . .
there are no references to Nature"; Sir Charles Grandison
has "two interesting passages concerning the estate of
Sir Charles"; Vathek "is an extravaganza where there is no
pretense of representing Nature as it is".

Thacker, Christopher. "'Wish'd, Wint'ry, Horror': The Storm   2/54
in the Eighteenth Century", CL, XIX (1967), 36-57.

Traces the change of attitude toward storms. "At the time
of Bishop Burnet the storm was evidence of evil, of man's
sin and the Creator's anger, [but] by the time of the romantics it was the opposite, the crowning evidence of the
sublimity of nature and a symbol of man's most rarefied
poetic aspiration." Notes Smollett's use of a storm in
Ferdinand Count Fathom "to create a mood of fearful anticipation". Includes Mrs. Radcliffe among the "many lesser
writers" who used landscape to achieve the sublime.

Thorpe, Clarence DeWitt. "Two Augustans Cross the Alps: 2/55
Dennis and Addison on Mountain Scenery", SP, XXXII
(1935), 463-482.

Years before Gray travelled to Italy and before Shaftesbury published his Moralists, "both Dennis and Addison had
left in their writings evidence of deeply appreciative
emotional response to mountain scenery". Thorpe believes
that "Dennis experienced sublimity, and it was the sublimity of the Addisonian-Kantian type, which takes into
account the mysterious vast, rather than the merely terrifying vast of Burke." Addison was "the undeniable originator of the modern theory of the sublime", and although he did record physical discomfort on crossing the
Alps, he found them to produce that "aesthetic delight
he was later to label sublime".

Ware, Malcolm. "An Early Reference to the Sublime: Sir   2/56
Thomas Herbert's 'Travels'", N&Q, CCVII (1962), 378-379.

Notes that Monk (2/7) "shows clearly that Dennis was the
first critic to consider at length sublimity as an effect
inseparable from terror", but points out that Herbert, in
his 1634, Travels, predates Dennis. The traveller associates sublimity "with emotions of terror produced by
lofty mountains and great bodies of water, two perpetual
sources of the sublime in Burke's Enquiry".

Zucker, Paul. "Ruins -- An Aesthetic Hybrid", JAAC, XX   2/57
(1961), 119-130.

Looks at ruins in three ways: (1) "As a vehicle to create
a romanticizing mood"; (2) "as documents of the past";
(3) "as means of reviving the original concept of space and
proportion of periods past". Traces depiction in art from

Nativity scenes of Lippi, Botticelli, and Ghirlandajo, through Rosa, Poussin, Ruisdael, to Thomas Cole. Covers artificial ruins and landscape gardens; mentions Shaftesbury, Pope, Gray, Walpole's Modern Gardening, but omits the Graveyard poets and the Gothic novelists. With thirteen plates.

III

THE LITERARY BACKGROUND

a.

Early Literary Theories

Addison, Joseph. Spectator, No. 44 (April 20, 1711), in   3/1
    Donald F. Bond, ed., The Spectator. 3 vols. Oxford:
    Clarendon, 1965.

    Discusses methods of raising terror and pity on the stage.
    Opposes scenes of violence; recommends the use of a toll-
    ing bell or thunder and lightning. "But there is nothing
    which delights and terrifies our English theatre so much
    as a ghost, especially when he appears in a bloody shirt.
    A spectre has very often saved a play, though he has done
    nothing but stalked across the stage, or rose through a
    cleft of it, and sunk again without speaking one word."

--------. Spectator, No. 110 (July 6, 1711).   3/2

    Deals with ghosts and Locke's theory of association of
    ideas. Mr. Spectator describes an allegedly haunted area,
    and interestingly, offers a Gothic-like picture of "one of
    the most proper scenes in the world for a ghost to appear
    in". "The Ruins of the Abbey", he writes, "are scattered
    up and down on every side, and half covered with ivy and
    eldar-bushes, the harbours of several solitary birds which
    seldom make their appearance till the dusk of the evening.
    The place was formerly a church-yard, and has still several
    marks in it of graves and burying places. There is such an
    echo among the old ruins and vaults, that if you stamp but
    a little louder than ordinary you hear the sound repeated.
    At the same time the walk of elms, with the croaking of the
    ravens which from time to time are heard from the tops of
    them, looks exceedingly solemn and venerable."

--------. Spectator, No. 419 (July 1, 1712).   3/3

    Asserts that the English excel at "the fairy way of writ-
    ing" and sees Shakespeare as the master in this field.
    Descriptions of spirits, witches, magicians, and demons
    "raise a pleasing kind of horror in the mind of the reader,

and amuse his imagination with the strangeness and novelty
of the persons who are represented in them. They bring up
into our memory the stories we have heard in our childhood, and favor our secret terrors and apprehensions to
which the mind of man is naturally subject."

Allott, Miriam. Novelists on the Novel [1959]. New York: 3/4
Columbia Univ. Press, 1966.

An anthology of extracts from the great novelists on various aspects of their art. "The Novel and the Marvellous"
offers 21 commentaries on the use of the supernatural and
the marvellous, extracted from Richardson, the Fieldings,
Smollett, Reeve, Rousseau, Holcroft, Cumberland, Anna Barbauld, Scott, Hawthorne, Sarah Green, Flaubert, Maupassant,
Stevenson, Conrad, Henry James, and Thomas Hardy.

Baillie, John. An Essay on the Sublime [1747]. Introduction   3/5
by Samuel Holt Monk. Augustan Reprint Society, No. 43.
Los Angeles: Clark Memorial Library, UCLA, 1953.

Baillie says "the sublime in writing is no more than a
description of the sublime in nature" and asserts that
sublimity derived from architecture is associated with
feelings of "great riches, power, and grandeur", and the
columns are connected with "strength and durableness".
He denies that terror itself can be sublime. "The sublime
dilates and elevates the soul, fear sinks and contracts it:
yet both are felt upon viewing what is great and awful.
And we cannot conceive a Deity armed with Thunder without
being struck with a sublime terror."

[Barbauld, Anna Letitia]. "On the Pleasure Derived from Ob-   3/6
jects of Terror", in John and Anna Letitia [Barbauld]
Aikin, Miscellaneous Pieces in Prose. London: J. Johnson, 1773.

Ponders why people seem fascinated by objects of terror
when "no passion seems to be excited but the depressing
one of fear". Tragedy, "the most favourite work of fiction", is filled with terror; and indeed, the ancient
critics thought that tragedy was to inspire terror. The
essayist wonders whether the answer might not rest with
curiosity for "we rather chuse to suffer the smart pang
of a violent emotion than the uneasy craving of an unsatisfied desire." Thus, she confesses she has read many an
"insipid narrative" just to satisfy her curiosity. But
the real reason, she suggests, is the new dimension.

32

"This is the pleasure constantly attached to the excitement of surprise from new and wonderful objects." She
suggests that the "wild, fanciful, and extraordinary",
as in Arabian Nights and Otranto, are more pleasing than
the "mere natural horror" of Ferdinand Count Fathom.

Burke, Edmund. A Philosophical Enquiry into the Origin of   3/7
our Ideas of the Sublime and Beautiful [1757]. Edited
by J.T Boulton. London: Routledge & Kegan Paul, 1958.

Boulton's introduction which is almost the length of the
Enquiry itself, traces Burke's sources and influences and
points out just how he differed from contemporary aesthetic theory. Boulton brushes aside the usual oversim-
plifications and rejects the watershed approach. Burke
is seen as a neo-classicist whose "sole reference to Gothicism reveals the common Augustan prejudices", and whose
linking of terror with sublimity was not original.

Cooke, Arthur L. "Some Side Lights on the Theory of the   3/8
Gothic Romance", MLQ, XII (1951), 429-436.

(1)Warburton justified the Gothic romance by the same
principles as the classical drama -- Aristotelian cathar-
sis. (2)Dr. Aikin was "the first to apply to the new
Gothic genre those theories of terror which earlier critics
like Dennis and Burke had developed in their discussion of
the sublime". (3)Clara Reeve pointed out that the glori-
fication of bygone days could be a weapon of propaganda
against the new ideas of the French revolution. (4)Ex-
plained supernatural transformed the Gothic romance "from
a kind of ghost story into a kind of elaborate brain
teaser". (5)Drake unsuccessfully attempted to revive "the
'sportive' branch of medieval superstition", the lighter
supernatural of Chaucer, Spenser, and Shakespeare.

Dennis, John. The Critical Works of John Dennis [1939].   3/9
Edited by Edward Niles Hooker. 2 vols. Baltimore:
Johns Hopkins Univ. Press, 1964.

Dennis, in "The Grounds of Criticism in Poetry" (1704),
claims that terror if rightly managed can give the greatest spirit to poetry. Terror is associated with religion,
the greatest terror coming from an angry God, but it can
also be produced by demons, spirits, witchcraft, monsters,
violent storms, natural disasters, etc. His "Essay on the
Genius and Writings of Shakespeare" (1712) praises the

playwright's use of terror, and in "The Usefulness of the
Stage" (1698), he defends the use of devils in drama.

Drake, Nathan. "On Gothic Superstition", in his Literary   3/10
Hours: or Sketches, Critical, Narrative, and Poetical
[1798]. 3 vols. 4th ed. London: Longman, 1820.

Asserts the superiority of the Gothic superstitions which
trace back to Chaucer and Spenser. Shakespeare mastered
the art and raised "the most awful, yet the most delightful species of terror". Drake places Celtic next to
Gothic "in point of sublimity and imagination", and notes
that Ossian's ghosts "are not the ghosts of Shakespeare,
yet they are equally solemn and striking". Even though
critics oppose any introduction of the supernatural,
Drake urges poets to employ "simple yet powerful superstitions", warning "that if at any time these romantic
legends be totally laid aside, our national poetry will
degenerate into mere morality, criticism, and satire;
and that the sublime, the terrible, and the fanciful in
poetry, will no longer exist".

--------. "On Objects of Terror", in his Literary Hours.   3/11

In order to avoid creating horror and disgust rather than
terror, Drake recommends "either to interpose picturesque
description, or sublime and pathetic sentiment, or . . .
to stimulate curiosity". He praises Mrs. Radcliffe who
intermixes beautiful description or pathetic incident so
that "the impression of the whole never becomes too
strong, never degenerates into horror, but pleasurable
emotion is ever the predominating result."

Dryden, John. "Of Heroic Plays: An Essay". Prefixed to his   3/12
Conquest of Granada (1672). In Montague Summers, ed.,
Dryden: The Dramatic Works [1932]. 6 vols. New York:
Gordian, 1968.

Dryden defends the use of the supernatural in heroic plays
claiming that "an heroic poet is not tied to a bare representation of what is true, or exceeding probable. . . ."
He does not see the need of elaborate justification for
"'tis enough that in all ages and religions the greatest
part of mankind have believed the power of magic, and that
there are spirits or spectres which have appeared."

34

Duff, William. _An Essay on Original Genius and Its Various_   3/13
Modes of Exertion in Philosophy and the Fine Arts, Par-
ticularly in Poetry [1767]. Edited, and with an introduction by John L. Mahoney. Gainesville: Scholar's
Facsimiles & Reprints, 1964.

Duff considers witches, ghosts, fairies "and such other
unknown visionary beings" to be well-worth the poet's
attention. "The invention of the supernatural characters . . . and the exhibition of them, with their proper
attributes and offices, are the highest efforts and the
most pregnant proofs of truly original genius."

Gerard, Alexander. _An Essay on Taste_ (1759). _Together with_   3/14
Observations Concerning the Imitative Nature of Poetry.
Edited by Walter J. Hipple, Jr. Gainesville: Scholar's
Facsimiles & Reprints, 1963.

Says beauty is intellectual, sublimity emotional. Explains
that sublimity in architecture comes from association:
"The columns suggest ideas of strength and durableness,
and the whole structure introduces the sublime idea of the
riches and magnificence of the owner." Gothic architecture has "novelty" but not "perfect beauty" because of
the "disproportion . . . [and] deviation from simplicity".
"Objects exciting terror are", he says, "in general sublime, for terror always implies astonishment, occupies
the whole soul, and suspends all its motions."

Hume, David. "Of Tragedy", in his _Essays, Moral, Political,_   3/15
and Literary [1741]. London: Oxford Univ. Press, 1963.

"Objects of the greatest terror and distress please in
painting and please more than the most beautiful objects
that appear calm and indifferent." Thus, with the painter
as well as with the poet and tragedian, a pleasure arises
from pain. Hume remains unsatisfied with earlier theories
which attempt to explain this paradox and believes that
the answer lies in the depiction of these objects and is,
therefore, tied up with eloquence, genius, force of expression, and comes as the result of conversion. "The
affection, rousing the mind, excites a large stock of
spirit and vehemence; which is all transformed into pleasure by the force of the prevailing movement."

Hurd, Richard. Letters on Chivalry and Romance [1762] with   3/16
the Third Elizabethan Dialogue [1759]. Edited by Edith
J. Morley. London: Henry Frowde, 1911.

Twelve letters dealing with Gothic writing, architecture,
manners, chivalry, and other topics. Compares Gothic
writing with classic; concludes Gothic is superior and
more sublime. Shakespeare was at his greatest when he
employed "Gothic manners and machinery"; Fairy Queen
must be judged by Gothic, not Grecian rules, for Fairy
Queen has a unity of design, not of action. In following
nature, a poet need not be confined to "the known and
experienced" but has "a supernatural world to range in".
Also, in "the more sublime and creative poetry", the poet
need not observe "those cautious rules of credibility".

--------. Letters on Chivalry and Romance (1762). Edited,   3/17
and with an introduction by Hoyt Trowbridge. Augustan
Reprint Society, Nos. 101-102. Los Angeles: Clark Memorial Library, UCLA, 1963.

A facsimile reprint of the first edition of 1762. In the
introduction, Trowbridge contends that critics have misinterpreted the Letters. "Hurd is not defending the
medieval romances. . . . The subject of the Letters is
Renaissance narrative literature, including the Italian
epics as well as Spenser, Milton, and Shakespeare, and
Hurd's purpose was to defend the romance element in that
literature as conducive to the sublime." (See also 3/25.)

Kames, Henry Home, Lord. Elements of Criticism [1762].   3/18
Introduction by Robert Voitle. Anglistica and Americana
Reprint Series. 3 vols. New York: Georg Olms, 1970.

In "Narration and Description", Kames writes: "Objects
that strike terror in a spectator have in poetry and
painting a fine effect. The picture, by raising a slight
emotion of terror, agitates the mind, and in that condition
every beauty makes a deep impression. May not contrast
heighten the pleasure by opposing our present security to
the danger we would be in by encountering the object represented?" "Objects of horror must be excepted from the
foregoing theory for no description, however masterly, is
sufficient to overbalance the disgust raised even by the
idea of such an object. Every thing horrible ought therefore to be avoided in a description."

Moore, Theodore McGinnes. "The Background of Edmund Burke's 3/19
Theory of the Sublime (1660-1759)." Unpublished doctoral
dissertation, Cornell, 1933.

Does not concentrate as much on Burke as the title seems
to suggest. "Background" is simply what comes before,
and indeed, the thesis embodies a history of the sublime,
terminating with Burke. Moore contends that "where
Burke differs from earlier writers on the sublime is in
restricting the effects of the sublime to the single
emotion of terror", and points out what he terms as three
errors: (1)"The selection of self-preservation as the
principle upon which to establish his theory of the sublime"; (2)"failure to form a consistent concept of his
own meaning of pain"; and (3)"failure to consider possible
differences between degrees of pain". Concludes that
Burke's "philosophical principles are historically, logically, and practically unsatisfactory".

Park, William. "Changes in the Criticism of the Novel after 3/20
1760", PQ, XLVI (1967), 34-41.

Sees Tristram Shandy (1759) as a watershed. Prior to this
date novels and criticism were concerned with truth, true
history, nature and probability, but with the new wave,
feeling became more important, and although novels were
still to instruct, "the limitations of probability became
a nuisance and a bore".

Smith, Audley L. "Richard Hurd's Letters on Chivalry and 3/21
Romance", ELH, VI (1935), 58-81.

A long, traditional explanation of Hurd's purpose and
place in the history of criticism. Smith says that Hurd,
at first an orthodox classicist, "yielded to the romantic
spell" and became a pioneer in Romanticism. His letters
provide "critical justification for the literature of the
Middle Ages and the use of romance material in modern
poetry by insisting that the chivalric manners and Gothic
superstitions are more poetic than those of the Greek
heroic age; by arguing that the greatness of Spenser and
the Italian renaissance poets lies in the romantic rather
than the classical features of their epics and by defending imagination and the 'fairy way of writing'".

Spacks, Patricia Meyer. "Horror-Personification in Late   3/22
Eighteenth-Century Poetry", SP, LIX (1962), 560-578.

The late 18th century saw a shift in the use of personification. Drawing on Burke and Milton, poets suggested
rather than delineated, and emphasized function rather
than appearance. Thus, for Blake, personification "must
be created in emphatic detail", but for Shelley, "only
the most allusive details are necessary".

Stroup, Thomas B. "Supernatural Beings in Restoration   3/23
Drama", Anglia, LXI (1937), 186-192.

Divides Restoration supernatural beings into two classes:
natives of earth and natives of spiritual regions. The
former, ghosts of departed mortals, were organic and used
much the same as the Elizabethans had employed them --
warning, foreshadowing, even instigating the whole action
of the play. But the second type were "mere parts of
operatic and masque-like scenes growing chiefly out of
masques and operas, and introduced for the 'diversion'
of the audience". In a footnote, Stroup adds that "it
is worth noting that by the time of Venice Preserved and
The Massacre of Paris the ghost had become somewhat
'psychologized', or explained away."

Swedenberg, H.T. "Fable, Action, Unity, and Supernatural   3/24
Machinery in English Epic Theory, 1650-1800", Englische
Studien, LXXIII (1938), 39-48.

"Most critics were distinctly in favor of using some form
of supernatural machinery. Dryden, Blackmore, Temple,
Dennis, Addison, Pope, Rolli, Trapp, Spence, Wilkie, Hurd,
Blair -- in fact, an impressive array of writers definitely
accepted machinery as a part of epic structure." Contrary
minded were Cowley; Fielding, who "admitted only the use of
ghosts"; Lyttleton; and Kames, who "was unequivocal in
rejecting machinery in a modern poem, on the grounds that
a modern mind cannot accept it".

Trowbridge, Hoyt. "Bishop Hurd: A Reinterpretation", PMLA,   3/25
LVIII (1943), 450-465.

Asserts that Hurd's views have been misinterpreted. In
the Letters on Chivalry "he is not attacking reason, the
rules, or the doctrines of imitation. Far from laying
the axe to the neo-classical tree, Hurd is engaged in
extending and supporting it." Trowbridge places him in

38

the tradition of Hume, Kames, Reynolds, and Burke. In
Letters, "he is not defending the medieval romances,
which he had not read, nor is he writing on poetry in
general. His purpose is to defend the poetical value
of chivalric manners and medieval superstitions as material for epic poetry; more particularly, he justifies
the romance element in renaissance epic."

Wichelns, Herbert A. "Burke's Essay on the Sublime and its   3/26
Reviewers", JEGP, XXI (1922), 645-661.

Discusses three contemporary reviews: Arthur Murphy's in
Johnson's Literary Magazine, Oliver Goldsmith's in the
Monthly Review, and an anonymous account in the Critical
Review. Traces their influence on Burke's second edition.

b.

Verse Precursors

Aubin, Robert Arnold. "Some Augustan Gothicists", Harvard   3/27
Studies and Notes in Philology and Literature, XVII
(1935), 15-25.

Aubin states his purpose as "simply to adduce more data
concerning the exceptional appreciation of Gothic pricr
to the 'revival' of the 1740's". Provides extracts from
Simon Ford (1667), Sir John Harington (1676), Henry
Keepe (1682), Thomas Hearne (1722), John Dart (1726),
Dr. Thomas Herring (1728), and from several anonymous
poems. Notes the connection with landscape gardening and
Chinese gardening; discusses the quest for "variety" and
"contrast".

--------. "Three Notes on 'Graveyard' Poetry", SP, XXXII   3/28
(1935), 103-109.

Note one views James Wright's The Ruins, Writ in the Year,
1668 as anticipatory of the Graveyard poems. Note two
presents an overlooked opponent of the school, Henry
Jones, author of The Relief; or, Day Thoughts: A Poem
(1754). The final note calls the Rev. George Gilfillan's
Night: A Poem (1867), "perhaps the latest specimen of
that ancient genre".

Draper, John W.   The Funeral Elegy and the Rise of English   3/29
Romanticism [1929]. New York: Octagon, 1967.

Contends that Gothicism has roots in the funeral elegy,
a form which originated with the Cavaliers. When the
Puritans used the tradition, it became part of the atmosphere of melancholia with emphasis shifting from Heaven
to earth, from immortality to decay. Sees Gothic ruins
as associated both with funeral services and burial vaults.
Regards Blair's Grave as the natural course of poetry, not
a new and unique departure. Notes that "at the very beginning of the 18th century, the Scotch elegist per-
ceived that realistic nature forms an admirable background for the stimulation of the emotions, and supplies
at the same time a grateful variety to moralizing and the
horrors of the grave."

Kurtz, Benjamin P.   "Gifer the Worm: An Essay toward the   3/30
History of an Idea", University of California Publications in English, II (1929), 235-261.

Sets out to trace the sources and history of the Address
of the Lost Soul, a poem on the putrefaction of the body,
found in both the Vercelli and Exeter codices. Notes
relevant themes in theology; looks at burial customs and
at the literature of various countries throughout the
ages. Concludes: "Straight from Job . . . and a few
passages scattered in Ecclesiasticus, The Wisdom of Solomon, and other books of the Old and New Testaments --
with no tradition bridging the centuries between, and
with no important source in any other ancient literature
of the West -- comes a theme that, misunderstood, ignobly
transformed, and applied to a new purpose, develops into
the Gifer-theme of the Middle Ages."

Moore, C.A.   "John Dunton: Pietist and Impostor", SP, XXII   3/31
(1925), 467-499.

A full coverage of the life and works of John Dunton
(1659-1733), "author, compiler, hack-master, publisher,
and factotum". This man, says Moore, represents "an
important link of connection between the poets of death
in the pre-Restoration period and their grave-yard successors in the 18th century".

Reed, Amy Louise. The Background of Gray's Elegy: A Study   3/32
in the Taste for Melancholy Poetry 1700-1751 [1924].
New York: Russell & Russell, 1962.

Sees the "Elegy" as representative of the contemporary
mood. "This mood was partly an implication in the classic
and in the English literary tradition, partly the result
of the political and religious upheavals of the 17th century, and partly the by-product of contemporary philosophic
and scientific thought. It was a sentiment widely dif-
fused among everyday, average people, and had been repeat-
edly the subject of poetical effusions by authors who had
found the largest popular audience."

Samoorian, Vahe. "The Way to Otranto: Gothic Elements in   3/33
Eighteenth Century English Poetry, 1717-1762". Unpublished doctoral dissertation, Bowling Green Univ., 1971.

Regards Otranto as the natural outgrowth of the times.
Its originality lies in that "it was the first prose
work of the century to employ Gothic effects within the
background of the Middle Ages". Investigates poetry beginning with "Eloisa to Abelard"; pulls out "Gothic elements" and proposes some specific influences on the novelists. Goes through Pope, Parnell, Young, Blair, the War-
tons, Collins, Gray and Macpherson.

Sickels, Eleanor M. The Gloomy Egoist: Moods and Themes of   3/34
Melancholy From Gray to Keats. Columbia University
Studies in English and Comparative Literature. New York:
Columbia Univ. Press, 1932.

Intended as a continuation of Reed's Background (3/32),
this study traces the melancholy theme into the 19th century, deals extensively with the Graveyard school, and
notes a very early attachment between melancholy poetry
and the infant Gothic revival. Suggests the physical
proximity of the Gothic church to the burial ground is
responsible for the association. Devalues the influence
of Milton in this sphere; sees "a psychological connection
between religious and romantic terror" and believes the
Protestant-sin-guilt-expiation graveyard-poetry theme
surfaces anew in the remorse of the Byronic hero.

41

Spacks, Patricia Meyer. <u>The Insistence of Horror: Aspects</u>   3/35
<u>of the Supernatural in Eighteenth-Century Poetry</u>. Cam-
bridge: Harvard Univ. Press, 1962.

On the aesthetics of terror/horror sublimity. Covers
poetry of Lewis, Burns, Blake, Coleridge; looks into
Dennis, Hurd, Duff, Drake, and Aikin. Shows that although
witchcraft laws were repealed in 1736, credence remained
widespread, especially with dissenters and non-conformists.
Also, in the period 1700-1740, "a surprisingly large group"
of poets used the supernatural for its own sake and not as
part of the Christian scheme.

c.

Prose Precursors

Almirall, Catherine L. "Smollett's 'Gothic': An Illustra-   3/36
tion", <u>MLN</u>, LXVIII (1953), 408-410.

Claims that Smollett's Gothic scene in Chs. 62 and 63
of <u>Ferdinand Count Fathom</u> (1753) is taken, consciously
or unconsciously, from Congreve's <u>Mourning Bride</u> (Act II,
Sc. ii), a play staged thirteen times in 1750-51, twice
in 1751-52, and twice in 1752-53. Says the passages have
parallels both in action and phrasing, and notes that with
Smollett, this scene "is dramatic beyond what is generally
characteristic of the author".

Baine, Rodney M. <u>Daniel Defoe and the Supernatural</u>. Athens: 3/37
Univ. of Georgia Press, 1968.

When the Salem witchcraft executions were carried out in
1692, Defoe was 33 years old and had just entered bank-
ruptcy. His <u>True Relation of the Apparition of Mrs. Veal</u>,
written in 1706, came six years before the last death
sentence for witchcraft was handed down in England. For
Defoe, the Devil was real, and rejection of the supernatural was a type of atheism. Thus, in <u>Robinson Crusoe</u>
(1719), <u>Captain Singleton</u> (1720), <u>Moll Flanders</u> (1722),
and <u>Roxana</u> (1724), the Devil has an actual role, and
Baine's study places these works in their historical and
literary perspectives.

Leland, Thomas. Longsword, Earl of Salisbury: An Historical   3/38
Romance. Edited, and with an introduction by John C.
Stephens, Jr. New York: New York Univ. Press, 1957.

Stephens regards Longsword as the first historical novel,
and via the Old English Baron, a strong influence on
the Gothic novel. Says it contains "virtually all the
ingredients of Gothicism . . . except the supernatural".
It features "the persecuted hero, the cunning villain,
the distressed maiden, the faithful retainer, and (present here only in touches) the architectural scene and
ornate description of external nature".

--------. Longsword, Earl of Salisbury: An Historical Ro-   3/39
mance. Edited, and with a foreword by Devendra P. Varma.
Introduction by Robert D. Hume. New York: Arno, 1974.

Hume disagrees with Stephens (3/38) and sees little
"Gothic" in Longsword. But, although L "has little or
no direct effect on the Schauerromantik Gothic school",
there is an influence via Clara Reeve and Sophia Lee on
Mrs. Radcliffe. Offers a long discussion of the 18th
century's concern with realism and didacticism in fiction.

Parsons, Coleman O. "The Interest of Scott's Public in the   3/40
Supernatural", N&Q, CLXXXV (1943), 92-100.

"Scott's own conflict and resultant indecision arise from
the fact that his religion cannot deny apparitions and
that his mature reason will not accept them; earlier in
life, it was his imagination which could not give them
up." But, it seems that for many of Scott's contemporaries, especially in Scotland, witchcraft and demonology
was still not a dead issue. Parsons notes that "political
unrest, attended as it is by increased fear, usually re-
animates belief in the grosser superstitions" and adds
that "to many orthodox minds, Napoleon's meteoric career
suggested the frenzy of Satan because his time was short".

Spector, Robert Donald. Tobias George Smollett. Twayne's   3/41
English Author Series. New York: Twayne, 1968.

Asserts that the Gothic episodes in Ferdinand Count Fathom
are part of the satiric framework, and argues that Smollett
was never seriously interested in the novel of terror.
"Smollett's apparitions", Spector says, "invariably turn
out the tools of the humorist; his supernatural, the material to evoke laughter."

Sutherland, James. "The Relation of Defoe's Fiction to his   3/42
Non-Fictional Writing", in Maynard Mack and Ian Gregor,
eds., Imagined Worlds: Essays on Some English Novels
and Novelists in Honor of John Butt. London: Methuen,
1968.

Shows how Defoe retouched an allegedly true ghost story in
order to make Mrs. Veal more credible.

Westcott, Isabel M., ed. Seventeenth-Century Tales of the   3/43
Supernatural. Augustan Reprint Society, No. 74. Los
Angeles: Clark Memorial Library, UCLA, 1958.

Four short tales written between 1675 and 1698. "Ann
Jeffries" tells of a servant girl and little green fairies;
"Six Seamen" deals with demonic possession, owes to the
Cambridge Platonists, and is a possible source for Coleridge's Ancient Mariner; "Houses Under Ground" discovers
the Devil's dwelling place; and "O-Brazile", the most
novel-like, offers a story of sailors, an enchanted island, a necromancer's curse, and features groans from a
castle.

d.

The Continental Background

Coleridge, Samuel Taylor. Collected Letters. Edited by   3/44
Earl Leslie Griggs. Oxford: Clarendon, 1956.

In a letter to Southey, dated 3 Nov., 1794, Coleridge
writes: "I sat down at 12 o'clock to read The Robbers of
Schiller -- I had read chill and trembling until I came
to the part where Moor fires a pistol over the robbers
who are asleep -- I could read no more -- My God! Southey!
Who is this Schiller? This convulser of the heart? Did
he write his tragedy amid the yelling of fiends? -- I
should not like to be able to describe such characters --
I tremble like an aspen leaf -- Upon my soul, I write to
you because I am frightened -- I had better go to Bed.
Why have we ever called Milton sublime? That Count de
Moor -- horrible wielder of heart-withering virtues --!
Satan is scarcely qualified to attend his execution as
gallows chaplain -- "

Grieder, Josephine. "The Prose Fiction of Baculard D'Arnaud   3/45
in Late Eighteenth-Century England", FS, XXIV (1970),
113-126.

Between 1772 and 1786 D'Arnaud was extremely popular in
England and some thirty translations of his works appeared, mainly in magazines. In France he was praised
for le sombre which he used "as a means of reintroducing
into a desiccated classicism the renewed spirit of pity,
terror, and wonder", but this side was not entirely known
to his English audience. His dramas, the chief vehicle
for le sombre were never translated; translators picked
novels "more notable for their sentiment than for their
horror", and scenes of violence were often cut out, or
cut down.

Havens, George R. The Abbe Prévost and English Literature   3/46
[1921]. Elliot Monographs on the Romance Languages and
Literatures. New York: Haskell, 1965.

Offers biography and examines Prévost's literary criticism. Of no value for a study of the Gothic novel.

Mackenzie, Henry. "Account of the German Theatre", Trans-   3/47
actions of the Royal Society of Edinburgh, II (1790),
154-192.

Read by Mackenzie on 21 April, 1788, this paper surveys
German literature, deals with Lessing, Goethe, Klopstock,
Brandes, and others, but reserves the highest praise for
Schiller. He notes that German drama disregards "the
regularities and the decorum of the stage" and uses murder and madness "as often as that of the ancient English
tragedy". No restraint appears. "Its horrors and its
distress assault the imagination and the heart of the
reader with unsparing force; it loves to trace those horrors and that distress through every scene and every situation in which they can be found. . . ." Die Räuber,
he calls "one of the most uncommon productions of un-
tutored genius that modern times can boast", and notes
its thrills, horrors, chills, and "horrid sublimity".

McKillop, Alan D. "The First English Translator of Werther",   3/48
MLN, XLIII (1928), 36-38.

Claims that the Rev. Richard Graves produced in 1779 the
first English translation of Werther. (See also p. 467.
McKillop is informed of a prior discovery by Wm. Speck.)

Morgan, Bayard Quincy. A Critical Bibliography of German 3/49
Literature in English Translation 1481-1927 [1938].
2nd ed., revised. New York: Scarecrow, 1965.

A valuable tool for tracing crosscurrents. Unfortunately,
print is small, close, and difficult to read. Two later
supplements (1965; 1972) extend the range to 1960.

--------, and A.R. Hohlfeld, eds. German Literature in Brit- 3/50
ish Magazines 1750-1860. (Walter Roloff for 1750-1810;
Morton E. Mix for 1811-1835; and Martha Nicolai for 1836-
1860.) Madison: Univ. of Wisconsin Press, 1949.

Includes an excellent short survey of English interest in
German literature and has notes on groups and authors.
Examines 164 British magazines and gives summaries or ex-
tracts of reviews and articles on German literature.

Stockley, V[iolet]. German Literature as Known in England 3/51
1750-1830. London: Routledge, 1929.

The author concerns herself with the actual work of translation, the translators, and the critical and popular reception of these translations. She avoids the topic of
influence upon English literature since Stokoe (3/52) has
already covered this. Includes extracts and paraphrases
of articles in contemporary reviews. Appends a chronological list of translations and a bibliography.

Stokoe, F[rank] W. German Influence in the English Romantic 3/52
Period 1788-1818 [1926]. New York: Russell & Russell,
1963.

A list of vague, general information which proves what is
already known -- that German literature became popular or
was popular. Stokoe seems embarrassed about the Schauerromane, calls it one of the "inferior productions of German literature" and says that Lewis's use of German stories
"contributed no doubt to bring about the disrepute which
attached so long to German literature in England".

Waterhouse, G. "Schiller's Räuber in England Before 1800", 3/53
MLR, XXX (1935), 355-357.

Reproduces an anonymous account of Schiller's Räuber
from the Dublin Chronicle of 29 Nov., 1788, which "ante-
dates in publication, if not in composition, what has

46

hitherto been regarded as the first English criticism of
this play, viz. Henry Mackenzie's 'Account of the German Theatre' read before the Royal Society of Edinburgh
on April 21st, 1788, and first published in 1790".

Woodbridge, Benjamin M.   "Romantic Tendencies in the Novels   3/54
of the Abbe Prévost", PMLA, XXVI (1911), 324-332.

Notes several "romantic" characteristics in Cleveland
(1732) which are not thought to have found expression
until a later date. These include subjective sensibility, a pleasurable melancholy, confession, belief in
uniqueness of one's misery, feeling of persecution of
a malign deity, cult of pessimism, suicidal feelings,
cult of the restless wanderer, and a "gruesome horror . . .
[which] would do credit to the romances of Mrs. Anne
Radcliffe".

IV

THE PSYCHOLOGICAL, SOCIAL, AND SCIENTIFIC BACKGROUND

a.

Pathological Studies

Bartel, Roland. "Suicide in Eighteenth-Century England: 4/1
The Myth of a Reputation", HLQ, XXIII (1960), 145-158.

In the 18th century, the English "acquired a reputation
that they came to regard as a major national problem.
They were accused of committing suicide at the slightest provocation and of having the highest suicide rate
in the world." Rev. Charles Moor's study on suicide
(1790) "concluded that England's reputation was more
apparent than real and that English tragedians were partly
to blame because of the way they glamorized suicide on
the stage". Encyclopedia Britannica of 1797 denied that
England had a high rate and attributed the reputation to
"the custom of publishing in the newspapers every instance
of suicide which is known".

Doughty, Oswald. "The English Malady of the Eighteenth Cen-   4/2
tury", RES, II (1926), 257-269.

During the 17th century, that malady called spleen, the
vapours, depression, or low spirits, was regarded as "a
physical evil, the bad temper induced by colds, fogs, lack
of warmth and sun". Later, towards the close of the 18th
century, the spleen became poetic and merged into "the
romantic love of the sombre and mournful". With the Romantics, this melancholy "sprang from a realisation of the
discrepancy between reality and ideal life as pictured by
the romantic imagination".

Freud, Sigmund. "The 'Uncanny'" [Das Unheimliche], in James   4/3
Strachey, et al., eds., The Standard Edition of the Com-
plete Psychological Works of Sigmund Freud. 23 vols.
London: Hogarth, 1955.

Freud rejects the simple solution that uncanny = unfamiliar
= fear-producing and takes his lead from Schelling who
says "everything is unheimlich that ought to have remained

48

secret and hidden but has come to life". Freud looks at
Hoffmann's Sand Man, sees the fear of being robbed of
one's eyes as a fear of castration and equates the Sand
Man with the terrible father. He links the double with
the fear of death, premature burial to prenatal existence.
Neurotic men, Freud believes, feel there is something
uncanny about the female genital organs. He concludes
that "an uncanny experience occurs either when infantile
complexes which have been repressed are once more revived by some impression, or when primitive beliefs
which have been surmounted seem once more to be confirmed."

Jones, Ernest. On the Nightmare. The Internation Psycho-   4/4
Analytical Library, No. 20. London: Hogarth, 1931.

Attempts "to estimate the part that nightmare experiences
have played in the production of certain false ideas . . .
incubus, vampire, werewolf, devil and witchcraft". The
nightmare stems from "the burden of guilt and fear every-
one inherits in his unconscious from the deepest stirrings
of mental life, the primordial conflict over incest" and
displays three cardinal features: "agonizing dread;
sense of oppression or weight at the chest . . .; con-
viction of helpless paralysis", and among "less conspic-
uous features" there exists "sometimes a flow of seminal
or vaginal secretions". Jones stresses that "even in the
most terrifying nightmare the Angst often has a distinctly
traceable voluptuous character." All five -- incubus,
vampire, werewolf, devil, and witch are closely related
but with differences. "The masochistic component of the
sexual instinct comes to expression in the incubus belief, the sadistic in the werewolf", and the vampire theme
displays a much larger share of guilt and hate. The Oedipal concept fosters the Devil -- the bad as opposed to the
good father, and the feminine counterpart of this infantile
situation is bound up with the witch -- a being noted for
causing impotence. This study does not restrict itself to
the medical and psychiatric aspects, but deals also in
literature, theology, real life monsters, criminals, and
ranges widely through time and space.

Miyoshi, Masao. The Divided Self: A Perspective on the   4/5
Literature of the Victorians. New York: New York Univ.
Press, 1969.

Says the Gothic villain reappears in the late 19th century as the divided self, the double, the doppelgänger,
or as the Romantic ideal. Notes that two currents run

49

through the 19th century, the "realistic" novel and the
Gothic romance, and "by the time of Dickens and the Brontë
sisters, it was the'unrealistic' romance that suggested
new ways of exploring the unconscious and the irrational,
the other self, within the framework of the novel". Looks
at Otranto, The Monk, Vathek, Caleb Williams, Frankenstein,
and many other romances. Sees the Gothic villain as "a
modern archetype for alienated man divided against himself";
notes the obsession with sex, especially incest; discusses
the homosexual elements. Shows that early Gothicists bequeathed much more than squeaky doors and mechanical devices.

Praz, Mario. The Romantic Agony [1933]. Translated by Angus   4/6
    Davidson. Cleveland: World, 1968.

    Deals with the new erotic sensibility of the 19th century
    and traces the influence of Byron and De Sade. Notes the
    inseparability of pleasure and pain and the strange at-
    traction of horror. "The Horrid, from being a category
    of the Beautiful, ended by becoming one of its essential
    elements and the 'beautifully horrid' passed by insensible
    degrees into the 'horribly beautiful'".

Rank, Otto. The Double: A Psychoanalytic Study [1925].   4/7
    Translated, and with an introduction by Harry Tucker,
    Jr. Chapel Hill: Univ. of North Carolina Press, 1971.

    Discusses the persistence of the doppelgänger as a Roman-
    tic theme; looks at Hoffmann, Poe, and Maupassant, noting
    problems in sexual matters, in personal relations, with
    alcohol and drugs, and with egocentric orientation. Con-
    cludes that the double represents elements of self-love
    which preclude a balanced personality -- that the indi-
    vidual transfers to his double, responsibility for guilt
    and fear of death. Accepts Freud's link of paranoia with
    homosexuality and sees the homosexual love object chosen
    with a narcissistic attitude. "The literary representa-
    tions of the double-motif which describe the persecution
    complex confirm not only Freud's concept of the narcis-
    sistic disposition toward paranoia, but also, in an in-
    tuition rarely attained by the mentally ill, they reduce
    their chief pursuer to the ego itself, the person formerly
    loved most of all, and now direct their defense against
    it."

Thorslev, Peter L., Jr. "Incest as Romantic Symbol", Com-   4/8
parative Literature Studies (Univ. of Md.), II (1965),
41-58.

Traces the theme of incest from Sophocles to O'Neill, but
deals mainly with the Romantics. Credits the Gothic
novelists with reintroducing the theme and says that with
these first practitioners, there was a "significance beyond its appeal to the sensibilities of excitable female
readers". Thus, "a good deal of credit must go to these
Gothic forerunners of Romanticism, who were exploring
sibling rivalry, father-hatred, and Oedipal love well
before the Romantic poets came on the scene."

Tymms, Ralph. Doubles in Literary Psychology. Cambridge: 4/9
Bowes & Bowes, 1949.

While Rank (4/7) uses a psychoanalytical approach, Tymms
pursues the literary aspects of the doppelgänger. He
finds a source for the double in Locke and traces the development of the motif in its own dual roles of realism
and allegory. He rejects Rank's interpretation of the
double as based on narcissism. This, says Tymms, may apply to Dorian Gray, Elixiere, and a few others, but is
only part of the story. The study devotes the most attention to Hoffmann, Dostoevsky, and Poe, but deals also
with Jean Paul Richter, Goethe, Fouqué, Hauff, Hans Andersen, Dickens, Hawthorne, Bulwer-Lytton, R.L. Stevenson,
and Maupassant.

b.

Criminal Studies

De La Torre, Lillian, ed. Villainy Detected: Being a Col-   4/10
lection of the Most Sensational True Crimes and the Most
Notorious Real Criminals that Blotted the Name of Britain
in the Years 1660 to 1800. New York: Appleton-Century,
1947.

Accounts of crimes taken from various sources both contemporary and modern. Includes Andrew Lang's "The Camp-
den Mystery", Defoe's "The Ride of Swift Nicks", Scott's
"The Gipsy Foot-pad", Swift's "Clever Tom Clinch Going to
be Hanged", plus extracts from Newgate Calendar, a chap-

book story of Jack Sheppard, an anonymous ballad, and
other assorted tales of villainy.

Hibbert, Christopher. The Road to Tyburn: The Story of   4/11
Jack Sheppard and the Eighteenth Century Underworld.
Toronto: Longmans, Green, 1957.

A biography of Jack Sheppard with chapters on Newgate,
Tyburn Fair, the general background of crimes and punish-
ments and conditions of the poor. Includes a bibliography with many works on crime, criminals, prisons, etc.,
and a glossary of cant terms.

Howson, Gerald. Thief-Taker General: The Rise and Fall of   4/12
Jonathan Wild. London: Hutchinson, 1970.

This new biography of Wild draws extensively on original
records, has many illustrations and a long annotated
bibliography.

Kerman, Sandra Lee, ed. The Newgate Calendar or Malefactor's 4/13
Bloody Register. New York: Capricorn, 1962.

A paperback, "illustrated profusely from the original
editions". Offers an introduction dealing with 18th-cen-
tury crime, criminals, and prison conditions.

Masters, R.E.L., and Eduard Lea. Perverse Crimes in History 4/14
Evolving Concepts of Sadism, Lust-murder, and Necro-
philia -- from Ancient to Modern Times. New York:
Julian, 1963.

A horrifying account of real-life monsters: vampires,
werewolves, rippers, necrophiles, necrosadists, necro-
phagists, and other assorted types. Mentions theory of
erotic excitation produced by fear; sees vampirism as a
disguised inversion of necrophilia; says Praz's Romantic
Agony (4/6) should be a required text for every student of
sexual crime. Has case histories of several vampires including the cave-dwelling Argentinian who, attired in a
black hat and cloak, in a single week in 1960, crawled
through open windows to attack, bite the throats of, and
suck blood from fifteen women.

Sherwin, Oscar. "Crime and Punishment in England of the   4/15
Eighteenth Century", American Journal of Economics and
Sociology, V (1946), 169-199.

A survey covering infant mortality, disease, drinking,
gin shops, the multitude of poor, workhouses, dangers of
the streets, pickpockets, footpads, highwaymen, linkboys,
watchmen, capital offences, transportation, state of
prisons, reformers, debtors, the spectacle of an execution,
and rogue biographies. A gathering together of secondary
sources.

c.

Wanderers, Witches, Devils, and Demons

Addison, Joseph. Spectator, No. 117 (July 14, 1711), in   4/16
Donald F. Bond, ed., The Spectator. 3 vols. Oxford:
Clarendon, 1965.

This paper on the witch, Moll White, indicates that belief
in the powers of darkness remained strong. Addison
writes: "I believe in general that there is and has been
such a thing as witchcraft, but at the same time can give
no credit to any particular instance of it."

Anderson, George K. The Legend of the Wandering Jew. Prov-   4/17
idence: Brown Univ. Press, 1965.

Long, scholarly, well-documented, undoubtedly the definitive work on the Wanderer. Traces the changing conception
of this figure from his earliest beginnings until the Romantics elevate him to symbol. Discusses Schiller, Lewis,
Coleridge, Goethe, Godwin, and others, but stress of
study falls in post-Gothic period. Comments on all Wandering-Jew tales and provides critical evaluation of
scholarship in that field.

--------. "The Neo-Classical Chronicle of the Wandering   4/18
Jew", PMLA, LXIII (1948), 199-213.

Discusses the role, function, and didactic elements in the
Wandering-Jew stories of the 17th and 18th centuries, eras
which did not view the outcast as a Byronic rebel. Ap-

pendix lists 44 topics which were "considered important
enough to be included in the neo-classical Chronicle of
the Wandering Jew".

Andrews, S.G. "The Wandering Jew and the Travels and Adven-   4/19
tures of James Massey", MLN, LXXII (1957), 39-41.

Cites a previously unnoted reference to the Wandering Jew
in 18th-century literature: Simon Tyssot de Patot's
Voyages et Aventures de Jacques Masse, translated to English in 1733 as The Travels and Adventures of James Massey. Here, for the first time, the Wanderer appears "in
order to make an authoritative pronouncement upon a . . .
fine point of medieval theology".

Gaer, Joseph. The Legend of the Wandering Jew. Mentor Books. 4/20
New York: New American Library, 1961.

Popular and semi-scholarly; brief and sketchy. Contains
illustrations by Gustave Doré and a brief annotated bibliography.

Glanvill, Joseph. Saducismus Triumphatus: or, Full and   4/21
Plain Evidence Concerning Witches and Apparitions [1689].
Introduction by Coleman O. Parsons. Gainesville:
Scholar's Facsimiles & Reprints, 1966.

A facsimile reprint of the third edition of 1689. No
notes or index have been added, but Parsons does offer an
excellent introduction and appends a brief bibliography.
The introduction treats Glanvill's influence on literature, but unfortunately, says nothing about the Gothic
period. Addison, Defoe, Poe, Hogg, and Scott are mentioned; attention is paid to Henry More, George Sinclair
and John Dunton.

Hansen, Chadwick. Witchcraft at Salem [1969]. Signet Books. 4/22
New York: New American Library, 1970.

Professor Hansen of Penn. State contends that witches and
witchcraft existed at Salem, their spells worked, the
victims suffered real symptoms, Puritanism played little
part in the persecutions; in fact, the clergy opposed the
proceedings. Illustrated, and with a very brief annotated bibliography.

Hole, Christina. A Mirror of Witchcraft. London: Chatto &   4/23
Windus, 1957.

"An attempt to show, by means of extracts from contemporary writings and trial-reports, what was in fact
thought and felt by educated or illiterate people during
the hey-day of the witch-creed." Ranges from Anglo-
Saxon times to the 1950's, but for the most part, concerns itself with the 16th century. Says some English
witches worshipped Satan, others, survivors of pagan fer-
tility cults, worshipped a much older god.

Kittredge, George Lyman. Witchcraft in Old and New England   4/24
[1929]. New York: Russell& Russell, 1958.

Kittredge says he is no believer, tackles the topic from
the viewpoint of folklore, and seems more amused than
repulsed. The study extends from Anglo-Saxon days to the
20th century, covers England and the Continent, and although it does touch on New England, the title seems to
suggest more coverage than is offered. Amusing anecdotes
and quaint cures are brought forward, and demon lovers,
curses, charms, sabbaths, trials, laws, etc., are covered.
Kittredge rejects the idea that English witchcraft represents vestiges of pagan rituals; says there was no organization, the sabbath came over from Europe after 1612.
Notes the lack of ritual and denies all social, political,
and theological complications. The Salem cases he sees
as typical, not exceptional, and in no way a part of
Puritanism or a result of Colonial living.

Langton, Edward. Essentials of Demonology: A Study of Jew-   4/25
ish and Christian Doctrine, Its Origin and Development.
London: Epworth, 1949.

Langton, a Doctor of Divinity and author of several works
on Satan, spirits, and supernaturalism, offers here a
theologian's examination of demonology. Jesus, he asserts,
accepted the Jewish beliefs in the existence of Satan and
demons but this cannot be taken as proof of their existence since Christ suffered human limitations.

Lea, Henry Charles. <u>Materials Toward A History of Witch-</u>   4/26
<u>craft</u> [1939]. Arranged and edited by Arthur C. Howland.
Introduction by George Lincoln Burr. 3 vols. New York:
Yoseloff, 1957.

Professor Lea of the University of Pennsylvania died in
1909, leaving 2,000 foolscap pages (longhand on both sides
of the page) of notes on witchcraft. Burr received the
notes, but later handed them on to Howland who worked
miracles in organizing, arranging and editing. Finally,
thirty years after Lea's death, his <u>Materials</u> saw publication. A storehouse of information encompassing
three volumes and 1550 pages, the work is certainly for
the specialist, and when one begins to read, the reason
for the title becomes apparent. The volumes contain no
index and the old-fashioned "Table of Contents" simply
doesn't compensate.

Mackenzie, Henry. <u>Lounger</u>, No. 41 (Nov. 12, 1785),in <u>The</u>   4/27
<u>Works of Henry Mackenzie, Esq</u>. 8 vols. Edinburgh:
Ballantyne, 1808.

Prints a letter from "Antiguo-Modernus", who, unlike the
young people of his day, has more reverence for the penetration of his forefathers and asserts that indeed, witchcraft does exist. Cites examples which "still continue
to be practiced in modern times" -- image magic, pins and
dolls, nightly meetings of witches, pacts with the Devil,
and invisible transportation.

Parsons, Coleman O. "Ghost-Stories Before Defoe", <u>N&Q</u>, CCI   4/28
(1956), 293-298.

Says that towards the end of the 17th century, there oc-
currs a shift in ghost-stories "from propaganda to pas-
time, from indoctrination to literary entertainment".
This trail becomes investigated with emphasis on Glanvill,
More, Sinclair, and Baxter. Lists eight "devices of his
predecessors which Defoe artfully combined" in <u>Mrs. Veal</u>.
Says "both Scott and Stevenson did much prospecting in
the 17th century and refined narrative gold from neglected
ores"; claims George MacDonald "appropriated" two vampire
stories from More.

Prior, Moody E. "Joseph Glanvill, Witchcraft, and Seven-   4/29
teenth-Century Science", MP, XXX (1932), 167-193.

Asserts that Glanvill's Sadducismus Triumphatus (1666),
"by a Member of the Royal Society", is not a contradiction
of scientific scruples and remains entirely consistent
with 17th-century thought since a defense of witchcraft
represented a defense of Christianity against atheism.
Says, of all the English thinkers of "first rate importance" of that century, only Hobbes opposed the belief in
witchcraft.

Robbins, Rossell Hope. The Encyclopedia of Witchcraft and   4/30
Demonology [1959]. London: Peter Nevill, 1964.

Draws on the "biggest and best collection in the world
for a study of witchcraft", the holdings assembled by
Cornell's first president, Andrew Dickson White. The next
best collection, Robbins says, is the Henry Charles Lea
Collection at the University of Pennsylvania, but Lea's
Materials (4/26) is limited as it does not utilize the
Cornell holdings, and "is best appreciated by the reader
who knows Latin, French, and German, and already is acquainted with the subject". This present study represents
"a distillation of more than 1000 primary works on witchcraft" and attempts a rational, balanced history of three
centuries" of witchcraft, a subject "in the province of
theology". Robbins does not share Summers' credulity
(4/33; 4/34), or Kittredge's humor (4/24) and presents a
horrid, disturbing picture of persecuting clergymen, false
accusations, rape, torture, and mutilation, and explains
how witch hunting made money and brought business to the
communities.

Rudwin, Maximilian. The Devil in Legend and Literature.   4/31
Chicago: Open Court, 1931.

"Satanism is not a part of Romanticism. It is Romanticism." The French Revolution caused a revival of interest in supernaturalism, and Rudwin contends that the
Romantics worshipped Satan. "The spirit of revolution
is at the very root of Romanticism", he claims, and asserts that the poets saw Satan as an object of devotion
"staggering beneath the unjust condemnation of a superior
power". Also, he says that "the Romantics could never
speak of Satan without tears of sympathy. . . . They
pitied the fallen angel as an outlaw; they applauded him
as a rebel."

Shorr, Philip. Science and Superstition in the Eighteenth   4/32
Century: A Study of the Treatment of Science in Two
Encyclopedias of 1725-1750. (Chamber's Cyclopedia:
London, 1728 and Zedler's Universal Lexicon: Leipzig,
1732-1750). No 364, Studies in History, Economics and
Public Law. Edited by the Faculty of Political Science
of Columbia University. New York: Columbia Univ. Press,
1932.

Looks at two 18th-century encyclopedias, one English,
the other German, and turns up much that seems to indicate
that this era was not quite the rational, scientific one
we usually picture. Much of medieval science remains.
Chambers believes in alchemy, the philosophers' stone,
amulets, witchcraft, physiognomy, and advances absurd
treatments for physical ills, i.e., the moss of a dead
man's skull applied to the skin cures nosebleeds. Zedler's work shares this belief in magic, the devil, and
witchcraft; asserts that animals can speak, reason, and
forecast weather; suggests anyone rendered impotent by
witchcraft might: (1)step over a broom, (2)urinate
through his wife's wedding ring, (3)boil urine in a
tightly closed pot.

Summers, Montague. The History of Witchcraft and Demonology.   4/33
New York: Knopf, 1926.

Says he attempts to show the witch as "an evil liver, a
social pest and a parasite; the devotee of a loathly and
obscene creed; an adept at poisoning, blackmail, and
other creeping crimes, a member of a powerful secret organization inimical to Church and State; a blasphemer in
word and deed; swaying the villagers by terror and superstition; a charlatan and a quack sometimes; a bawd, an
abortionist; the dark counsellor of lewd court ladies and
adultorous gallants; a minister to vice and inconceivable
corruption; battening upon the filth and foulest passions
of the age". Includes a chapter entitled "The Witch in
Dramatic Literature".

--------. The Geography of Witchcraft [1927]. New Hyde   4/34
Park: University Books, 1965.

"The present work", Summers says, "may be regarded as a
complementary volume to or even a second volume of, my
History of Witchcraft and Demonology. There I spoke of
general principles; here I give particulars." He examines
witchcraft in Greece, Rome, England, Scotland, New England, France, Germany, Italy and Spain, offers accounts,

anecdotes, and his own firm opinions. Says some of accused witches were innocent, but "there were many who belonged to that dark and anarchical company which seeks to destroy all social order, to corrupt and to pollute, to replace Christianity by the worship of the Devil. Nor must we suppose that this is wholly a thing of the past."

Summers, Montague, trans. and ed. <u>Malleus Maleficarum</u>   4/35
[1928]. New York: Benjamin Blom, 1970.

Summers calls <u>MM</u> "one of the most pregnant and most interesting books I know in the library of its kind", notes that it was once "used as a standard text-book" but has since been abused and ridiculed by writers who haven't read it. Written in the late 15th century by the German clerics, Sprenger and Kramer, this work represents an ecclesiastical investigation into witches and witchcraft, notes cures and preventatives for spells, discusses legal action, tortures, and is, says Summers, a "mighty treatise" even if it does contain misogynic passages.

d.

Ghosts, Vampires, and Werewolves

Baine, Rodney M. "Daniel Defoe and <u>The History and Reality</u>   4/36
<u>of Apparitions</u>", <u>PAPS</u>, CVI (1962), 335-347.

"Through his <u>History and Reality of Apparitions</u> and its frequently reprinted narratives, Defoe helped to shape the popular thinking of his century concerning apparitions, for his stories were reprinted, usually without acknowledgement, far into the following century." Shows where Defoe obtained his materials, how he reshaped and reformed them; notes his unswerving Christianity, his concern with moralizing, his view that apparitions are an intermediate type of spirit, beneficent yet not Heavenly, and not of the Devil.

Grant, Douglas. <u>The Cock Lane Ghost</u>. New York: St. Mar-   4/37
tin's, 1965.

An entertaining account, based on contemporary news items, pamphlets, and the trial transcript, but unfortunately, devoid of footnotes. Devotes special attention to John-

son, Boswell, Goldsmith, Churchill, Walpole, Garrick, and
Hogarth. Notes that Walpole mocked the Cock Lane ghost,
but two years later offered Otranto to the public.

Lavater, Lewes. Of Ghosts and Spirites Walking by Nyght.   4/38
Edited by J. Dover Wilson and May Yardley. Printed for
the Shakespeare Association. Oxford: Univ. Press, 1929.

A treatise written in 1570 by Lavater, a Swiss Protestant
theologian and published in London in 1572, in a translation by "R.H.", which sets forth the Protestant view
and attacks the Catholic doctrine of Purgatory. J. Dover
Wilson's introduction covers "The Ghost-scenes in Hamlet
in the Light of Elizabethan Spiritualism" and Miss Yardley
appends an essay, "The Catholic Position in the Ghost Controversy of the 16th Century, with Special Reference to
Pierre Le Loyer's IIII Livres des Spectres (1586)".

McNally, Raymond T. and Radu Florescu. In Search of Dracula: 4/39
A True History of Dracula and Vampire Legends. Greenwich:
New York Graphic Society, 1972.

Two professors collaborated to present this triple treat --
a study of the historical Dracula and his castle; a look
at the Dracula of Stoker; and an investigation of vampire
lore in Transylvania, present and past. Includes a chapter on the vampire in fiction and film and has valuable
bibliographies of vampire novels, studies, films, etc.

"The Man-Wolf, From the Portuguese of M. D'Oliveira",   4/40
Monthly Mirror, XII (1801), 241-244.

Reports that in Portugal, the people believe in the Lup-
tus-homo, "a man who at night changes his natural form
for that of a wolf or a great dog. . . . It is called a
Fado, or a destiny which he cannot avoid, if he is a
seventh son of the same father and mother, without the
intervention of any daughter." The wolf-man roams the
streets by night, carefully avoiding man, pursued by dogs
against which he must protect himself until he becomes
restored. If blood can be drawn from the loupgaron, an
instant and permanent transformation will be effected.
The author says that although he slashed at "a great number" of dogs, he cannot say that he "ever had the good
fortune to rid any poor devil of his fado".

Masters, Anthony. The Natural History of the Vampire.   4/41
London: Rupert Hart-Davis, 1972.

An introductory work with little interest for learned
vampirists, this book draws heavily on Summers and other
men and offers little in the way of an original contribution. Two noteworthy chapters look at the vampire in
literature, the movies, and television. Masters sees the
vampire as a sexual deviate and points out that homosexuality was a common trait in many of the "real vampires".
Contains a long bibliography and many illustrations.

Speculum Linnaeanum: or Linnaean Zoology. . . . , by George   4/42
Shaw. Reviewed in Analytical Review, IX (1791), 191-
192.

Reviewer explains why the vampire bat bears this name.
"The Vampyre is an imaginary monster, supposed to suck
the blood of sleeping persons. It also alludes to one
of the most absurd superstitions that ever entered the
human mind. About the year 1732, an idea arose amongst
the vulgar, in some parts of Poland and Hungary, that
certain bodies, when interred, became possessed of a
power of extracting blood from the bodies of those who
were so unlucky as to pass over, or stand near their
graves; and that by this means they swelled to an enormous degree, with the blood thus absorbed from the various persons, who were themselves weakened in proportion.
Such bodies were called Vampyres. It was supposed to be
necessary to disinter and open them, or wound them with
a sword, by which means this pernicious power was put a
stop to, and the blood they had unjustly gained was
evacuated."

Summers, Montague. The Vampire, His Kith and Kin. New York: 4/43
Dutton, 1929.

"The first serious study in English of the Vampire, and
kindred traditions from a general, as well as from a
theological and philosophical point of view." Concludes
that "it is hard to believe that a phenomenon which has
had so complete a hold over nations both old and young,
in all parts of the world, at all times of history, has
not some underlying and terrible truth however rare this
may be in its more remarkable manifestations." The study
covers appearance, characteristics, causes for, feeding
habits of, and precautions to be taken against. Includes
case histories, ancient accounts, an anthropological-type

survey of various nations, asides on premature burial, necrophilia, and various perverse and antisocial acts. Contains a chapter on the vampire in literature and a bibliography of both true and fictitious vampires. A fascinating account which proves the old adage about truth and fiction.

Summers, Montague. The Werewolf [1933]. New Hyde Park: 4/44
University Books, 1966.

Asserts that werewolves exist and are the victims of demonic possession. Complete with case histories of ferocious, ravenous wolves, house cats assisted by Satan, and with a bibliography containing books in various and sundry languages.

Wolf, Leonard. A Dream of Dracula: In Search of the Living   4/45
Dead. Boston: Little, Brown, 1972.

A half-hip, widely ranging look at the Dracula scene, with attention to its sexual roots. Highly appreciative of Stoker's novel. Has comments on Walpole, Lewis and Mrs. Radcliffe.

V

EIGHTEENTH-CENTURY GOTHIC, IN GENERAL STUDIES

a.

Surveys of the Novel

Allen, Walter. The English Novel: A Short Critical His-   5/1
tory. London: Phoenix, 1959.

Offers a very brief coverage of the Gothic novel. Highly
critical of Walpole. Praises Mrs. Radcliffe and Mrs.
Smith. Denies that the latter is a Gothic writer.

Baker, Ernest A. The Novel of Sentiment and the Gothic Ro-   5/2
mance. Vol. V of The History of the English Novel. London: Witherby, 1934.

Provides a lengthy coverage of Walpole, Reeve, the Lees,
Smith, Radcliffe, Lewis, Beckford, C.B. Brown, Mary Shelley, and Maturin. Rejects Walpole as father of the Gothic
novel; puts the start "either earlier or later" -- via
Prévost to Smollett and Leland, or to the Lee sisters.
Sees Recess as important. Praises Mrs. Smith; praises
Mrs. Radcliffe's atmosphere but sees her flaws. Almost
contemptuous of Lewis. Notes Gothic parodies; looks at
influence on Scott.

Cross, Wilbur L. The Development of the English Novel. New   5/3
York: Macmillan, 1899.

Says the Gothic novel bears traces of the newer "realistic novel" and is not a step backwards; however, since
it lacks plausible psychological motivation, it represents
melodrama -- not true tragedy. Credits Smollett with
pioneering a return to "magic, mystery, and chivalry".
Says he "gave to the romance its method of dealing with
the superstitious. Walpole gave it its machinery, its
characters, its castle, and its Gothic name." Notes contributions of the genre; offers a chapter on 19th-century
Gothic.

Neill, S. Diana. A Short History of the English Novel.   5/4
    London: Jarrolds, 1951.

    Chapter V, "The Gothic Romances", advances a brief and
    unimportant survey. Otranto is regarded as "amusing
    rather than frightening". Radcliffe becomes praised, but
    the implication seems that Lewis and German horror bring
    debasement. Chapter VI opens with the line: "The Novel
    of Terror -- by its repulsive themes and creaking arti-
    fices -- brought novel-reading into disrepute."

Phelps, William Lyon. The Advance of the English Novel.   5/5
    New York: Dodd, Mead, 1916.

    Dislikes Gothic; says "not one of these books is worth
    reading for its own sake". Otranto, "a worthless hodge-
    podge of gloom and tinsel that threw England into a fever
    of excitement . . . is more responsible than any other
    one book for releasing the flood of tales of mystery".

Raleigh, Walter. The English Novel: A Short Sketch of Its   5/6
    History From the Earliest Times to the Appearance of
    "Waverley" [1894]. London: John Murray, 1929.

    Chapter VIII, "The Revival of Romance", treats Gothic.
    Walpole he finds too crude, Mrs. Radcliffe too timid,
    Lewis too vulgar, but Maturin just right -- at "the head-
    ship of the School of Terror".

Saintsbury, George. The English Novel. London: Dent, 1913. 5/7

    Otranto is regarded as "preposterous, desultory, tedious,
    clumsy, dull"; the Monk "as preposterous as Otranto" and
    indecent; and The Old English Baron "is rather a bore".
    Highly critical also of Dacre, Wilkinson and the Lees.
    Has some good to say about Mrs. Smith; praises Mrs. Rad-
    cliffe.

Stevenson, Lionel. The English Novel: A Panorama. Boston: 5/8
    Houghton Mifflin, 1960.

    Regards Gothic as a development, not an invention. Otranto
    seems a pre-Richardson reversion; Reeve followed the
    Richardsonian moralizing; Smith's novels are based primar-
    ily on Richardson; Radcliffe's "imprisoned heroine came
    straight from Pamela and Clarissa". Says Mrs. Radcliffe

"stumbled upon the whole realm of the unconscious" and
her central theme of persecution   represents a "powerful sex symbol". Calls Mrs. Smith "the most respectable
novelist of the period (1790-1800)".

Tuckerman, Bayard. A History of English Prose Fiction From   5/9
Sir Thomas Malory to George Eliot. New York: Putnam's,
1882.

   "The works of Walpole, Clara Reeve, and particularly of
   Mrs. Radcliffe, contain very decided merits. They made
   a school which has found many admirers and has given a
   vast deal of pleasure. But the school was founded on
   wrong principles and could not endure. It is impossible
   for the mind to enjoy the supernatural while it is chained
   down to every-day life by realistic descriptions of
   scenes and persons."

Wagenknecht, Edward. Cavalcade of the English Novel [1943].   5/10
2nd ed. New York: Holt, Rinehart, and Winston, 1954.

   Denies that Otranto is the first Gothic novel; says Walpole "was fundamentally right in his preference for real,
   as opposed to a sham, supernaturalism, as his successors,
   Clara Reeve and Mrs. Radcliffe, were fundamentally wrong".
   Sees both merits and defects of Mrs. Radcliffe; calls
   Vathek "one of the minor classics of English literature";
   says "excepting the work of the acknowledged masters,
   [Old Manor House]   is surely one of the best romances in
   the whole realm of English fiction". Contains a valuable
   bibliography.

b.

Period Studies

Beers, Henry A. A History of English Romanticism in the   5/11
Eighteenth Century [1898]. New York: Henry Holt, 1926.

   Beers looks at architecture and aesthetics and traces the
   growth of melancholia, gloom, decay, and the Gothic
   spirit. Of Otranto, he says that nowadays "instead of
   keeping us out of bed, it sends us there -- or would, if
   it were a little longer". The Mysterious Mother he finds

"more absurd than horrible"; Old English Baron "is infinitely tiresome", but the Monk "is not a wholly contemptible work". It stands superior to the works of Mrs.
Radcliffe as "it has neither the excess of scenery nor of
sentiment which distinguishes that very prolix narrator".

Elton, Oliver. A Survey of English Literature 1780-1830.   5/12
2 vols. London: Edward Arnold, 1912.

Offers a general and undistinguished survey of Gothic
from Walpole to Maturin.

Foster, James R. History of the Pre-Romantic Novel in Eng-   5/13
land. Modern Language Association of America. Mono-
graph Series XVII. Baltimore: Waverley, 1949.

Aim is "to give an account of the pre-romantic narratives
which appeared in England during the eighteenth century
and to describe the French novels influencing them".
Provides good coverage of Prévost and asserts that either
directly or through D'Arnaud, he influenced Reeve, the
Lees, Bage, and Radcliffe. Gives extended coverage of
Reeve, the Lee sisters, Mrs. Smith, and Mrs. Radcliffe.
Offers shorter coverage of Mackenzie, Eliza Parsons, Mrs.
Helme, and Mrs. Roche.

Oliphant, Mrs. [Margaret]. The Literary History of England   5/14
in the End of the Eighteenth and Beginning of the Nineteenth Century. 3 vols. London: Macmillan, 1889.

Finds Udolpho old-fashioned in style and technique but
praises its characters and decorum. Says Beckford's
mixed style represents a defect, and the Monk "is hardly
up to the mark of a 'penny dreadful', even in point of
literary merit".

Saintsbury, George. A History of Nineteenth Century Litera-   5/15
ture (1780-1895). New York: Macmillan, 1896.

Says the Gothic novel, in general, represents a low literary value, but Mrs. Radcliffe is "not without glimmer-
ings". Praises Beckford, a writer esteemed superior to
Blake. Vathek, "in the florid kind of supernatural . . .
has no equal", and Travels has "extraordinary merits".

66

Saintsbury, George. The Peace of the Augustans: A Survey   5/16
of Eighteenth Century Literature as a Place of Rest and
Refreshment [1916]. New York: Oxford Univ. Press, 1951.

Contains but a brief and general outline of the Gothic
novel.

Steeves, Harrison R. Before Jane Austen: The Shaping of   5/17
the English Novel in the Eighteenth Century. New York:
Holt, Rinehart, and Winston, 1965.

Emphasis on biography, plot summary, and extracts. Sees
Vathek as outcome of Beckford's evil and perversion; can't
take Walpole seriously; says Reeve lacks inspiration.
Credits Ann Radcliffe with influencing the Romantics;
praises her descriptive effects but objects to the padding,
poor plots, delays, transparent suspense, slow and labored
explanation. Says "what Lewis attempted to do with the
Monk, and with no small success, was to raise sexual violence to the level of tragic significance".

Tompkins, J[oyce] M.S. The Popular Novel in England 1770-   5/18
1800 [1932]. Bison Books. Lincoln: Univ. of Nebraska
Press, 1962.

Important for the backgrounds of Gothic. Shows the growth
towards exotic, erotic, foreign, and sensational. Counters
the common notion that Gothic was an independent invention
or an offshoot of the sublime. Discusses also the status
of the novel, readers, publishers, reviewers, sales promo-
tions, etc. Tracks influences of Richardson and Fielding.
Sorts out French and German crosscurrents. Provides significant studies of Radcliffe, Reeve, Smith, Sophia Lee,
Walpole. A valuable source of information on relatively
obscure writers.

Williams, Ioan, ed. Novel and Romance 1700-1800: A Docu-   5/19
mentary Record. London: Routledge & Kegan Paul, 1970.

An anthology of 101 entries consisting of "prefaces to
collections, translations, and original novels; essays
written for journals modelled on the Spectator, passages
from miscellanies and from books written primarily for
some purpose unconnected with the novel; reviews from the
monthly reviews; and introductions to the collected works
of certain authors". Includes prefaces to Otranto and
Old English Baron, three essays by the Aikins, and reviews
of novels by Charlotte Smith and Ann Radcliffe.

Wright, Walter Francis. "Sensibility in English Prose Fic-   5/20
tion 1760-1814:   A Reinterpretation", ISLL, XXII (1937),
Nos. 3-4.

Purpose is to study the emotional impulses which inspired
the novelists and to show "how an author's emotions led
him to choose the devices he did choose and how they de-
termined his use of them". Sophia Lee was the first English novelist to unite the new forms of sensibility (Prévost, D'Arnaud, Burke, Hurd) with that descending from
Richardson. Charlotte Smith expanded sensibility further,
adding a sentimental depiction of nature, but it was Mrs.
Radcliffe who "polished the novel of sensibility to a
high degree". However, this same lady also brought on
the decadence of sensibility by sameness of incident and
character, overuse of scenery, and monotony.

c.

Studies in Women's Literature

Horner, Joyce M. "The English Women Novelists and their Con-   5/21
nection with the Feminist Movement (1688-1797)", Smith
College Studies in Modern Languages, XI (1929-30), Nos.
1-3.

A Smith College M.A. thesis which surveys the female
writers and looks in depth at Behn, Manley, Haywood, Len-
nox, Burney, D'Arblay, and Sarah Fielding. Mrs. Radcliffe
rates a few pages and many praises.

Kooiman-Van Middendorp, Gerarda Maria. The Hero in the Femi-   5/22
nine Novel [1931]. New York: Haskell, 1966.

States that "investigations . . . have proved that the female intellect is certainly not behind the male", and sets
out to see if the female novelists have created a new type
of hero. Looks at Clara Reeve in a 3 1/2-page chapter and
devotes another 3 1/2-page chapter to Mrs. Radcliffe. Concludes that "the hero is always a young lover, a noble,
generous gentleman of high birth, with whom the heroine
falls in love because of his amiable manners and capti-
vating appearance". Does not consider the villain as
hero.

MacCarthy, B[ridget] G. The Later Women Novelists, 1744-1818. 5/23
Dublin: Cork Univ. Press, 1947.

Consists mainly of old-fashioned criticism; examines plot
realism, looks for well-drawn characters and anachronisms.
Critical of Walpole and Reeve; likes the Lees and Mrs.
Smith. Sees good in Ann Radcliffe, but finds she suffered
because of sexual discrimination. Mrs. Radcliffe represents "the supreme example of genuine literary power mis-
directed for want of education".

Whitmore, Clara H. Woman's Work in English Fiction From the 5/24
Restoration to the Mid-Victorian Period. New York: Putnam's, 1910.

"Written from a woman's viewpoint", and asserts that men
and women have different taste in novels. Notes that many
fine novels written by women have "sunk into oblivion because literary scholarship is a man's domain. Discusses
Reeve, Smith, and Radcliffe, but offers only plot summary
and generalities.

d.

Books and Publishers

Ashton, John. Chap-Books of the Eighteenth Century [1882].   5/25
New York: Benjamin Blom, 1966.

An anthology of extracts from about 100 chapbook tales.
Stories include "The Wandering Jew", "Faustus", and several
tales of witches, ghosts, and various and sundry monsters.
With many original illustrations.

Blakey, Dorothy. The Minerva Press 1790-1820. Oxford: 5/26
Univ. Press, 1939.

A study of William Lane, his press, circulating libraries,
book production, sales practices, and the authors who contributed to him. Minerva handled much sensational and
Gothic, including the works of Mrs. Kelly, Mrs. Parsons,
Frances Lathom, Mrs. Meeke, Mrs. Roche, and Mrs. Sleath.
Also, Lane printed the British editions of C.B. Brown
and sold later editions of Mrs. Radcliffe and Charlotte

Smith. Appendix lists the Minerva output for 1773-1820, and shows the Gothic glut.

Mayo, Robert D. The English Novel in the Magazines 1740-   5/27
1815. With a Catalogue of 1375 Magazine Novels and
Novelettes. Evanston: Northwestern Univ. Press, 1962.

Between 1740 and 1815, 470 different periodicals carried
fiction of some sort, but as each tended to specialize,
no generalizations can be offered. About "a third of all
fiction published in volume form between 1796 and 1806
was frankly 'Gothic' in character, or at least included
important scenes of sentimental terror". Mayo investigates these magazines, defines Gothic tale and fragment,
looks at serial chapbooks, plagiarized abridgements, redactions, etc.

Varma, Devendra P. The Evergreen Tree of Diabolical Know-   5/28
ledge. Washington: Consortium, 1972.

Varma calls his work "a literary-curio, the jig-saw pieces
of a broken mirror reflecting some vignettes of 18th century life and literary movement". He describes the origins and growth of the circulating libraries, discusses
reading vogues, book-clubs, literary societies, and provides fascinating details on printing, binding, lending
rules and clientele. The work contains also an inventory
of circulating libraries in London, and offers many facsimiles from extant catalogues.

Weiss, Harry B. A Book About Chapbooks: The People's Liter-   5/29
ature of Bygone Times [1942]. Hatboro: Folklore Assoc.,
1969.

Deals with all types of chapbooks, both British and American. Of special interest are the chapters "Demonology
and Witchcraft", "Crimes and Criminals", and "Prose Fiction Chapbooks". Has a full coverage of size, shape,
price, printers, sellers, and a chapter devoted to each
variety -- from religious to joke book. Includes a bibliography, notes on chapbook collections in the U.S. and
Britain, and reproduces many original illustrations.

e.

Special Studies

Booth, Michael R. English Melodrama. London: Herbert   5/30
Jenkins, 1965.

Sees two kinds of Gothic melodrama: "The earlier the cas-
tle-dungeon-ghost variety, the later the bandit-forest-
cottage sort". Says "what the melodramatists did with the
Gothic novel was to simplify and intensify: wherever possible sensations were elaborated and the supernatural emphasized. Improvements in stage mechanics facilitated a
full display of ghosts, and where the novelists tended to
suggest horrors the playwrights made a satisfying physical
show of them." Looks at plays of Lewis, adaptations of
Mrs. Radcliffe's romances, vampire and monster melodramas,
the dog-dramas, and exotic Eastern plays.

Fiedler, Leslie A. Love and Death in the American Novel   5/31
[1960]. 2nd ed. New York: Dell, 1966.

Discusses "the failure of the American fictionist to deal
with adult heterosexual love and his consequent obsession
with death, incest and innocent homosexuality". Drawing
heavily on Freud and Jung, Fiedler has an intensely sex-
ual/mythical view of literature and sees the Gothic guilt
as "the guilt of the revolutionary haunted by the (paternal)
past which he has been striving to destroy". The maiden
in flight, the villain, the castle -- all are viewed as
symbols and the Gothic novel is regarded as avant-garde.

Fletcher, Angus. Allegory: The Theory of a Symbolic Mode.   5/32
Ithaca: Cornell Univ. Press, 1964.

Sheds new light on the Gothic novel and shows that there
is much more to the sublime and picturesque than physical
nature. Allegory is viewed as the "very life blood" of
romance. Allegorical protagonists are always demonic, and
existing between the human and the divine levels, touch at
times in either plane and, if viewed as "real people",
seem one-sided, possessed, obsessed, controlled by an external agency.

Frye, Northrop. Anatomy of Criticism: Four Essays [1957].   5/33
New York: Atheneum, 1969.

Discusses the Gothic villain as alazon. The obsessed
figure need not be restricted to comedy, but can be "one
aspect of the tragic hero as well". "The result as a
rule is not tragedy so much as the kind of melodrama
which may be defined as comedy without humor. When it
rises out of this, we have a study of obsession presented
in terms of fear instead of pity: that is, the obsession
takes the form of an unconditioned will that drives its
victim beyond the normal limits of humanity. One of the
clearest examples is Heathcliff, who plunges through death
itself into vampirism." In the essay, "Archetypal Criticism", Frye places the Gothic romance in the sixth phase
of comedy, a phase in which "secret and sheltered places,
forests in moonlight, secluded valleys, and happy islands
become more prominent, as does the penseroso mood of romance, the love of the occult and the marvellous". Here,
in the last phase, "myths closely connected psychologically
with a return to the womb are appropriate".

Knight, G[eorge] Wilson. The Golden Labyrinth: A Study of   5/34
British Drama. London: Phoenix, 1962.

A history of drama from "Greeks" to "Georgian" with a
chapter devoted to Gothic. Coverage is rather general
and draws on Evans (6/15) and Varma (6/31), but there are
original points. Gothic drama is called "a fusion of the
Faust myth and the Don Juan myth". The guilt of the Gothic
villain, says Knight, is sexual, "and for many of the authors, and some spectators or readers, we may suggest the
trouble was probably homosexual".

Matthews, J.H. Surrealism and the Novel. Ann Arbor: Univ.   5/35
of Michigan Press, 1966.

Part I, "Anticipation", includes a chapter on the Gothic
novel, makes some observations, and corrects the miscon-
ceptions put forward in Summers' Gothic Quest (6/29). The
Gothic novel, Matthews says, has limited appeal and simply
cannot be judged by critics obsessed with realism, historical accuracy, and logical consistency. The castle is a
privileged locale, free from restrictions of reality; characters need not be logical and psychologically motivated;
marvellous is beautiful; an atmosphere indifferent to logic
and reason is exciting. Thus, surrealists have always applauded the Gothic novel for the same reasons that conventional critics have rejected it.

Shepperson, Archibald Bolling. The Novel in Motley: A   5/36
    History of the Burlesque Novel in English. Cambridge:
    Harvard Univ. Press, 1936.

    Surveys the burlesque novel and apportions one chapter to
    Gothic. Heavy on plot summaries and parallels. Deals
    with Azemia, Modern Novel Writing, Effusions, Impartial
    Strictures, Pursuits of Literature, New Monk, Northanger
    Abbey, Heroine, Haunted Tower, and others.

VI

STUDIES DEVOTED TO EIGHTEENTH-CENTURY GOTHIC

a.

Meanings of Gothic

Holbrook, William C. "The Adjective Gothique in the XVIIIth   6/1
Century", MLN, LVI (1941), 498-503.

Traces the attitude of 18th-century France toward the Middle Ages by noting shifts in the use of the adjective
gothique. In the first half of the century it was a
sneering word meaning "old-fashioned" or "barbaric", and
was applied most often to manners. Later, gothique came
to be synonymous with melancholy moods and Romanticism,
but in France never developed the meaning of "ghastly,
supernatural, or superhuman".

Kliger, Samuel. "The 'Goths' in England: An Introduction to   6/2
the Gothic Vogue in Eighteenth-Century Aesthetic Discussion", MP, XLIII (1945), 107-117.

Investigates the use and shifts in meaning of the term
Gothic. This label became extended from the name of a
single tribe to mean "German", and things medieval or
non-Roman were called "Germanic". England was believed
to have inherited Germanic political institutions; therefore, Gothic came to signify "free", "liberal", or "democratic". Gothic freedom was opposed to Roman tyranny, and
in the 18th century, a taste for things Gothic was associated with the Whig faction.

--------. The Goths in England: A Study in Seventeenth and   6/3
Eighteenth Century Thought. Cambridge: Harvard Univ.
Press, 1952.

Concerned with the various meanings and connotations of
Gothic in the 17th and 18th centuries. Gothic originated
in the 17th century as a political term, became equated
with Whig politics, and a fondness for Gothic depended
on political affiliations. Explains that "terrible"
Gothic or the schauerromane is part of the cult of the

sublime; "sportive" Gothic is steeped in the traditions which Goths brought in their migration from east to north.

Kliger, Samuel. "The Gothic Revival and the German Trans-   6/4
latio", MP, XLV (1947), 73-103.

The translatio imperii ad Teutonicos, a "thought current set in motion by the Reformation . . . suggested force-fully an analogy between the breakup of the Roman Empire by the Goths and the demands of the humanist reformers of northern Europe for religious freedom, interpreted as lib-eration from Roman priestcraft". Thus, the Goths were viewed as bearers of enlightenment, and "England progressed confidently toward the double ideal of Anglo-Saxon democ-racy and Protestantism".

Longueil, Alfred E. "The Word 'Gothic' in Eighteenth Century   6/5
Criticism", MLN, XXXVIII (1923), 453-460.

Traces changes in meaning and the "ups and downs of 'Gothic', from a race-term to a sneering word, from a sneering word to a cool adjective, from a cool adjective to a cliche in criticism". Runs through meanings "bar-barous", "medieval", "supernatural", "grotesque", "ghost-ly". Says that for Horace Walpole, Clara Reeve, Barbauld, and Maturin, Gothic meant medieval.

b.

Character Portrayal

oyer, Clarence. The Villain as Hero in Elizabethan Tragedy.   6/6
New York: Dutton, 1914.

Traces the villain-hero from his origins in Seneca's Medea, through Machiavelli and Marlowe's Machiavellian heroes, down to the Elizabethan villains. Concludes Aristotle was mistaken in asserting that the character of the hero must be good; pity and fear can be inspired by certain villain-heroes. "For the highest degree of terror cannot be aroused unless the villain's power of evil is extraordinarily great; nor can sadness accompany a vil-lain's downfall unless splendid powers perish with him."

Danziger, Marlies K. "Heroic Villains in Eighteenth-Cen-   6/7
tury Criticism", CL, XI (1959), 35-46.

The moral 18th century took a favorable view of villain-
heroes because aestheticians linked the villain to the
sublime. John Baillie opposed Longinus and argued that
the desire for wealth, honors, and power can be sublime
even when it is far from virtuous. Gerard admitted that
some vices could appear sublime, but he condemned this
taste as inferior. Hugh Blair saw great daring in great
villainy. These critics often confused life and art,
aesthetic and moral experiences. "Nevertheless, it is
noteworthy that there was a tradition in the 18th century
of relating heroic villains to the sublime in order to
explain their appeal. The interest in heroic villainy
perhaps reflects, in a small way, the more general interest in genius which grew as the century progressed."

Graham, John. "Character Description and Meaning in the Ro-   6/8
mantic Novel", SIR, V (1966), 208-218.

Credits the Gothic novelists with making the use of physiognomy "a standard technique and approach to reality".
Defoe, Richardson, Fielding, and Smollett reserved physical descriptions "for comedy or satire of aberrant figures",
but the use of physiognomy and pathognomy rose with the
sentimental heroine and the Gothic villain. "One might
say that Lewis, with Mrs. Radcliffe, forced the reader to
believe that it was important to know what the character
looked like and what that 'appearance' meant."

Hart, Francis Russell. "The Experience of Character in the   6/9
English Gothic Novel", in Roy Harvey Pearce, ed., Experience in the Novel. New York: Columbia Univ. Press,
1968.

Romance characters, Hart argues, are intended as symbolic,
illustrative, and closely allied to allegory while characters in the novel are governed by rules of mimesis.
But it is in error to view Gothic characters as symbols
and to deny them mimetic status, for then the point is
lost -- "the demonic is no myth, no superstition, but a
reality in human character or relationship, a novelistic
reality". Misunderstanding results from this intentional
paradox, this shifting between the symbolic and the psychological mimetic.

Hazlitt, William. "Why the Heroes of Romance are Insipid",   6/10
in W. Carew Hazlitt, ed., Sketches and Essays. London:
Bell, 1872.

It is taken for granted that heroes of romance are "amiable
and interesting"; therefore, all the author need do is
present them. Lack of delineation assures that they will
not destroy this pose. Secondary characters, however,
need to act, to speak, to distinguish themselves. "Mrs.
Radcliffe's heroes and lovers are perfect in their kind;
nobody can find any fault with them, for nobody knows anything about them. They are described as very handsome,
and quite unmeaning and inoffensive."

Mise, Raymond Winfield. "The Gothic Heroine and the Nature   6/11
of the Gothic Novel". Unpublished doctoral dissertation,
Univ. of Washington, 1970.

"This study explains why the heroine is generalized to
the extent that she is and shows that she does experience,
in Radcliffe's and Lewis' novels, a character change
which is crucial in understanding the novel. Most important, though, is the fact that the heroine's nature and
function provide needed insight into misunderstood aspects
of the gothic mode, e.g., the central image of the castle
and the themes of filial duty and incest." The erotic
nature of the Gothic novel becomes emphasized, and the
change in the heroine, says Mise, is that after being
threatened sexually, she triumphs and gains "new sense
of sexual adequacy". The castle "is symbolic of the mind.
It suggests the buried accumulation of childhood fantasies.
Thus, once in the castle, the heroine experiences the return of the repressed, a recall of the forgotten." The
incest theme "is a means of discrediting parent figures and
is, thus, related to the theme of filial duty". Concludes that the Gothic mode "can be understood as being
subversive" since it emphasizes "an unofficial and inner
reality as opposed to an official and collective reality".

Saagpakk, Paul F. "A Survey of Psychopathology in British   6/12
Literature From Shakespeare to Hardy", Literature and
Psychology, XVIII (1968), 135-165.

Surveys the theme of "morbidity of the mind" and devotes
attention to the Gothic hero created by Walpole, "a flat
literary type . . . a personage of pronounced psychopath-
ological traits". Discusses characters of Lewis, Reeve,
the Lees, Beckford, Moore, Maturin, Godwin, Bulwer, the
Brontës, Dickens, and others.

Thorslev, Peter L., Jr. The Byronic Hero: Types and Proto-   6/13
types. Minneapolis: Univ. of Minnesota Press, 1962.

Devoted mainly to Byron, but has a chapter on the Gothic
villain. Considers Gothic a low level of literature;
sees the villain's origins in the "flood of subliterary
pseudo-historical 'romances'" which existed at that time.
Puts emphasis on psychology, not physiognomy. With attention to the heroic tradition, 18th-century sensibility,
Satanism, Scott's contribution, and offers a look into
Nietzsche.

c.

Gothic Drama

Adelsperger, Walter Charles. "Aspects of Staging of Plays of   6/14
the Gothic Revival in England". Unpublished doctoral dissertation, Ohio State Univ., 1959.

A highly technical investigation into the physical aspects of staging Gothic plays. Looks at the exact nature and use of scenery: stock vs. special, two vs. three
dimensional, deep vs. shallow settings, the placing of
elements, the use of furniture, etc. Studies special
effects including the vampire trap, the ghost glide, the
flying machines. Covers in detail, Grecian Daughter,
Castle Spectre, Bertram, Adelgitha, Thalaba, but looks at
many minor dramas. Compares the Gothic drama's properties
with those of the later melodramas. Includes several illustrations and a list of Gothic plays.

Evans, Bertrand. Gothic Drama from Walpole to Shelley.   6/15
University of California Publications in English, XVIII.
Los Angeles: Univ. of California Press, 1947.

Cites Home's Douglas (1757) and Hartson's Countess of
Salisbury (1787) as antecedents; discredits Elizabethan
and/or Jacobean drama as sources and traces both Gothic
novel and Gothic drama from Otranto. Calls The Mysterious
Mother the first Gothic drama, yet says it is not the
source of inspiration of later plays. Gothic drama
flourished before Die Räuber was translated, maintained
the Gothic tradition in England, and is responsible for
turning the Gothic tyrant into the hero-villain. Evans

78

also studies English-German crosscurrents, presents a
chapter on Joanna Baillie, notes the influences on Scott
and the Romantics, and appends a list of Gothic plays.

Evans, Bertrand. "Manfred's Remorse and Dramatic Tradition", 6/16
PMLA, LXII (1947), 752-773.

Asserts that Manfred's character was shaped by the Gothic
playwrights before Byron's own birth. Critics who see
sources for Manfred in the Gothic novel neglect the fact
that there, the Gothic villain is villain -- in Manfred,
the villain is hero. Calls the Countess in The Mysterious
Mother the "first Gothic villain in dramatic literature";
shows how in the 1780's the "villain grew in stature and
gradually assumed new functions". The switch from villain
to hero was to attract name actors. To please the moralists, a marked remorse was the necessary atonement for evil.
Says Mrs. Radcliffe "lagged behind the playwrights in ex-
panding the villain's earliest functions and stature" and
she gave the best part to the persecuted heroine.

Loomis, Emerson Robert. "Gothic Drama as a Source for Gothic 6/17
Fiction in the Magazines", N&Q, XV (1968), 28-29.

Suggests that Gothic drama offered a source of inspiration
and material for writers of magazine fiction. Points out
that the anonymous "The Clock Has Struck", Lady's Magazine,
1809, has parallels in Lewis's The Wood Demon, or, The
Clock Has Struck, unpublished, but performed in 1807 and
1808, also with his Bravo of Venice, published and performed in 1805.

Thorp, Willard. "The Stage Adventures of Some Gothic 6/18
Novels", PMLA, XLIII (1928), 476-486.

Many Gothic novels were staged but their horrors became
minimized and frequently perverted into comedy. Authors
and producers were uncertain whether audiences would
tolerate ghosts, and so, James Cobb thought that if an
audience wouldn't show alarm at a ghost, it might be induced to laugh at one. Later, in the early 19th century,
Lewis became the leader of the new school of Romantic
dramatists which did succeed in bringing terror and the
supernatural to the theater.

Whitmore, Charles Edward. The Supernatural in Tragedy.   6/19
Cambridge: Harvard Univ. Press, 1915.

Surveys the supernatural in tragedy from Aeschylos,
Sophocles and Euripides to Beddoes and Ibsen but devotes
only fifty of the 350 pages to the post-Restoration
period. The Elizabethan ghost, he says, was at first derived from Seneca,but took on native traditions until "the
desire for revenge which appeared sporadically in the
classical ghosts became the dominant trait of their English successors". Shakespeare made the ghost organic,
and with time, the charnel house aspects grew. Castle
Spectre "represents the lowest conceivable point in the
degradation of the supernatural, and has not the remotest
affiliation to genuine tragedy. With it the English
tradition reached its lowest ebb."

                              d.

              Full-Length Studies of Gothic

Birkhead, Edith. The Tale of Terror: A Study of the Gothic   6/20
Romance [1921]. New York: Russell & Russell, 1963.

A broad survey extending from earliest times up to the
1920's, with emphasis upon classifications. Coverage
includes also American Gothic and Gothic satires. Relies
on plot summary and biography; lacks a specific thesis.
Has no bibliography and footnotes are rather incomplete,
but despite its limitations, essential reading.

Church, Elizabeth. "The Gothic Romance: Its Origin and   6/21
Development". Unpublished doctoral dissertation, Harvard,
1913.

Heavy on plot summaries and concerned with classifications.
In Chapter I, "Types of Prose Fiction Before 1764", says
that the pastoral gave the low-life comedy to Walpole, the
oriental tale prepared the way for the marvellous, and
the heroic romance lacked only the supernatural. Chapter
II, "Influences Tending to Produce Gothic Romance", doesn't
always distinguish between Gothic and Romantic and cites
Warton, Hurd, Macpherson, Percy, Gray, Leland, Ferdinand
Count Fathom, the Graveyard poets, supernatural on the
stage, and belief in witchcraft. Chapter III, "Walpole

                              80

and Otranto", devotes over 80% of its space to biography
and Strawberry Hill. Says HW had no literary source for
Otranto. The final three chapters are concerned with
classification of novels into (1)HW's historical-type,
or (2)Radcliffe-type, or (3)Lewis-type. There is little
in this section other than cataloguing and long plot summaries. An appendix lists 399 romances read for this
thesis and includes an early Summers-type bibliography.

Coleman, William Emmet. "On the Discrimination of Gothi-   6/22
cisms". Unpublished doctoral dissertation, City Univ.
of New York, 1970.

The opening chapter discusses and evaluates the criticism
of Gothic fiction and notes that there are two schools --
those who see the Gothic novel as "bad literature" and
those who see it "fit for serious study" but either "limited in its intent or lacking it its accomplishments".
Coleman explains that Gothic was a complex and developing
form which "could express The Enlightenment certainties,
the ironic vision of the Age of Sensibility, and the trans-
cendent world view of Romanticism". Thus, Englightenment
Gothic (C of O, OEB, FCF, "Wandering Willie") has supernaturalism to advance the plot to a standard conclusion.
Mysteries are solvable and the relationship between cause
and effect is clear. Gothicism of Sensibility (MU, Italian,
Monk, Lammermoor, Caleb W, St. Leon, Melmoth, Manfred) has
a world completely devoid of certainties with good and
evil "ambiguously related, if not indistinguishable". The
cosmos "may be a threatening and evil one", and man's reason
is incapable of making sense of the world around him. Mrs.
R, "despite her professed intentions . . . leads us to
ambiguous and ironic conclusions about man and the world
around him". The final division, Romantic Gothicism (Borderers, Frankenstein, Ancient Mariner, Christabel, Cenci,
Zastrozzi, St. Irvyne) as the first, "describes a world of
justice and resolution but suggests fulfillment and resolution in some 'other' world".

Hudson, Randolph Hoyt. "Hence, Vain Deluding Joys: The   6/23
Anatomy of Eighteenth-Century Gothicism". Unpublished
doctoral dissertation, Stanford, 1961.

Sees Gothicism as a reaction to purified pastoral. Previous to the 18th century, pastorals often contained
"stated or implied contrasts" or "anti-pastoral " features
but neo-classical criticism purged these elements. Anti-
pastoral poetry and short stories appeared in the magazines, and from these pre-Gothic short stories, the Gothic

81

novel emerged. "Gothic fiction took over the cliches of
anti-pastoral aspects of nature, added them to cliches
used in accounts of anti-pastoral urban and religious
life, and amalgamated them all into the huge debate between pastoral good and Gothic evil." Treats Romance of
the Forest, Mysteries of Udolpho, and the Monk.

Loomis, Emerson Robert. "The Anti-Gothic English Novel".   6/24
Unpublished doctoral dissertation, Florida State Univ.,
1957.

Consists of nine chapters covering background, history,
characters, plots, themes, settings, style and diction,
and the final chapter offers something of a brief recap.
"Exaggerated imitation" is the recurring phrase, and
Loomis shows both why and how the anti-Gothic novelists
wrote. Neo-classical, conservative, and realists, they
used "exaggerated imitations" of the stereotyped characters and plots, weakened the Gothic vogue, and offered an
entertaining sub-genre which lasted for 25 years. Works
with scores of obscure parodies as well as with Northanger
and Heroine; devotes much attention to Beckford's Modern
Novel Writing and Azemia. Calls the latter "the most
brilliant example of burlesque by extreme exaggeration
among anti-Gothic novels". Contains a valuable bibliography.

Penzoldt, Peter. The Supernatural in Fiction [1952]. New   6/25
York: Humanities, 1965.

A study of the English short story of the supernatural.
Traces the supernatural from the drama to the novel to
the short story and concludes that the short story is the
proper container since this type of tale is plotless and
since belief cannot remain suspended indefinitely.

Railo, Eino. The Haunted Castle: A Study of the Elements   6/26
of English Romanticism [1927]. New York: Humanities,
1964.

Railo follows Birkhead (6/20) by six years, offers a
longer and more detailed study, and works from a different
approach. His concern is with components rather than with
theme or author. Thus, while Birkhead devotes chapters to
authors, Railo has such divisions as "The Byronic Hero",
"The Young Hero and Heroine", and "The Criminal Monk".
Shakespeare is seen as the father of Gothic and many, many
themes from tolling bells to the dark hero are traced back

to him. Undeniably, this is a fascinating work and
contains a wealth of information, yet retrieval seems a
problem. There exists no index, no separate bibliography, and little organization.

Scarborough, Dorothy. The Supernatural in Modern English   6/27
Fiction. New York: Putnam's, 1917.

Although literature does receive some attention it becomes subordinated to folklore or perhaps to demonology.
Similarly, authors receive less treatment than themes.
Professor Scarborough distills pictures of the Devil,
determines character traits of vampires, witches, etc.,
and shows how descriptions of these beings have changed
over the years. Perhaps it might be said that she shows
how literature has handled the supernatural. There are,
however, some remarks on the castle as hero, Gothic machinery, use of weather and scenery, characteristics of
the hero and heroine, etc., which seem to originate here,
yet are often credited to critics who wrote at a later
date.

Smith, Warren Hunting. Architecture in English Fiction   6/28
[1934]. [Hamden]: Archon, 1970.

Clarifies much about the sublime and the picturesque;
shows exactly how ruins and castles fit into these categories; traces three distinct phases of the Gothic revival: historical, pictorial, emotional. Thinks Clark
(2/21) "not precisely correct" in saying Gothic revival
and Gothic novel "were utterly divergent", and doubts
that literary sources were main impetus of revival. Examines influence of Shakespeare, Percy, Ossian, Richardson,
Leland. Discusses Walpole, Reeve, the Lees, Smith, Radcliffe, Roche, Parsons, Drake, Horsley Curties, Beckford,
Scott, Bulwer, Dickens, Ainsworth, and Hawthorne.

Summers, Montague. The Gothic Quest: A History of the   6/29
Gothic Novel [1938]. New York: Russell & Russell, 1964.

Overwhelms with a surfeit of knowledge and abounds with
indiscriminate praise. Intended as a first volume, and
the second, never produced, would have covered Radcliffe,
Smith, Godwin, Mary Shelley, Maturin, and others. This
work deals with the rise of Romanticism, the circulating
libraries, influences from abroad, surrealism, and looks
in depth at Lewis, Lathom, the Lees, Horsley Curties,
Ireland, and others. No separate bibliography, but

features both a general index and an index of novels.
Valuable for a study of the lesser-known Gothic writers.

Tarr, Sister Mary Muriel. Catholicism in Gothic Fiction: A   6/30
Study of the Nature and Function of Catholic Materials
in Gothic Fiction in England (1762-1820). Washington:
Catholic Univ. of America Press, 1946.

Notes that of the 121 Gothic romances examined, 107 make
use of things Catholic. Some works are anti-Catholic
novels of propaganda, but the bulk use Catholicism for
its emotional appeal. Objections to Catholic dogma come
from Deists. "Sense rejects the dogma; sensibility re-
vels in the decorations." These decorations: masses,
cowls, candles, convents, and catacombs, provide both
dramatic flourishes and emotional heightening.

Varma, Devendra P. The Gothic Flame. Being a History of   6/31
the Gothic Novel in England: Its Origins, Efforescence,
Disintegration, and Residuary Influences [1957]. New
York: Russell & Russell, 1966.

The most recent of the full-length studies of Gothic, this
work sets out to trace the origins, discover the causes
of decline and outline the residuary influences. Earlier
works are heavily drawn upon, Summers' theories of continental influences are contested, and the complicated
crosscurrents are sorted out. The final chapter, "Quest
of the Numinous: The Gothic Flame", is especially recommended. Here Varma speculates and raises some interesting points on Freud, Jung, Gothic symbolism, and
the reasons which made the western world ripe for the tales
of terror. Includes an extensive bibliography.

Watt, William W. Shilling Shockers of the Gothic School: 6/32
A Study of Chapbook Gothic Romances. Cambridge: Harvard Univ. Press, 1932.

A pamphlet which describes the appearance, price, circulation and content of the blue books of the period 1800-
1820. Includes a four-page version of the Monk, discusses
abridgements, plagiarisms, etc.

Yardley, Edward. The Supernatural in Romantic Fiction.   6/33
London: Longmans, Green, 1880.

This is not a work covering the Romantic or Gothic eras.
The author writes: "I have used the word romantic in
opposition to classical, and possibly have made the word
unduly comprehensive by treating of all supernatural fiction, except that of ancient Greece and Rome, and even
that I have occasionally noticed for the sake of comparison." Among authors and books mentioned are --
Ovid, Petronius, Orlando Furioso, Arabian Nights, H.C.
Andersen, Grimm, Shakespeare, Milton, Spenser, Jack and
the Bean Stalk, Hoffmann, Goethe, etc. Forty-eight
topics are presented. Examples: "Enchanted Persons",
"Enchanted Places", "Magicians", "Supernatural Animals",
"Vampires and Animated Corpses", "The Evil Eye", "Invis-
ibility", etc. Each topic covers a few pages and consists mainly of a cataloguing process -- writers who
touched upon these themes are listed and coverage often
extends from the Greeks to the Victorians.

                              e.

          Articles, Essays, Introductions, Etc.

Andersen, Jorgen. "Giant Dreams: Piranesi's Influence in   6/34
England", EM, III (1952), 49-59.

Both Walpole and Beckford were familiar with Piranesi's
Carceri and its influence is seen in Otranto's overpower-
ing aspects, huge helmet, sword, etc. In Vathek, the
tortures of the prisoners, the highly imaginative conceptions, and the obsession with exaggeration owe to that
Italian artist and architect.

Axton, William F. Introduction to Melmoth the Wanderer by   6/35
Charles Robert Maturin. Bison Books. Lincoln: Univ.
of Nebraska Press, 1966.

Views the Gothic novel as highly symbolic with "a number
of obsessive archetypes to depict the historical situation
of the age". Contends that the villain is intended as
"more a psychological projection than a realistic representation".

                              85

Black, Robert K. The Sadleir-Black Gothic Collection. An   6/36
Address Before the Bibliographical Society of the Univer-
sity of Virginia. Charlottesville: Univ. of Virginia
Press, 1949.

Michael Sadleir began to purchase Gothic novels in 1922.
Later, Arthur Hutchinson bequeathed to him 140 packing
cases of books, contents unclassified, some novels still
in the mailing wrappers. Black purchased the combined
collection from Sadleir, added some 80-100 volumes of his
own, and gave the "Sadleir-Black Gothic Collection" to
Virginia in 1942.

Bland, D.S. "Endangering the Reader's Neck: Background   6/37
Description in the Novel", Criticism, III (1961),
121-139.

Discusses the function of background description in the
novels of Fielding, Walpole, Radcliffe, Austen, Scott,
Dickens, and others. Notes that Walpole's "Theodore
actually seeks a setting for his melancholy, and this
deliberate association of mood and situation with setting
remains a staple feature of fictional description there-
after." Points out Mrs. Radcliffe's debt to landscape
painters; says Dickens was "one of the first English
novelists (if not the first) to raise description to a
symbolic level".

Blondel, Jacques. "On 'Metaphysical Prisons'", DUJ, NS,   6/38
XXXII (1971), 133-138.

Looks at the theme of imprisonment in the 18th-century
Gothic novel; views it as both symbol and sign of im-
patience with order. Concludes that Gothic dug "beneath
the level of conscience and consciousness, questioning
the order of the age of Englightenment which had unwit-
tingly planned those historical 'tidy prisons' with the
horror of which the world of concentration camps has made
us all too familiar, and which Huxley's Brave New World
had so lucidly anticipated".

Cordasco, Francesco. "A Poetic Stricture of the Gothic   6/39
Romance Craze", N&Q, CXCVI (1951), 258.

Critics have questioned the existence of the poem The
Age, from which Summers (6/29) quotes in his GQ (pp. 33-
37). Cordasco has found the poem, says the quotation "is

exact", and notes that "there is no copy of the book in
the British Museum, and Halkett and Laing make no mention
of it."

Fiske, Christabel Forsythe. "The Tales of Terror", _Conser-_   6/40
vative Review (March, 1900), pp. 37-74.

A lengthy early account which suggests three categories
of Gothic: Conventional, Reactionary, and Historical.
Asserts that a Gothic novel should not be judged by ordinary standards but by its ability to "stimulate us to
a mental state of fearsome delight". Bad characterization
should be overlooked since the real heroine is the reader.
Calls _Otranto_ "extravagantly absurd", the _OEB_ "stupid and
powerless", _The Monk_ "one of the worst books in the English language", but likes _Vathek_ and the works of Radcliffe.
Includes coverage of many figures, both British and American; appends a list of Gothic novels.

Gross, Harvey. "The Pursuer and the Pursued: A Study of   6/41
Caleb Williams", _TSLL_, I (1959), 401-411.

Sees the Gothic novel as "a story of the pursuer and the
pursued; a man of passionate and relentless energy hunts
down some helpless female", but denies any symbol or allegory in these figures. Godwin was the first to use "the
empty Gothic" horrors for political and social purposes.
Notes that in the traditional Gothic novel, the strict
middle-class morality becomes considerably relaxed. "Un-
qualified true love is often replaced by shadowy hints of
incest; courtship frequently becomes demoniacal persecution." Inversions abound.

Henderson, James. "The Gothic Novel in Wales", _NLWJ_, XI   6/42
(1960), 244-254.

Traces some fifty novels whose titles seem to identify
them as Welsh-Gothic, but concludes that "in fact not
even one of the many novels in English with some sort of
Welsh background can justly be termed fundamentally Gothic".
There exist only, he says, some Gothic parts in mannered
novels set in Wales. Notes that Summers' _Gothic Bibliog-_
raphy (1/39) lists "many" novels which simply are not what
they are claimed to be. Includes a "Check-List of Novels
Connected with Wales (1790-1820)".

"The Historical Romance", Blackwood's,LVIII (1845), 341-   6/43
356.

Writing in 1845, the essayist says that "the novels of
Charlotte Smith, Miss Radcliffe, and Miss Burney . . .
are now wellnigh unreadable". The reason for the present
state is because they were not founded on real life, "because they were confined to one circle and class of society", and because they employ "artificial and often
ridiculous" ideas.

Hume, Robert D. "Gothic Versus Romantic: A Revaluation of   6/44
the Gothic Novel", PMLA, LXXXIV (1969), 282-290.

Asserts that a Gothic novel is not one which uses certain
stock machinery, but rather one which is marked by the
use of atmosphere for psychological purposes. Notes the
change from terror-Gothic to horror-Gothic and explains
that this is part of the concern with moral ambiguity.
Distant settings, complex villain-heroes, and the anti-
clerical elements all add to this ambiguity. "In its
highest forms romantic writing claims the existence of
higher answers where Gothic can find only unresolvable
moral and emotional ambiguity." Looks at Walpole, Beckford, Reeve, Radcliffe, Lewis, Mary Shelley, Maturin;
calls Moby Dick "perhaps the greatest of Gothic novels,
and an almost perfect example of the form"; sees Faulkner's
Sanctuary as traditional Gothic.
      See also "'Gothic Versus Romantic': A Rejoinder",
PMLA, LXXXVI (1971), 266-274, in which Hume defends his
article against Robert L. Platzner.

Loomis, Emerson Robert. "The Problem of the Gothic Novel in   6/45
Wales", NLWJ, XIII (1963), 67-69.

Henderson (6/42) suspected that Mrs. Isabella Kelly's The
Abbey of St. Asaph might be Welsh-Gothic but could not
procure a copy to pursue the suspicion. Loomis reports,
indeed it is. He notes that Mrs. Kelly seems to equate
Wales and Gothicism since all her Gothic episodes occur
there, but suggests that the almost complete absence of
Welsh-Gothic may indicate that "perhaps most Gothic novelists felt that Wales was not remote enough to serve as an
effective setting for their novels."

Lovecraft, H[oward] P. "Supernatural Horror in Fiction"   6/46
[1927], in his Dagon and Other Macabre Tales. Edited,
and with an introduction by August Derleth. Sauk City:
Arkham, 1965. ("S.H." reprinted separately, N.Y.:
Dover, 1973; E.F. Bleiler, ed.)

Concentrates on mood, atmosphere, and emotion -- not
properties. Says "we must judge a weird tale not by the
author's intent, or by the mere mechanics of the plot;
but by the emotional level which it attains at its least
mundane point." Radcliffe had a "genuine sense of the
unearthly in scene and incident which closely approached
genius"; Walpole was "tedious, artificial, and melodramatic". Praises Lewis, Maturin, and Beckford, but almost
worships Poe, whom he considers the first of the line of
true artists.

Lund, Mary Graham. "The Century of De Sade", Modern Age,   6/47
VIII (1963-1964), 38-44.

On the Sadian dream, the confessional, Durrell, Miller,
Céline, Rousseau, Diderot, but with passing references
to the Gothic novel. Offers the thought that "the primary meaning of the Gothic Romance is terror, and in an
age which was attempting to shake off the horror of hell-
fire, what could more inspire terror than sin, unspeakable
sin?"

McC., H. "Tales of Terror, Old and New", More Books, 6th   6/48
ser., XV (1940), 337-338.

Introduces two new first-editions which the Boston Public
Library has just acquired -- Udolpho and Dracula.

McKillop, Alan D. "On the Acquisition of Minor English Fic-   6/49
tion, 1740-1800", Newberry Library Bulletin, 2nd ser.,
IV (1956), 70-74.

States that "the minor fiction of the period extending
from Samuel Richardson to Jane Austen has never been completely surveyed or studied" and cites "the inaccessibility
of the novels themselves" as a principal reason for this
neglect. Says there is not even a satisfactory checklist
of the novels of that period and "our conclusions and generalizations in the field are as yet inadequate."

Mayo, Robert D. "Gothic Romance in the Magazines", <u>PMLA</u>,   6/50
LXV (1950), 762-789.

Mayo examined 118 periodicals to find that "only about
twenty offered original Gothic fiction at all, and some
of these only a single example or two". Curiously, this
neglect occurs during a time (1765-1806) when "at least
one-third of all novels published in Great Britain were
Gothic in character". Concludes that "the traditional
Gothic romance, with its longdrawn suspense, slow un-
folding of a central mystery and labored 'explanations',
its sustained episodes of terror, and its 'atmosphere'
and prolix background detail, undoubtedly suffered more
than other species of fiction from the special limitations
of the short-instalment form."

--------. "The Gothic Short Story in the Magazines", <u>MLR</u>,   6/51
XXXVII (1942), 448-454.

Refutes two of Birkhead's (6/20) points: (1)That the
<u>Blackwood's</u> type of short tale of terror descends from
the Gothic chapbooks and, (2)that between 1797 and 1820
Gothic romance maintained but "a disreputable existence".
Points out that about a score of reputable magazines
carried either Gothic tales or fragments, and the <u>Lady's
Magazine</u>, between 1791 and 1812, serialized 21 Gothic romances.

--------. "How Long Was Gothic Fiction in Vogue?", <u>MLN</u>,   6/52
LVIII (1943), 58-64.

Examines fiction in the <u>Lady's Magazine</u> and calculates
the Gothic content as follows:

1791-1798	1799-1802	1803	1804-1806	1805	1807-09	1810-12
52%	62%	23%	72%	84%	44%	19%

Gothic started in <u>LM</u> with a translation of Ducray-Duminil's
<u>Alexis</u> in 1791, the year of Mrs. Radcliffe's first success,
and continued popular as long as a decade after Mrs. Radcliffe ceased to write. Attributes the decline of Gothic
not to parodies or the Waverley novels but to "twenty years
of unimaginative repetition".

Nelson, Lowry, Jr. "Night Thoughts on the Gothic Novel",   6/53
    YR, LII (1962), 236-257.

    Looks at the works of the early Gothicists and sees Frank-
    enstein as an important turning point. Here, characters
    take on full psychological reality and Gothic begins to
    move from claptrap machinery toward symbolism and myth.
    Asserts that the Gothic novel foreshadows future interests
    in "contradictory impulses, irrational and gratuitous
    evil [and], the intimacy of love and hate". Discusses
    importance of the accursed Cain-like wanderer and his
    heirs Ahab and Heathcliff.

Peterson, Clell T. "Spotting the Gothic Novel", Graduate   6/54
    Student of English, I (1957), 14-15.

    A fairly accurate even if somewhat tongue-in-cheek list
    of sixteen Gothic features. "If a given novel has ten
    of these characteristics, it is Gothic; and the more Goth-
    ic qualities it has, the more Gothic it is." (1)Acute
    sensibilities, (2)swooning, (3)long-lost children, (4)co-
    incidences, (5)south Europe, (6)inexplicable but apparently
    natural/supernatural incidents, (9)spooky settings,
    (10)excessively genteel and abstract conversations, (11)a
    Cook's-type tour, (12)lack of gainfully employed persons,
    (13)picturesque posers, (14)mysterious messages, (15)es-
    cape via secret passage, (16)curious female explorers
    who swoon at the last moment.

Piggott, Stuart. "Prehistory and the Romantic Movement",   6/55
    Antiquity, XI (1937), 31-38.

    Notes the parallel tastes for prehistoric archaeology and
    things Gothic. Says that the "morbid interest in graves
    and skeletons" seen in Graveyard poems and tales of terror
    is paralleled in the "conscious gloating over the para-
    phernalia of Death in some of the early archaeological
    records".

Preu, James A. "The Tale of Terror", EJ, XLVII (1958), 243-   6/56
    247.

    An introduction to the Gothic novel, designed for high-
    school teachers and devoid of originality. Covers meaning
    of Gothic, the machinery, the two schools, summarizes The
    Monk, mentions Lake Leman 1816, touches on Melmoth and
    Dracula. Very shallow and views Gothic as camp and corn.

Quennell, Peter. "The Moon Stood Still on Strawberry Hill", 6/57
Horizon, XI (1969), 113-119.

A general introduction to the Gothic novel, probably in-
tended for the non-specialist or the undergraduate.
Covers Pope's "Unfortunate Lady" and "Eloisa to Abelard",
Otranto, Vathek, Udolpho, Monk. Notes De Quincey's The
Avenger (1838) is still in the Gothic stream, but says
Dickens' "Cockney realism" ended the genre. The final two
pages, "Do-it-yourself Gothic -- A Few ideas for the Back
Yard", features eight pictures of Gothic edifices, sham
and serious.

Roberts, R. Ellis. "The Other Side", Life and Letters, X 6/58
(1934), 691-701.

In a rather roundabout way, deals with the power of words
and with the tale of terror. Makes two points: (1)The
genre was synchronized with the highly evocative Ossian,
and, (2)"the Gothic novelists showed their successors how
not to try to suggest mystery or the supernatural". Asserts "the early Gothic novelists forgot that the mind,
keyed up to the wonderful and the unexpected, was less
likely to be terrified by magnificent and horrible monsters in monstrous surroundings than by lesser terrors
when encountered amid everyday scenes." Says that Poe
transformed modern fiction, for he could make "suspense
out of any incident in life, and all his suspense is in-
tolerable".

Rogers, Winfield H. "The Reaction Against Melodramatic Sen- 6/59
timentality in the English Novel, 1796-1830", PMLA, XLIX
(1934), 98-122.

A general survey of parodies and satires directed against
the "pseudo-Richardsonian and gothic writers". Includes
more plot summary than critical insight. Says that in
Modern Novel Writing, Beckford "abstains almost entirely
from making sense". Believes Barrett's Heroine "undoubtedly had a considerable influence in turning the course
of fiction". Asserts that Northanger Abbey "singled out
Udolpho for particular ridicule".

Sade, [Donatien Alphonse François] Marquis de. "Reflections   6/60
    on the Novel" [1800], in his The 120 Days of Sodom and
    Other Writings. Edited and translated by Austryn Wain-
    house and Richard Seaver. Introductions by Simone de
    Beauvoir and Pierre Klossowski. New York : Grove, 1966.

    Asserts that the Gothic novel was "the inevitable result
    of the revolutionary shocks which all of Europe has suf-
    fered". "There was not a man alive who had not experienced
    in the short span of four or five years more misfortunes
    than the most celebrated novelist could portray in a cen-
    tury. Thus, to compose works of interest, one had to
    call upon the aid of hell itself, and to find in the world
    of make-believe things wherewith one was fully familiar
    merely by delving into man's daily life in this age of iron.
    Ah! but how many disadvantages there are in this manner
    of writing! The author of The Monk has avoided them no
    more than has Mrs. Radcliffe. Here, there are perforce
    two possibilities: either one resorts increasingly to
    wizardry -- in which case the reader's interest soon
    flags -- or one maintains a veil of secrecy, which leads
    to a frightful lack of verisimilitude. Should this
    school of fiction produce a work excellent enough to at-
    tain its goal without foundering upon one or the other of
    these two reefs, then we, far from denigrating its methods,
    will be pleased to offer it as a model." Calls The Monk
    "foremost" and "superior in all respects to the strange
    flights of Mrs. Radcliffe's brilliant imagination".

Sadleir, Michael. Introduction to The Heroine by Eaton   6/61
    Stannard Barrett. New York: Frederick A. Stokes, 1927.

    Offers a very general introduction to Romanticism which
    is seen as "a fierce reaction against the exhausted clas-
    sicism, which . . . lay like a tired blight upon the civi-
    lization of Western Europe". Gives some generalizations
    about Gothic and the reasons for its decline. Sees
    Heroine as "the most violent" of the contemporary satires
    of Gothic.

Saintsbury, George, ed. Tales of Mystery: Mrs. Radcliffe--   6/62
    Lewis -- Maturin. New York: Macmillan, 1891.

    Defends the Gothic genre, wonders if the "horrid novels"
    really existed, admires Mrs. Radcliffe, "the acknowledged
    queen of the style", praises Vathek, likes Frankenstein,
    places P.B. Shelley's Gothic "among the greatest rubbish
    ever written by a man of genius", calls Melmoth "execrably

93

bad" in structure but containing genius, sees Ambrosio
not as a character but "only a label, or series of labels,
used to designate the perpetrator of divers more or less
atrocious deeds".   Text contains extracts from Melmoth,
Monk, Sicilian Romance, Romance of the Forest, Udolpho,
and Italian.

Sholl, Anna McClure.   "Goose Flesh in Literature", The   6/63
    Catholic World, CL (1939), 306-311.

    A brief general survey of the ghost story which comes
    closer to being an annotated checklist than an article.
    Covers Scott, Bulwer, Dickens, Kipling, De la Mare, Black-
    wood, the two Jameses, Hugh Walpole, E. Bowen, Bierce,
    Alarçon, Mrs. Gaskell, and others.   Says that "from Shake-
    speare to H.G. Wells nearly every author of note has
    written at least one ghost story, or has made some reference
    to spectral matters in his letters or memoirs, or has,
    himself, been involved in an uncanny experience."

Smith, Warren Hunting.   "Recent Acquisitions in Gothic Fic-   6/64
    tion", YULG, VIII (1934), 109-111.

    Notes how the British Museum and Bodleian had neglected
    to collect Gothic novels; says Harvard was among the
    first to begin a collection; lists a few volumes which
    Yale has recently acquired.

Solomon, Stanley J.   "Subverting Propriety as a Pattern of   6/65
    Irony in Three Eighteenth-Century Novels: The Castle of
    Otranto, Vathek, and Fanny Hill", ErasmusR, I (1971),
    107-116.

    Views these novels as ironic yet lacking "the typical
    didactic impulse of the neoclassical author".   Each "tends
    to be both a serious example of the kind of novel which it
    professes to be on the surface as well as a sustained ex-
    ample of comic irony at the expense of some established
    notions of propriety".   All three books are devoted to the
    overthrow of the 18th-century ideal of a rational world
    order.   In each of the novels, reason disappears as a
    controlling approach to life and is replaced by the un-
    restrained cultivation of imagination (Otranto), of feeling
    and sensibility (Vathek), or of physical passion (Fanny
    Hill)."

"Some Remarks on the Use of the Preternatural in Works of   6/66
Fiction", Blackwood's, III (1818), 648-650.

Says the late 18th-century Gothic novel craze arose "partly from the revival of old ballads, and partly from the
importation of German books". The "unskillfulness of the
artists, and the unsparing manner in which their resources
were employed" caused the genre to fall into disrepute.
But adds that the great poets of the day use the supernatural -- Scott, Wordsworth, Coleridge, Byron. Cautions
against using the marvellous to produce the ludicrous.
Because of this, Vathek "has never been very popular in
this country".

Spector, Robert Donald, ed. Seven Masterpieces of Gothic   6/67
Horror [1963]. New York: Bantam, 1970.

In his introduction, notes that critics have not done justice to the genre as they use "standards alien to the irrational nightmare world of the Gothic". Praises both
Mrs. Radcliffe and Lewis. Says Monk "characterizes the
rebellion against authority which both the French Revolution and the subsequent Reign of Terror had given political and social expression to in France". Sees connection
with works of De Sade. Looks also at the American tradition from Brown to Faulkner. Text includes: Otranto,
OEB, "Mistrust", "Heir of Mondolfo", "White Old Maid",
"House of Usher", and "Carmilla".

Stern, Philip Van Doren. "Tales of Terror", Saturday Review   6/68
of Literature, XXV (March 14, 1942), 3-4, 20.

Views the ghost story as "genuine literature"; calls it
"an exceedingly difficult and delicate form to master";
says that "a superlatively well-told tale acting upon a
sensitive audience can result in greater emotional heightening than that produced by almost any other kind of literature." Recommends a story be vague about its ghosts.
Fear can be of long duration, but "horror is necessarily
climactic in effect", and most of us meet horror only in
nightmares. "The horror found in supernatural literature
is closer to that experienced in dreams than to anything
encountered in our waking life", and the horror story, he
says, "is even more difficult to handle than the ghost
story".

Summers, Montague. "Architecture and the Gothic Novel",   6/69
Architectural Design, II (1931), 78-81.

A general article which ties Otranto to Strawberry Hill
and Cambridge and credits Walpole with the mode of garden
ruins. With brief mention of architecture in Reeve, Radcliffe, Ainsworth and others.

--------. "Byron's 'Lovely Rosa'", in his Essays in Petto   6/70
[1928]. Essay Index Reprint Series. Freeport: Books
for Libraries, 1967.

Treats Charlotte Dacre or "Rosa Matilda", the author of
Zofloya, Confessions of the Nun of St. Omer and various
other Gothic novels. Sees her as a competent writer,
highly imitative of Lewis, and in turn, an influence on
P.B. Shelley.

--------. "The Illustrations of the 'Gothick' Novels",   6/71
Connoisseur, LXXV (1936), 266-271.

Does not deal exclusively with illustrations although
thirteen are offered. Notes, but doesn't explain how
"romantic architecture . . . exercised a tremendous influence on the Gothic novel". Offers comments on Ferdinand Count Fathom, Longsword, and some of the Gothic
devices.

--------, ed. The Supernatural Omnibus, Being a Collection   6/7
of Stories of Apparitions, Witchcraft, Werewolves, Diab-
olism, Necromancy, Satanism, Divination, Sorcery, Goetry,
Voodoo, Possession, Occult Doom, and Destiny [1931].
London: Gollancz, 1950.

An anthology of 38 stories together with a long introduction which surveys the supernatural tale from ancient time
to the present, but concentrates on the 19th century, "the
hey-day of the good old-fashioned ghost story". Valuable
for the cataloguing of novels, novelists, and short stories of various sub-species. A glut of information, highly compressed.

arma, Devendra P., ed.   Gothic Novels.   40 vols.   New York: 6/73
Arno, 1971 --.

Facsimile reprints, each with a new introduction.   In 1971,
ten volumes were issued: Varney the Vampire, Confessions
of the Nun of St. Omer, St. Leon, Recess, Bravo of Venice,
Athlin & Dunbayne, Gaston de B., Sicilian R., Nocturnal
Minstrel, and Manfrone.   Scheduled for 1974:   Libertine,
Passions, Zofloya, Abbess, Longsword, Grasville Abbey,
Netley Abbey, Romance of the Forest, Fatal Revenge and
Albigenses.

-------, ed.   The Northanger Set of Jane Austen Horrid   6/74
Novels.   7 vols.   London: Folio, 1968.

The Castle of Wolfenbach contains a general introduction
to the series and gives the background complete with
various critical estimates.   Each volume contains in addition, its own individual introduction which fits it into
the Gothic galaxies and offers extracts from contemporary
reviews.   These introductions provide welcome information
on rather obscure literary figures.

ilson, Angus.   "Evil in the English Novel", The Listener,   6/75
LXIX (Jan. 10, 1963), 63-65.

In four papers, Wilson works with evil from Richardson to
the moderns, and in this the third, offers a few remarks
on the Gothic novelists, seeing them as the influence
which enabled Dickens and Brontë "to break through the
shell of the novel".

ilson, Edmund.   "A Treatise on the Tales of Horror", in his   6/76
Classics and Commercials: A Literary Chronicle of the
Forties.   London: Allen, 1951.

Writing in 1944, Wilson notes the "sudden revival of the
appetite for tales of horror" and suggests two reasons
for the resurrection of this genre in the age of the
electric light.   (1) "The longing for mystic experiences
which seems always to manifest itself in periods of social
confusion, when political progress is blocked", and (2)
"the instinct to inoculate ourselves against panic at
the real horrors loose on the earth."   He passes opinion
on Hawthorne, Poe, Melville, Gogol, Kipling, Henry and
M.R. James, Machen, Blackwood, De la Mare, and Kafka.

f.

Early Opinions and Miscellaneous Reviews

1. <u>Longsword</u> (1762)

<u>Critical Review</u>, XIII (1762), 252-257.   6/77

"We are indebted to the author of this work for the introduction of a new and agreeable species of writing, in
which the beauties of poetry, and the advantages of history are happily united." Praises language, sentiments,
characters, descriptions, events. "The conduct resembles
that of an epic poem; and had it the advantage of measure
we should not scruple to call it by that name."

<u>Monthly Review</u>, XXVI (1762), 236-237.   6/78

"The truth of history is artfully interwoven with agreeable fictions, and interesting episodes; and the whole
has the appearance of being the production of some elegant
female pen, formed on an intimate acquaintance with those
paragons of literature, the Romances of the 15th and 16th
centuries: which, however extravagant and <u>above</u> nature,
were always favourable to the cause of honour and virtue;
and, so far, preferable to many of the more natural productions of later times." Concludes that although "the
good old Romance may be now laughed out of doors . . . no
species of writing could ever <u>amuse</u> with less injury to
the <u>morals</u>, and <u>virtuous manners of</u> the Reader".

<u>Scots Magazine</u>, XXIV (1767), 145-148.   6/79

Includes the identical review which appears in the <u>MR</u>
(6/78), plus additional comments and a long extract.
Calls <u>L</u> "a new and agreeable species of writing, in which
the beauties of poetry and the advantages of history are
happily united" (cf. 6/77). Notes that "the events . . .
without deviating from probability, are very powerfully
interesting".

ermons on Various Subjects, by the late Rev. Thomas Leland.   6/80
Reviewed in English Review, XII (1788), 121-123.

Notes that a biographical sketch is appended and "one
piece of information it contains which we believe is
new, and which will probably be acceptable to the curious
. . . is that the well-known romance of Longsword, Earl
of Salisbury was the production of Dr. Leland."

2. Sophia and Harriet Lee

ecess, by Sophia Lee. Reviewed in English Review, I (1783),   6/81
417-418.

"Miss Lee has imitated in this novel some of the French
romance writers of the last age. She has taken her chief
personages from history. But, more attentive to character than her precursors in this walk, she has, for the
most part, made them think, speak, and act, as they probably would have done in the situations in which she has
placed them."

-------. Gentleman's Magazine, LVI (1786), 327.   6/82

"We cannot entirely approve the custom of interweaving
fictitious incident with historic truth; and, as the
events related approach nearer the era we live in, the
impropriety increases; for the mind, pre-occupied with
real fact, rejects, not without disgust, the embellishments of fable --".

e Mysterious Marriage or the Hermitage of Roselva. A Play   6/83
in Three Acts, by Harriet Lee. Reviewed in Analytical
Review, XXVII (1798), 295-296.

Asserts that "the characters are not supported with sufficient spirit, and . . . the dialogue is feeble and un-
dignified". Highly critical of the use of a ghost, the
reviewer says that "supernatural agency is the taste of
a barbarous age, and ought to be banished from our
theatres at once". "No, no; let ghosts and hobgoblins
people the pages of a romance, but never let their forms
be seen to glide across the stage."

Mysterious Marriage. Reviewed in British Critic, XII   6/84
(1798), 73.

"To us, the originality [of the female spectre] appears
not worth contending for. We would interdict the production of any new spectre on the stage. This 'reign of
terror' is over: 'incredulus odi'. In a modern play,
ghosts cannot be tolerated: they are generally mere sub-
stitutes for good sense and good writing."

--------. Monthly Mirror, V (1798), 166-169.   6/85

Says that the play had been written two years earlier,
but "the present rage for ghosts" now brings it to the
stage. Calls her style "evidently an imitation of Shakespeare -- and in some places the resemblance is remark-
ably striking". Offers plot summary, and, "as many of our
readers may be curious to know what use Miss Lee has made
of her GHOST, we have transcribed a greater part of the
scene in which it is introduced."

--------. Monthly Review, XXVI (1798), 96.   6/86

Quotes Miss Lee as saying that her play had been written
two years earlier (1795) and read privately. Reviewer
wonders "whether the ghost conjured up by Miss Harriet
Lee was known to the author of the Castle Spectre".

"Sophia Lee". Obituary notice in Gentleman's Magazine, NS,   6/8
XVII, pt. 2 (1824), 88-89.

Cites the Recess as "the first romance in the English
language which blended history with fiction, and enriched
both by pathos and descriptive scenery". Says "Mrs. Rat-
cliffe [sic] (then Miss Ward), resident at Bath, and acquainted in Miss Lee's family, though too young to have
appeared herself as a writer, was among the warmest admirers of the Recess."

C., C. "Mrs. Harriet Lee", Living Age, XXXI (1851), 329-330.   6/8

A general tribute to the Lee sisters, written in the year
of Harriet's death. Gives biography and lists works.
Discusses influence of The Recess on Scott, and influence
of "Kruitzner, or the German's Tale", on Byron.

3. The Northanger Novels

Castle of Wolfenbach, by Mrs. Eliza Parsons. Reviewed in 6/89
British Critic, III (1794), 199-200.

"This novel is opened with all the romantic spirit of the
Castle of Otranto, and the reader is led to expect a tale
of other times, fraught with enchantments and spells from
every page. As the plot thickens, they vanish into air --
into thin air, and the whole turns out to be a company of
well-educated and well-bred people of fashion. . . .
Taken as a whole, the C of W is more interesting than the
general run of modern novels, the characters are highly
coloured and the story introduced in a manner that excites
curiosity, and in the language of the drama, abounds with
interesting, though improbable situations."

-------. Critical Review, 2nd ser., X (1794), 49-52. 6/90

"We do not pretend to give this novel as one of the first
order, or even of the second; it has, however, sufficient
interest to be read with pleasure. The terrible prevails,
and the characters of the two heroes in crime, are too
darkly tinted. The two stories, besides, are not suf-
ficiently interwoven with one another. . . . There is no
fine writing in these volumes; and now and then we meet
with vulgarisms. . . ."

Necromancer, by Lawrence Flammenberg. Translated by Peter 6/91
Teuthold. Reviewed in Analytical Review, XX (1794),
52-53.

"To those who are pleased with tales that 'freeze the
blood', and harrow up the soul, the Necromancer will afford a delightful treat." "With such dreadful tales does
this work abound; and they are related with such variety
and minuteness of horrid description, that to readers of
delicate nerves the perusal might be too hazardous. . . ."

Necromancer. Reviewed in British Critic, IV (1794), 194.   6/92

Complete item: "A stranger farrago of Ghosts and Robbers was never put together. This work calls itself a
translation from the German: Out of respect to such of
our countrymen as are authors, we heartily wish it may be
a translation. We should be sorry to see an English original so full of absurdities. Errors of ignorance or of
the press occur perpetually, such as affect for effect,
adjectives used for adverbs, etc., etc."

--------. Critical Review, 2nd ser., XI (1794), 469.   6/93

"Exclusive of the entertainment arising from this narrative, it has in view an additional purpose, of greater
importance to the public. It exposes the arts which
have been practiced in a particular part of Germany for
carrying on a series of nocturnal depredations in the
neighborhood, and infusing into the credulous multitude
a firm belief in the existence of sorcery."

--------. English Review, XXIV (1794), 149-150.   6/94

"This tale is said to be founded on facts; but we must
suppose some embellishments have been added; or that the
people where the scene lies must have been wonderfully
credulous. To those who are fond of reading stories of
ghosts, this book may be entertaining, and also instructive, as it may tend to shew how easily superstition may
be worked upon without any foundation in reality." Concludes that "this piece is not defective in genius or
fancy; though, to most readers it will probably appear
wanting in just taste and design."

--------. Monthly Review, 2nd ser., XVI (1795), 465-466.   6/95

A vague, rambling review which devotes only eight lines
to the novel. Objects that the "extraordinary events"
of Volume I are "not very dexterously unravelled".

Horrid Mysteries, by P. Will. Reviewed in Critical Review,   6/96
2nd ser., XXI (1797), 473.

"More gross and absurd nonsense was surely never put together under the name of adventures. We suspect that this
work has been translated by another hand, and under another
name. The work from which the present appears to be taken,

as far as concerns the general outline, is entitled the
Victim of Magical Delusion [6/97]. . . ." Notes that
Mr. Will translated both and wonders why he did not point
out the similarities.

The Victim of Magical Delusion; or the Mystery of the Revo-   6/97
lution of P------l: a Magico-Political Tale, Founded on
Historical Facts, and Translated From the German of
Cajetan Tschink. By P. Will. Reviewed in Critical Review, 2nd ser., XV (1795), 63-74.

Says that "The Ghost-Seer is the German name of this
work". The "novel . . . is of very singular construction,
and . . . the reader will derive no common portion of entertainment, such as novels afford, and some intellectual
improvement, such as they seldom yield". The reviewer believes that P. Will is "assistant preacher at the German
chapel in the Savoy".

The Mysterious Warning, by Eliza Parsons. Reviewed in Criti-   6/98
cal Review, 2nd ser., XVI (1796), 474.

"The style of this novel is not splendid, yet it is not
defective, the character of Count Rhodophil is, we hope,
too coldly and deliberately atrocious to be natural; the
mysterious warnings, arraigned at the bar of a strict morality, are not perfectly justifiable; and the mystery is
but ill disguised." "The novels of Mrs. Parsons would be
more interesting, if her plans had more unity; when the
principal narrative is frequently broken in upon by different stories, however entertaining in themselves, attention flags, the mind experiences a kind of disappointment, loses the connection, proceeds languidly, and is
not easily reanimated."

Clermont, by Regina Maria Roche. Reviewed in Critical Review,   6/99
2nd ser., XXIV (1798), 356.

"This tale reminds us, without any great pleasure, of Mrs.
Radcliffe's romances. In Clermont, mystery is heaped upon
mystery, and murder upon murder, with little art, and
great improbability." "We have also the usual apparatus
of dungeons, long galleries, clanking chains and ghosts,
and a profusion of picturesque description which, though
it displays some merit, serves only to interrupt the narrative."

The Midnight Bell, a German Story , [by Francis Lathom].   6/100
Reviewed in Analytical Review, XXVII (1798), 644.

"This tale, which is amusing and not ill-written, branches
out into some episodical relations, that aid in keeping
alive attention, without destroying the interest of the
main plot: as a composition, it is not characterised by
that extravagance of passion that belongs to the majority
of German novels, and is calculated, perhaps rather to
entertain than to make any great impression upon the
reader."

--------. British Critic, XII (1798), 304.   6/101

"They who delight in being terrified, may, with much satisfaction, waste an hour or two in turning over this story,
or rather knots of stories, so intertwined, that it requires more attention than the matter is worth, to keep
in view the connection of the several characters."

--------. Critical Review, 2nd ser., XVIII (1798), 472.   6/102

"The authors of works on this plan seem not to care how
absurd and contradictory the story may be in its progress,
provided they can make all plain and evident at the conclusion; but, indeed, they do not always attend even to
this point."

--------. Monthly Mirror, VI (1798), 34-35.   6/10

Complete review: "To readers of a certain description
this specimen of the gloomy and the horrific, will be no
unacceptable present; we shall not seek to lessen the
pleasure it will afford them by anticipating the contents,
but merely observe, that it is as full of mystery, suspicion, and murder and other alarming ingredients of
modern romance, as the most ardent admirer of such compositions can wish. We have read, however, many worse
stories of the kind."

Orphan of the Rhine, by Mrs. Eleanor Sleath. Reviewed in   6/10
Critical Review, 2nd ser., XXVII (1799), 356.

Complete item: "The creative genius and the descriptive
powers of Mrs. Radcliffe have given considerable popularity to the modern romance; and, even as critics, we

have perused the productions of that authoress with no
small degree of interest and gratification. If, however,
we have sinned in suffering ourselves to be seduced by
the blandishments of elegant fiction, we endure a penance
adequately severe in the review of such vapid and servile
imitations as the Orphan of the Rhine, and other recent
romances."

4. Miscellaneous Items

The Abbey of Clugny, by Mrs. Mary Meeke. Reviewed in Criti-   6/105
cal Review, 2nd ser., XVI (1796), 473.

"The A of C, without having any claim to originality, is
superior to the common class of novels", says the reviewer,
and adds that "we were much entertained by a humourous
story of an apparition, which does not enter merely 'to
clank its chains', but bears a considerable share in the
winding up of the plot."

Academicus. "On the Absurdities of the Modern Stage",   6/106
Monthly Mirror, X (1800), 180-182.

Attacks the Gothic stage productions. "Are we to have
prodigies and monstrous omens, horrid shapes, and the
fruits of brooding darkness forced on us at a place to
which we resort to be instructed and amused? Are we to
expect to meet fiction instead of reality, on the stage?
Cannot sober melancholy be portrayed without the aid of
turrets and gloomy Gothic corridors haunted by ghosts?"
Urges that playwrights deal with "human follies" and
avoid presenting "examples for villainy".

Arabian Nights, translated from the French by Robert Heron.   6/107
Reviewed in Analytical Review, XVI (1793), 456-462.

"To those who are of opinion, with Dr. Johnson, that the
basis of all excellence in writing is truth, it may appear
strange, that a work so full of extravagant absurdities as
the Arabian Nights Entertainments, should have been generally read and admired. Critics, in endeavouring to account for this fact, have had recourse to contradictory
explanations. Some have said that these tales please,
because their wild and wonderful machinery has its laws,
and the magicians and enchanters perform nothing but what

was to be naturally expected from beings endued with such
powers. Whilst others have asserted that the pleasure
they afford is owing to their wildness and extravagance,
whence the reader's curiosity is supplied with such a
rapid succession of strange and surprising things, as
leaves his judgment no leisure to attend to their improbability."

Remarks on the Arabian Nights Entertainment, by Richard   6/108
Hole. Reviewed in British Critic, X (1797), 87.

Asserts that Hole errs "in supposing that the Arabian
Nights are 'held in contempt, more particularly by the
grave and learned.' This is so far from the fact, that
we have known some of the most grave, and the most learned
retain with delight the impression made by the perusal of
these volumes."

Austenburn Castle. Reviewed in Critical Review, 2nd ser.,   6/109
XVI (1796), 222.

"Since Mrs. Radcliffe's justly admired and successful romances, the press has teemed with stories of haunted
castles and visionary terrors; the incidents of which are
so little diversified, that criticism is at a loss to
vary its remarks."

"The Complaint of a Ghost", Lady's Monthly Museum, IV (1800),   6/110
365-370.

"Formerly, ghosts were as much an object of terror to the
ladies as gray hairs; but now, a lady's book (a novel),
destitute of barbarous murders, and dreadful apparitions,
is as rare a phenomenon as an author entirely free from
vanity." The ghost bewails his overuse by paltry scribes
and says, to Walpole "we owe the introduction of the fantastic herd of Ghosts, Goblins, etc." Accuses Lewis of
plagiarization -- CS from the Robbers and part of the Monk
from the Spectator.

Camilla,by Fanny Burney. Reviewed in British Critic, VIII   6/111
(1796), 529-536.

Includes a slap at Gothic. "To astonish by the marvellous,
and appal by the terrific, have lately been the favourite
designs of many writers of novels; who, in pursuit of those

effects, have frequently appeared to desert, and sometimes
have really transgressed the bounds of nature and possibility. We cannot approve these extravagances. The artful conduct of an interesting plot, and the dramatic delineation of character, are certainly the features that
give most dignity to this species of fiction. . . ."

The Castle of Hardayne: A Romance, by John Bird. Reviewed   6/112
    in Analytical Review, XXIII (1796), 55.

"Mrs. Radcliffe's Mysteries of Udolpho have given birth
to several humble imitations, which have resembled the
original in nothing, but in attempting to excite surprize
and terrour. The simple, natural, and often instructive
novel, founded upon real life, seems to be in some danger
of being abandoned for the extravagant and terrific romance.
If this taste be encouraged, the merit of a writer of fictitious tales may come to be measured, not by his power
of copying, but of departing, from nature. . . ."

The Castle of Mowbray, [by Mrs. Harley]. Reviewed in Ana-   6/113
    lytical Review, IV (1789), 350.

"A mass of intricate adventures and hairbreadth escapes
. . . [but] young females may peruse the book without im-
bibing any immoral sentiments, and be amused by the quick
succession of incidents, though they outstrip even that
lax kind of probability necessary to give interest to fiction, and weary instead of amuse. . . ."

he Castle of Ollada, [by Francis Lathom]. Reviewed in Cri-   6/114
    tical Review, 2nd ser., XIV (1795), 352.

"Another haunted castle! Surely the misses themselves
must be tired of so many stories of ghosts, and mur-
derers. . . ."

he Castle of St. Vallery: An Ancient Story. Reviewed by   6/115
    M.D. in Analytical Review, XV (1793), 183.

Complete item: "As the age of chivalry, so also the age
of ghosts, is past. For want of faith, which makes things
that are not to be as though they were; stories, in which
supernatural events are introduced, leave less impression
than formerly. Nevertheless, to those readers with whom
faith in ghosts still lingers, or whose lively imaginations
can supply the place of faith, the Castle of St. Vallery,

like the Castle of Otranto, and the Old English Baron, will
be an interesting tale. The story is well conceived, and
the language is correct and forcible."

The Cavern of Death, a Moral Tale. Reviewed in British Cri-   6/116
tic, III (1794), 444.

"This is not only a moral but an interesting Tale. The
scene is placed in Germany, and the Cavern is said still
to retain the name of Die Hole des Todes, and to be
dreaded by the neighbouring peasantry, who entertain many
wild and superstitious ideas respecting it. All this may
be true, though the Tale itself can not. The preternatural
events in it, carry us, however, into such a region of
fancy as we visit with pleasure. The incidents keep attention alive, which is repaid by a catastrophe, artfully
and pleasingly conducted. The language is elegant." "To
admirers of agreeable and moral fiction we recommend the
whole."

--------. Monthly Review, XIV (1794), 464-465.   6/117

"The story is told in correct and good language, and is
interesting and impressive: but we like not this mode of
impression, which fills the mind of the juvenile reader
with horrid ideas of supernatural agency, and makes him
fancy, like Macbeth, that he sees bloody spectres flitting
before his eyes, and ensanguined daggers streaming in the
air."

Clarissa: or, The Fatal Seduction: A Tragedy in Prose.   6/118
Founded on Richardson's Celebrated Novel of Clarissa
Harlowe. By Robert Porrett. Reviewed in English Re-
view, XIV (1789), 337-341.

Notes that "we find some things in this tragedy not to be
met with in Richardson, and which our author tells us are
intended to produce stage effect; such we suppose are the
madness of Clarissa, and the appearance of her spirit
after her death." Wonders also about the introduction
of "a banditti living in a cave" awaiting wealthy travellers.

Count Roderic's Castle; or, Gothic Times. Reviewed in Eng-   6/119
lish Review, XXIV (1794), 392-393.

Complete item: "This novel seems almost incomprehensible.
It contains a continued scene of terrors, battles, and
escapes; subterraneous vaults and men in irons; and ladies
in distress. There have been so many such castles in the
air, that this is by no means new. It seems to be the intention of many of the novelists of the present day, as
well as of former times, to outdo each other in the marvellous at any expense of probability."

The Count de Santerre. Reviewed in Critical Review, 2nd   6/120
ser., XXI (1797), 354.

"The usual furniture of modern romances, -- old castles,
-- long galleries, -- deep vaults, -- sullen echoes, --
flitting lights, -- murders and revivals, are jumbled
here in a confusion which forms a greater mystery than
any the authoress pretends to unravel. We cannot expect
that novel-writers will have any pity for reviewers: but,
for their own sakes, we could wish that they would cease
to build castles in the air, and return to terra firma,
to common life, and common sense."

--------. Monthly Mirror, IV (1797), 346.   6/121

Complete review: "The author of these volumes has suffered herself to be misled by the prevailing taste for
the mysterious and the horrid; which, unless they are
managed with great dexterity, do not even answer the purpose of amusing the fancy; but, on the contrary, provoke
the laughter, if not the contempt of the judicious reader.
This writer, notwithstanding, possesses abilities, which,
with proper cultivation, will place her on a level with
some of our most successful novelists."

usseldorf; or the Fratricide, by Anna Maria Mackenzie. Re-   6/122
viewed in Critical Review, 2nd ser., XXIV (1798), 236.

"It seems to be agreed that those who write on the horrific plan must employ the same instruments -- cruel German counts, each with two wives -- old castles -- private
doors -- sliding panels -- banditti -- assassins -- ghosts,
etc."

Earl Strongbow, [by James White]. Reviewed in Analytical   6/123
Review, III (1789), 343-344.

"We cannot help lamenting that we have not more romances
of this kind, which afford the most pleasing amusement to
the imagination, while they improve the heart. How far
preferable are these histories of deeds of chivalry to
the insipid love tales offered to the public. . . ."

Edmund; or, the Child of the Castle. Reviewed in Critical   6/124
Review, LXX (1790), 454.

Complete item: "Uncommon and unexpected incidents please
by their novelty and the surprize which they occasion;
but when what is uncommon is absurd, and what is unsus-
pected is highly improbable, disgust takes the place of
pleasure, and it is a Reviewer only, steeled by frequent
practice to inflexible perseverance, who does not throw
aside the work with contempt. The adventures before us
are not only absurd and improbable, but almost wholly
unintelligible."

The Enchanted Castle. Reviewed in European Magazine, X   6/125
(1786), 473.

The Enchanted Castle, a pantomime with scenes and "the
literary part" by Mr. Andrews tells of shipwreck on an
enchanted isle, "a formidable magician", a trespass attempted against chastity, and a hero who "ventures
through all the mazes of an enchanted castle, and a succession of scenes . . . presented to the audience, calculated to inspire awful terror".
    The European Magazine, in the same issue (pp. 399-400),
reprints "Sir Bertrand" and says Enchanted Castle "is
partly founded" upon this fragment.

Fatal Revenge; or, the Family of Montorio, a Romance, by   6/12
Dennis Jasper Murphy [Charles Robert Maturin]. Reviewed
by Sir Walter Scott in Quarterly Review, III (1810), 339-
347. (Reprinted in Ioan Williams, Sir Walter Scott on
Novelists and Fiction, New York: Barnes & Noble, 1968.)

A long article which surveys romances. Cites Charlotte
Smith as one of the better writers; notes that the imitators of Mrs. R and MGL, "to all the faults and extrav-
agancies of their originals, added that of dulness, with
which they can seldom be charged." Praises FR but cri-

ticizes the use of explained supernatural, the "mode introduced by Mrs. Radcliffe". "They must either confine
themselves to ordinary and natural events, or find adequate causes for those horrors and mysteries in which they
love to involve us."

The Ghost-Seer; or Apparitionist, by Frederick Schiller. Re-   6/127
viewed in Monthly Review, 2nd ser., XVIII (1795), 346-
347.

"The Ghost-Seer is a novel of great originality. It has
pointed out a new source of the TERRIBLE, -- the pursuit
of an influence over the invisible world, -- and has given
birth to imitations nearly as contemptible as they are
multifarious."

--------. English Review, XXVII (1796), 82.   6/128

"This interesting fragment will prove more interesting to
those, who are fonder of wonder-causing tricks, than to
those, who have a partiality for delineations of genuine
nature."

Grasville Abbey, [by George Moore]. Reviewed in Critical   6/129
Review, 2nd ser., XXI (1797),115-116.

Notes that the novel was first printed in Lady's Magazine
and reissued in book form. "The story is uninterrupted by
digressions, and the interest it creates is powerful.
The situations, likewise, have the merit of being new and
striking. Excepting that there is an abbey furnished
with caverns, ghosts, and dead bodies, there is no servile
imitation of former works of this kind; and, allowance
being made for a foundation of the mysterious sort, probability will not appear to be very grossly violated."

The Haunted Cavern: A Caledonian Tale, by John Palmer, Jr.   6/130
Reviewed in Critical Review, 2nd ser., XV (1795), 480.

"In truth, we are almost weary of Gothic castles, mouldering turrets and 'cloud enveloped battlements' -- The tale
of shrieking spectres, and bloody murders, has been repeated till it palls upon the scene. It requires the
genius of a Radcliffe to harrow up our souls with these
visionary terrors.'

The Haunted Cavern. Reviewed in English Review, XXVI   6/131
(1795), 468.

"Another ghostly story! This novel puts us in mind of
many others of the same kind, particularly the Romance
of the Forest, which the author has had in view when he
wrote the manuscript, said to be found in the haunted
cavern."

The Haunted Priory; or, the Fortunes of the House of Rayo;   6/132
a Romance, Founded Partly on Historical Facts, [by
Stephen Cullen]. Reviewed in British Critic, V (1795),
299.

"We can venture . . . to recommend it strongly to the
perusal of those who do not hesitate to wander beyond
the boundaries of nature, in search of objects which may
excite alarm and surprise; who are better pleased with
the vagaries of a ghost in a Baron's castle, than with
the usual trappings of a novel, sentimental misses, and
intriguing chambermaids."

Hubert de Sevrac, A Romance of the Eighteenth Century, by   6/133
Mary Robinson. Reviewed in Analytical Review, XXV
(1797), 532.

Says the romance is modeled after the works of Mrs. Radcliffe, and "she deserves to rank as one of her most successful imitators: still the characters are so imper-
fectly sketched, the incidents so unconnected, the changes
of scene so frequent, that interest is seldom excited,
and curiosity flags." But, "some of the descriptions are
evidently sketched by a poet."

A Jacobin Novelist. "Terrorist System of Novel Writing",   6/134
Monthly Magazine, IV (1797), 102-104.

An amusing tongue-in-cheek praise of Gothic novels. Says
"Maximilian Robespierre, with his system of terror, . . .
taught our novelists that fear is the only passion they
ought to cultivate, that to frighten and instruct were
the same thing. . . ." Gives instructions on how to write
-- use castle, pictures, decayed furniture, etc., and
presents a rather complete list of stock Gothic devices.

More Ghosts, [by Mrs. F.C. Patrick]. Reviewed in Critical   6/135
    Review, 2nd ser., XXIV (1798), 236.

"More Ghosts would have been superfluous in the present
state of novel-writing, had not the author of this work
conjured up her ghosts with a view of dissipating the
horrors, lately excited in the tender breast of many a
boarding-school miss, by the more artful and terrific
dealers in the article."

Priory of St. Bernard, an Old English Tale, being the first   6/136
    literary Production of a Young Lady [Mrs. Harley]. Re-
    viewed in Critical Review, LXVIII (1789), 75-76.

"There is, as may be expected, much fancy, a luxuriance
of description, and no little improbability in this work.
The young lady steps in the vestiges of Miss Lee and
other novelists and violates a little the truth of history. . . ."

R., E. "On Novels and Romances, With a Cursory Review of   6/137
    the Literary Ladies of Great Britain. Extracts of a
    Letter from a German Lady to Her Friend", La Belle
    Assemblee, I (1806), 531-533.

Alleges that "the mania of falling into the marvellous
is but too common among authoresses as well as authors.
We [Germans] may flatter ourselves with having given the
English a precedent of this, as the fictions of Mrs. Radcliffe, and the horrid dreams of Mr. Lewis, and all the
romances of ghosts that my ears are fatigued with, in-
cessantly prove. I should like to know in what respect
this reading is preferable to those novels that offer
us a true picture of life. . . ." Praises Burney, Ben-
nett, Inchbald, Robinson, Smith, Ann Yearsley, Barbauld,
and Hanna More.

Remarkable Trials and Interesting Memoirs of the Most Noted   6/138
    Criminals. Reviewed in Monthly Review, XXXII (1765),
    395.

Complete item: "These Newgate-annals will doubtless have
their admirers; and it is certain that no kind of reading
is more generally entertaining: whether any improvement
is to be drawn from a contemplation of the vices and
crimes of mankind, is a point that deserves consideration."

Rimelli. "Novels and Romances", Monthly Mirror, XIV (1802),   6/139
81-82.

On the question of whether novel reading corrupts youth.
"Yet, though a great part of our modern novels are flimsy
productions, without either good writing or good sense,
others mere catchpenny trash, and some immoral and even
impious; though the press teems with Midnight Bells,
Black Castles, Haunted Towers, Mysterious Monks, etc.,
etc., with a long train of ghosts, phantoms, etc., yet
I am inclined to think that many excellent precepts and
morals are inculcated in by far the greatest part of
them; and that the rest are to be censured rather as being
absurd, improbable, and illwritten, than tending to corrupt the mind." Cites the Monk as "immoral" and "blasphemous", but says Mrs. Radcliffe and Dr. Moore please
and instruct.

St. Julian's Abbey, a Novel, in a Series of Letters. Re-   6/140
viewed in Critical Review, LXVI (1788), 255.

Complete item: "These volumes are in the modern dress,
but the story is old, the manners are those of the last
century. Though there is much murder, there is scarcely
any pathos; St Julian's Abbey may amuse a winter's evening, if the reader looks not for probability, and is not
disgusted by absurdity."

The Secret, by Isabella Kelly. Reviewed in Monthly Review,   6/141
LI (1806), 207.

Complete review: "Those who delight in useless mysteries
and unnecessary horrors may perhaps be gratified by reading these volumes; but, in our judgment, the contemplation
of such stories is attended with worse consequences than the
mere waste of time. It tends to produce a sickly and
irritable state of mind, gives a temporary shock even to
intellects that are sound and healthy, but enervates and
permanently diseases those which are weak."

The Sorcerer: a Tale From the German of Veit Weber [Georg   6/142
P.L.L. Wachter]. Reviewed in Critical Review, 2nd ser.,
XVII (1796), 113.

"Supernatural agency, when judiciously managed, and where
philosophy and true religion have not wholly eradicated
its terrors from the popular mind, is a fine machine in

the hands of the poet and romance-writer. The terrible
and the sublime, perhaps, cannot be separated; but in
this advanced period of knowledge, it requires a writer
of genius to prevent the high-wrought feeling from too
suddenly subsiding, or from sliding (a not very difficult
transition) into burlesque. The catastrophe of the present
work harrows up the soul with emotions too shockingly
vivid to be gratifying; they exceed in a great degree all
the limits of pleasure which critics point out as the
sources of the satisfaction we receive from the perusal
of works of this nature, -- and we shut the book with a
sensation of horror bordering on disgust."

Sorrows of Werther; a poem, by Amelia Dickering. Reviewed in   6/143
    English Review, XIII (1798), 128.

"Will the sorrows of Werther never have an end? That
dangerous, though well-written book, seems to have fascinated the public mind, and that of the female sex in
particular. It is with regret we see this; for though
we do not apprehend that the reading of it, in the present
state of society, will produce many catastrophes similar
to that of Werther, yet we are afraid it may be productive
of much harm to the youth of both sexes."

W.W. "On Novels and Romances", Scots Magazine, LXIV (1802),   6/144
    470-474, 545-548.

Reading romances generates "imbecility of mind" and "the
female mind is more readily affected by the tendency of
such works". Calls the Gothic novels "literary abortions"; discusses and derides Rinaldo, Udolpho, Caroline
of Lichtfield, and The Monk. Objects to Mrs. Radcliffe's
suspense technique; says in MU "many passages occur, that
cannot but strike the most superficial reader, as being
particularly objectionable". Says Monk has "something of
merit in point of style", but possesses "all the faults
and immoralities ascribed to novels".

VII

THE GOTHIC LEGACY

a.

General Influences

Chew, Samuel C., Jr. The Dramas of Lord Byron: A Critical   7/1
Study [1915]. New York: Russell & Russell, 1964.

Notes the influence of the Gothic novel (a "style on the
verge of absurdity") on the new romantic drama, and sees
Byron working in this tradition. Asserts that there
exist in Byron's works, influences of Walpole, Lewis, and
Beckford. Sees Manfred as drawing on Prometheus, Don Juan,
and Faust.

Dutt, Sukumar. The Supernatural in English Romantic Poetry.   7/2
Being a Critical Survey of Supernaturalism: Its Growth
and Phases of Development in English Poetry During 1780-
1830 [1938]. [Folcroft]: Folcroft, 1972.

A long general treatment of the supernatural in poetry
from Beowulf to Shelley and Keats. Traces the changing
treatment of the marvelous from a superstitious, religious,
awe-inspiring motif to the Romantic revolt, the inner
vision, the mysticism, the extension of insight. Pays
some attention to Lewis's horror-romanticism, but the
Gothic novels receive little more than mention, and the
glut of cheap "pedlar literature" is viewed with disdain.

Dyce, A. "Plagiarisms of Lord Byron", Gentleman's Magazine,   7/3
NS, X, pt. 1 (1818), 121-122.

Points out specific "borrowings" in Lara from Radcliffe's
Udolpho, Parnell's "Night-Piece on Death", Voltaire's
Henriade, and from a letter of Pope, but says "no doubt,
the author was unconscious" of this plagiarism.
     This contradiction of terms is questioned by C.C. in
"Lord Byron Vindicated from Alleged Plagiarisms", Gentle-
man's Magazine, NS, X, pt. 1 (1818), 390-391.

Gilpatric, Mary Ellen Park. "Gothic Elements in English Ro-   7/4
mantic Poetry". Unpublished doctoral dissertation, Kent
State Univ., 1965.

"One of the influences of the age was the Gothic novel --
sensational, imitative, and superficial -- yet strangely
provocative to the Romantic poets, who found beneath its
crude surface an imaginative stimulus and materials to
objectify their conception of reality." Says that with
the exception of Shelley, the Romantic poets were openly
contemptuous of Gothic romances, yet although they damned
Gothicism, they were practitioners of it to some extent.
Shows how they borrowed and used certain key themes --
the romantic captive, the living dead, the veil of obscurity. These Gothic elements, this "imagery of its
nightmare world", became transformed into a "philosophical
context that gives these images a kind of meaning which
would have been all but incomprehensible to the author
of The Italian".

Heilman, Robert B. "Charlotte Brontë's 'New' Gothic", in   7/5
Austin Wright, ed., Victorian Literature: Modern Essays
in Criticism. Galaxy Books. New York: Oxford Univ.
Press, 1961.

Contests Montague Summers' (6/29) view of surrealism and
contends that Miss Brontë used "old"Gothic trappings,
some "anti-Gothic" to undercut, and contributed something
of her own. "In her flair for the surreal, in her plung-
ing into feeling that is without status in the ordinary
world of the novel, Charlotte discovers a new dimension
of Gothic."

Hollingsworth, Keith. "Vathek and the 'Ode to a Nightin-   7/6
gale'", TLS (Oct. 27, 1961), p. 771.

Keats read Vathek. Borrowings have been found in "En-
dymion", "Hyperion", and "The Fall of Hyperion", and now
it is suggested that "Ode to a Nightingale" may owe to
"The Flower and the Leaf", but "when he wrote the Ode,
Beckford's luxuriant arbor seems to have been there too".

Longueil, Alfred Edwin. "Gothic Romance: Its Influence on   7/7
the Romantic Poets Wordsworth, Keats, Coleridge, Byron
and Shelley". Unpublished doctoral dissertation, Harvard, 1920.

This pioneering work sets out to investigate the influence
of Gothic on Romantic, notes interrelations, and compares
the manner in which landscape description, horror, and
Gothic machinery are utilized. Concludes that the influence "was wide in the scope of material furnished; that
it was varyingly wide in the scope of time through which
this material exerted a power, the duration depending
upon the strength of the original stimulus, which differed
for each poet, being strongest apparently in Shelley and
Byron, next strongest in Coleridge and Keats, weakest in
Wordsworth: and that in the main, descriptions excepted,
it was not a wholesome influence, working against, rather
than for, the ends of poetic art."

Peck, Walter E. "Keats, Shelley, and Mrs. Radcliffe", MLN,   7/8
XXXIX (1924), 251-252.

Professor Shackford's article (7/10) pointing out that
Keats' "Eve of St. Agnes" draws on Mrs. Radcliffe caused
Peck to reread Mysteries of Udolpho, and he now suggests
that Keats also displays parallels in "Ode to a Nightingale". Shelley, Peck asserts, similarly drew on Udolpho
for names of characters in Zastrozzi and St. Irvyne and
for the poisoned goblet incident.

Rudwin, Maximilian. "Balzac and the Fantastic", SR, XXXIII   7/9
(1925), 1-24.

A general treatment of the influence of the English Gothic
novel in France, with special attention to Balzac and
his fantastic works.

Shackford, Martha Hale. "The Eve of St. Agnes and The Mys-   7/10
teries of Udolpho", PMLA, XXXVI (1921), 104-118.

Asserts that Keats drew upon MU for his poem and borrowed
for setting, plot, and character. Offers extensive quotations for comparison. Concludes that Keats was not
"slavishly imitative, but rather, intensely original" in
the way he handled the materials.

118

Young, A.B. "Shelley and M.G. Lewis", MLR, I (1906), 322-   7/11
324.

Shelley's Original Poems contain "St. Edmund's Eve",
"which is copied word for word from a poem entitled 'The
Black Canon of Elmham or Saint Edmund's Eve' from Lewis'
Tales of Terror, 1799 and 1808 editions". Also, "Ghasta"
"is nothing more or less than a versification by Shelley
of the tale of 'Don Raymond', 'The Bleeding Nun' and the
'Wandering Jew' as related in the Monk with some minor
alterations". Shelley's "The Revenge" follows "Castle
of Lindenberg", and "Alonzo the Brave" is from Alonzo the
Brave. Zastrozzi is not from German originals but rather
"nothing but a second version of certain portions of the
Monk, with, however, great alterations".

b.

Influence on American Literature

Arvin, Newton. "Melville and the Gothic Novel", in his   7/12
American Pantheon. Edited by Daniel Aaron and Sylvan
Schendler. New York: Delacorte, 1966.

Notes Melville's interest in the Gothic novel, points
out his allusions to Mrs. Radcliffe, isolates the Gothic
machinery in Moby Dick and certain short works. Concludes
that although Gothic influence seems slight, it is remarkable that it remained an influence for so long in
America. (On Melville, see also 8/87.)

Charney, Maurice. "Hawthorne and the Gothic Style", NEQ,   7/13
XXXIV (1961), 36-49.

Shows NH's love of Gothic architecture and points out
that he used Gothic and romantic as synonyms. Concludes
by saying that "one may . ◦ . posit a certain unity in
Hawthorne's sense of style, and it is not surprising
that he should have tried to achieve in his romances
qualities that moved him so deeply in gothic churches, or
that he should have seen in these churches stylistic
qualities that he admired as a romancer."

Coad, Oral Sumner. "The Gothic Element in American Litera-   7/14
ture Before 1835", JEGP, XXIV (1925), 72-93.

A survey of American Gothic in poetry, drama, and prose
fiction. Covers Brown, Cooper, Irving, Neal, Freneau,
Whittier, Dana and more than a score of lesser-known
writers. Notes that more than half the plays written in
the U.S. between 1794 and 1835 contained Gothic elements,
and four-fifths of these American Gothic dramas use the
explained supernatural of Mrs. Radcliffe. Playwrights
and poets used European settings, but prose writers,
following Brown, utilized native scenes and often used
gloomy natural settings in place of architectural gloom.
Novels also followed the explained supernatural.

Hartley, Lodwick. "From Crazy Castle to The House of Usher: 7/15
A Note Toward a Source", SSF, II (1965), 256-261.

Claims that Poe may have found his source for Roderick
Usher in the real life figure of John Hall-Stevenson,
friend of Sterne, and noted hypochondriac. Poe read
Sterne, but Hartley can not prove that he was familiar
with Sterne's Crazy Tales (1762) which describe, in verse,
a moated, mouldering castle.

Hawthorne, Nathaniel. Preface to The Marble Faun, or, The   7/16
Romance of Monte Beni [1859], in Norman Holmes Pearson,
ed., The Complete Novels and Selected Tales of Nathaniel
Hawthorne. Modern Library. New York: Random, 1937.

Sheds some light on his predecessors. "Italy, as the site
of his [NH speaking of himself] Romance, was chiefly
valuable to him as affording a sort of poetic or fairy
precinct, where actualities would not be so terribly in-
sisted upon as they are, and must needs be, in America.
No author, without a trial, can conceive of the difficulty
of writing a romance about a country where there is no
shadow, no antiquity, no mystery, no picturesque and
gloomy wrong, no anything but a commonplace prosperity,
in broad and simple daylight. . . . Romance and poetry,
ivy, lichens, and wall-flowers, need ruin to make them
grow."

Loshe, Lillie Deming. The Early American Novel, 1789-1830   7/17
[1907]. New York: Ungar, 1966.

Chapter II, "The Gothic and the Revolutionary", deals with
Charles Brockden Brown "who introduced to America, the
fashion then prevailing in British fiction", but concludes
that Brown "had no imitators in his genre, and he exerted
no immediate influence on American fiction". Calls The
Asylum, or Alonzo and Melissa "the only American product
of Mrs. Radcliffe's influence".

Lundblad, Jane. Nathaniel Hawthorne and the Tradition of   7/18
Gothic Romance [1946]. New York: Haskell, 1964.

Lists "the principal traits of the novel of terror and
wonder" as: (1)MS (2)Castle (3)Crime (4)Religion
(5)Italians (6)Deformity (7)Ghosts (8)Magic (9)Nature
(10)Armoured Knights (11)Works of Art (12)Blood. Goes
through NH's works and looks for these elements. Concludes that "Gothic Romance formed an important substra-
tum of Hawthorne's productions -- perhaps not always consciously used, but ever present and often employed for
definite artistic purposes." Notes that "Hawthorne's
use of the Gothic elements was comparatively profuse in
his first short stories; it waned during the middle period of his productions, to be revived in his latest
works."

Malin, Irving. New American Gothic. Preface by Harry T.   7/19
Moore. Carbondale: Southern Illinois Univ. Press,
1962.

Deals with six modern American Gothicists -- Capote, Mc-
Cullers, Hawkes, O'Connor, Salinger, and Purdy. The
symbolic use of the traditional themes of imprisonment,
the haunted castle, and the escape journey are discussed,
but Malin asserts that for the early Gothic novelists,
these were mere props. Narcissism, the family as micro-
cosm, Freudian themes, mechanical and animalistic imagery,
and distorted images are topics of study. "Flatness" of
character is viewed as a characteristic of Gothic, and
types, not individuals, people the novels. "In Gothic,
order often breaks down: chronology is confused, identity
is blurred, sex is twisted, the buried life erupts. The
total effect is that of a dream."

121

O'Connor, William Van. "The Grotesque: An American Genre",   7/20
in his The Grotesque: An American Genre and Other Essays.
Carbondale: Southern Illinois Univ. Press, 1962.

Of peripheral interest. Raises questions on the abnormal,
the violent, the sexual; comments on how the grotesque is
linked to the sublime. Emphasis falls on Algren, West,
and Faulkner, but the genre is traced to Poe. Explains
that characters are conceived as one dimensional, obsessed
with one thing, and in movement similar to the blocks of
a comic strip.

Pearson, Edmund. Queer Books. Garden City: Doubleday, 1928. 7/21

Contains plot summary and extracts from an American Gothic
novel of 1811 written "under the influence of The Mysteries
of Udolpho and the Gothic romance generally". This book,
Isaac Mitchell's The Asylum; or Alonzo and Melissa, "enjoyed a popularity and long life which few American
novels have ever known". It lasted for sixty years, un-
derwent various printings, and "there were periods when
a new edition of it seemed to come out every year, each
time in a different city".

Phillips, George L. "The Gothic Element in the American   7/22
Novel Before 1830", West Virginia University Bulletin:
Philological Studies, III (1939), 37-45.

"Since, by the turn of the century, Gothicism, was finding
increasing favor on the part of the American public in
architecture, painting, and imported English novels, why
did not the cult of the Gothic novel become fashionable
among the American writers of fiction?" Offers several
reasons: America lacked medieval props and aristocratic
families; American Puritans opposed a novel written for
amusement only; American patriotism demanded American
scenes and incidents. Includes comments on some American-
Gothic novels.

Redden, Sister Mary Mauritia. The Gothic Fiction in the   7/23
American Magazines (1765-1800). Washington: Catholic
Univ. of America Press, 1939.

Examines five English Gothicists and five American Gothicists. Isolates, catalogues, then compares their machinery; concludes there are differences -- for example,
Americans used terrors of plague, Indians, wild animals;

122

neglected use of nuns. Offers plot summaries of 75 stories. Says American magazine Gothic "exceeded in horror by far" the American-Gothic novel, which was its descendant. Includes bibliography, list of magazines, and a chronological list of stories from 1785 to 1800.

Whitt, Celia. "Poe and The Mysteries of Udolpho", University 7/24 of Texas Studies in English, XVII (1937), 124-131.

Poe's "The Assignation", first published as "The Visionary" in Godey's Lady's Book in 1843 shows some specific borrowings from Udolpho. In both name and character , Poe's Mentoni resembles AR's Montoni; Poe's unnamed young hero and his heroine resemble those of Mrs. R, and "in addition, the novel contains a surprising number of details that are similar to those of the story, including the very unusual one of Venetian glass that is sensitive to poison". Also it is suggested that Montresor in "The Cask of Amontillado" represents a later version of Montoni. Finally, since Poe, in "The Oval Portrait" refers to Mrs. Radcliffe, it seems certain that he was familiar with her work.

c.

Influence on Coleridge

Ainsworth, Edward G., Jr. "Another Source of the 'Lonesome 7/25 Road' Stanza in The Ancient Mariner", MLN, XLIX (1934), 111-112.

Suggests lines 56-70 of Blair's The Grave (1743) as the source for Coleridge's passage which begins: "Like one that on a lonesome road / Doth walk in fear and dread. . . ." (AM, 446-451.)

Basler, Roy P. Sex, Symbolism; and Psychology in Literature 7/26 [1948]. New York: Octagon, 1967.

Discusses Nethercct's Road (7/31) and argues that he is incorrect in glossing over the sexual theme in Christabel. Basler sees a sexual theme binding the two girls and sees also a Freudian daughter-father-dead mother problem in the relationship of Christabel and Sir Leoline.

123

Coburn, Kathleen. "Coleridge and Wordsworth and 'the Super-   7/27
natural'", <u>UTQ</u>, XXV (1956), 121-130.

Wordsworth said <u>Ancient Mariner</u> had "grave defects"; his
own <u>Peter Bell</u> is on the same theme but features no supernatural agency. Coburn says Wordsworth's poem "is a poem
of behaviour" while Coleridge's is "by direct emotional
evocation, a poem of the inner life". Or, <u>AM</u> "comes
deeply out of a troubled mind and the other out of a theory
of the supernatural". Says <u>Christabel</u> "is not an incomplete Gothic romance, but rather makes use of the medium
to project an inner experience".

Greever, Garland. <u>A Wiltshire Parson and His Friends: The</u>   7/28
<u>Correspondence of William Lisle Bowles, Together with Four</u>
<u>Hitherto Unidentified Reviews by Coleridge</u>. London: Con-
stable, 1926.

Includes a letter of March, 1797, from Coleridge to Bowles
which establishes the identity of a hitherto anonymous
reviewer. "I am almost weary of the terrible, having been
a hireling in the <u>Critical Review</u> for these last six or
eight months. I have been lately reviewing the <u>Monk</u>, the
<u>Italian</u>, <u>Hubert de Sevrac</u>, etc., etc., in all of which
dungeons, and old castles, and solitary Houses by the Sea
Side, and Caverns, and Woods, and extraordinary characters,
and all the tribe of Horror and Mystery, have crowded on
me -- even to suffering." Greever appends the reviews --
<u>Udolpho</u> (11/111), <u>Italian</u> (11/126), <u>Monk</u> (12/89), <u>Hubert</u>,
together with a short introduction in which he comments
upon Coleridge's debt to Mrs. Radcliffe. (But see 7/32.)

Lowes, John Livingston. <u>The Road to Xanadu: A Study in the</u>   7/29
<u>Ways of the Imagination</u>. Boston: Houghton Mifflin, 1922.

An exhaustive study of background sources and suggestions
for "Kubla Khan" and <u>Ancient Mariner</u>. Lewis's <u>Monk</u> im-
pressed Coleridge and may have furnished the Wanderer for
<u>AM</u>. Says <u>AM</u> not really part of Gothic tradition; admits
he can not find the track of <u>Christabel</u>.

<u>Lyrical Ballads</u>. Reviewed in <u>Analytical Review</u>, XXVIII   7/30
(1798), 583-587.

"The 'Rime of the Ancyent Marinere', . . . is written pro-
fessedly in imitation of the style as well as the spirit
of the ancient poets. We are not pleased with it; in our

opinion it has more of the extravagance of a mad German
poet, than of the simplicity of our ancient ballad
writers."

Nethercot, Arthur H. The Road to Tyermaine: A Study of the   7/31
History, Background, and Purposes of Coleridge's "Christabel". Chicago: Univ. of Chicago Press, 1939.

Contends that sources of Christabel are closer than Lowes
(7/29) thought. Says the poem has sources not in the
Gothic novels, but rather in essays by Calmet and Voltaire,
in Manchester Memoirs, and also may have the influence of
Goethe. Calls Ancient Mariner "supernatural", Christabel
"preternatural". Sees Christabel as a didactic poem fea-
turing beings from another world, and concerned with name-
less sin, suffering, and atonement. Discusses vampirism,
the lamia, mesmerism and the backgrounds of the 1790-1800
Gothic period. Examines Coleridge's Gothic reviews.

Patterson, Charles I. "The Authenticity of Coleridge's Re-   7/32
views of Gothic Romances", JEGP, L (1951), 517-521.

Refutes Greever's claim that Coleridge wrote the reviews
of Italian, Udolpho, and Hubert de Sevrac which appeared
in the Critical Review and are reproduced in Wiltshire
Parson (7/28). Says Coleridge did write reviews of these
three novels -- but they are not the reviews which appear
in the CR. In a previously unpublished letter of 1828,
STC claimed he burned reviews which he called "clever
and epigramatic and devilishly severe". In length, they
varied from a single sentence to half a page. Thus, these
three reviews were never published, but the piece on the
Monk (CR, Feb., 1797) is genuine.

Tuttle, Donald Revel. "Christabel Sources in Percy's Re-   7/33
liques and the Gothic Romance", PMLA, LIII (1938), 445-
474.

Calls Christabel "a versified Gothic romance"; says chief
sources "are works which The Road to Xanadu [7/29] notes
as contributing to Kubla Khan and The Ancient Mariner;
namely, Percy's Reliques, and the Gothic romances of Mrs.
Radcliffe, 'Monk' Lewis and Mrs. Robinson". Points out
parallels in Udolpho and Monk; sees Mrs. Radcliffe as
main influence.

125

d.

Influence on Jane Austen

Bradbrook, Frank W. "Sources of Jane Austen's Ideas About   7/34
Nature in 'Mansfield Park'", N&Q, NS, VIII (1961), 222-
224.

Sees as sources, Gilpin, Charlotte Smith, and Ann Radcliffe. Points out "a number of parallels between The
Mysteries of Udolpho and Mansfield Park" and notes also
that in MP, "Jane Austen occasionally appears to have
absorbed Shakespeare through the medium of Ann Radcliffe".
Also, sees a similarity in phrasing in Wordsworth's "It
is a Beauteous Evening Calm and Free" (1802), MP (ca. 1811-
1813), and MU (1794). Thinks JA drew directly on MU and
wonders if Wordsworth or his sister recalled the passage
in MU.

Davie, John. Introduction to Northanger Abbey and Persuasion. 7/35
Oxford English Novels. London: Oxford Univ. Press, 1971.

Discusses the Gothic parody thesis, offers a bibliography,
rejects the simple solution of Gothic burlesque and suggests a wider range of purposes.

Emden, Cecil S. "The Composition of Northanger Abbey", RES,   7/36
NS, XIX (1968), 279-287.

Contends that the bulk of NA was written in 1794 "and that
the sections burlesquing horror-novels, and Mrs. Radcliffe's
Mysteries of Udolpho in particular, were added some four
years later". Offers comments on opinions of other critics. Isolates and enumerates in an appendix some 38 "references to what appear to be the Gothic interpolations".

Litz, A. Walton. Jane Austen: A Study of Her Artistic De-   7/37
velopment. New York: Oxford Univ. Press, 1965.

Shows that NA is a very complex and subtle piece of irony
and not just another laughable parody of a ridiculous
genre. The Gothic elements are organic and serve as a
commentary on Catherine's character. The mature themes

126

of "the problem of accommodating reason and feeling, of
regulating sympathy without destroying it" are presented,
but Litz asserts that technical failure and inconsistencies
bring about confusion.

McKillop, Alan D.   "Jane Austen's Gothic Titles", N&Q, NS,   7/38
IX (1921), 361-362.

Identifies Necromancer, thus solving the last mystery of
the Northanger novels. Provides information on the authors and lists contemporary reviews. Notes that all of
the novels were written between 1793 and 1798, so "the
passage in question [in NA] was probably written in 1798,
and records strictly contemporary horrors".

Mayo, Robert D.   Introduction to Grasville Abbey by George   7/39
Moore. New York: Arno, 1974.

Shows that GA is "an important member of the Northanger
canon, though never mentioned by name". Discusses early
opposition to Gothic novels and looks at magazines and
serial publications.

Sadleir, Michael.   "'All Horrid?': Jane Austen and the   7/40
Gothic Romance", in his Things Past. London: Constable,
1944.

Sadleir says that "the Gothic romance and the French Sym-
bolist Movement were in their small way as much an expression of a deep subversive impulse as were the French
Revolution itself and the grim gathering of forces for
industrial war." Offers an essay on Gothicism, comments
on ruins, revivals, and architecture, and observes that
"Jane Austen's pick of Gothic novels was rather deliberate
than random, [and] was made for the stories' rather than
for their titles' sake." Copies of all seven have now
been located and each is briefly discussed and classified
according to "school". Gothic parodies are examined and
Beckford's Modern Novel Writing and Azemia are deprecated
as "buffooneries content to mock by exaggeration and without any pretence of creating a new intelligibility of
their own".

e.

Influence on Scott

Boatright, Mody C. "Scott's Theory and Practice Concerning   7/41
the Use of the Supernatural in Prose Fiction in Relation
to the Chronology of the Waverley Novels", PMLA, L (1935),
235-261.

In 1799 Scott was sympathetic to Gothic and shortly after
this date, established certain guidelines for the use of
the supernatural in fiction; but, by the time of Waverley,
he broke with Gothic. Professor Boatright isolates five
of Scott's theories, applies them to his novels, and attempts to establish chronology. Believes Black Dwarf
(pub. 1816) was first written shortly after 1797 as a
tale of terror "in the tradition of Ann Radcliffe". Similarly, The Monastery (pub. 1820) has serious violations
of rules laid down previous to publication. Believes
Guy Mannering (pub. 1815) and Redgauntlet (pub. 1824) are
also pre-Waverley.

Freye, Walter. The Influence of "Gothic" Literature on Sir   7/42
Walter Scott. Rostock: Winterberg, 1902.

A 62-page pamphlet which attempts to point out Scott's
debt to Mrs. Radcliffe, Lewis, and Coleridge. Asserts
influence is strongest on the earlier verse works, but
says that the novels owe something also. Offers parallel
passages from Scott and his masters to show similarity
in meter, handling of supernatural, and resemblance of
description, but this asserted similarity is not always
apparent and sometimes appears highly questionable. Has
some awkwardness in English, a lack of clear direction,
and a weak case.

Mayo, Robert Donald. "The Waverley Novels in their Relations   7/43
to Gothic Fiction". Unpublished doctoral dissertation,
Princeton, 1938.

A long, scholarly, thorough investigation of Scott's
Gothicism. Begins with definitions of Gothic; looks at
earlier attempts to classify the Gothic novel; suggests
that Gothic defines a novel which uses specialized, stand-
ardized, and stereotyped machinery. The first 140 pages

128

represent a study of the genre, and Mayo devalues Walpole
as "father", tracing the line from sentimental comedy,
through domestic tragedy, Richardson, Prévost, D'Arnaud,
and Smollett. Says Mrs. Radcliffe's works not rooted in
Burke's sublime, Tasso, Spenser, Milton, and Shakespeare,
but rather in 18th-century sentimental romance and 18th-
century melancholy poetry. Establishes that Scott was a
prolific novel reader, owned many Gothic novels, and was
thoroughly familiar with their conventions. Contends
that contrary to what Tompkins (5/18) and Mehrotra (8/43)
say, the Gothic novel remained popular till 1830. Scott
claimed to renounce Gothic sentimentalism, but borrowed
heavily. He claimed to write of real life, but portrayed
a heroic past. Bride of Lammermoor represents his most
Gothic and "may be regarded, in a sense, as the embodiment
of all that Walpole sought to do, and failed". In Scott's
other novels, Gothic machinery appears, but in subordinate
roles. Sometimes Scott revivified the old motifs by uti-
lizing materials drawn from real life, and at his best,
"he recreates the forms and imagery of Gothic romance in
terms of equivalents drawn from Scotch life." Scott's
last novels make increased use of supernatural -- both
real and explained -- in search for new materials and
popular appeal.

Parsons, Coleman O. Witchcraft and Demonology in Scott's   7/44
Fiction. With Chapters on the Supernatural in Scottish
Literature. London: Oliver & Boyd, 1964.

Relates Sir Walter's supernaturalism, not to the 18th-
century English Gothic novel, but to "the rich store of
Scottish literature and folklore which was at his disposal". Scatters ideas for two dozen dissertations and
examines other Scottish practitioners -- Boswell, Smollett,
Thomson, Mallett, Beattie, Macpherson, Burns, Mackenzie,
Hogg, John Galt, George MacDonald, Margaret Oliphant,
R.L. Stevenson, John Buchan, Neil Gunn, and Eric Link-
later.

Pandy, Stephen Merrill. "Studies in the Form of the Romantic   7/45
Novel: Otranto to Waverley". Unpublished doctoral dissertation, Harvard, 1963.

Asserts that a good part of Sir Walter Scott's talent was
that of a syncretist. Scott was influential on 19th-
century fiction, and he himself "drew together the path-
less diversity into which the novel had strayed". Studies
eight novels: Otranto, Old English Baron, Recess,

129

Ethelinde, Udolpho, Thaddeus of Warsaw, Scottish Chiefs, Waverley. Sees the Freudian interpretation of Otranto, the thematic concern with a protagonist limited by society, and makes a penetrating investigation into the sparse style of prose writing. Attention is paid to Mrs. Radcliffe's aesthetic concern and her debt to Burke and Burnet. Contends that even though Scott depreciated Mrs. Radcliffe's value, he owes her a debt for his isolated protagonist moving through a carefully chosen landscape.

Scott, Sir Walter. General Preface to the Waverley Novels.   7/46
Edinburgh: [n.n.], 1854.

Records his early ambition of "attempting a work of imagination in prose", of "composing a tale of chivalry, which was to be in the style of the Castle of Otranto, with plenty of Border characters, and supernatural incident".

--------. "On the Supernatural in Fictitious Composition;   7/47
and Particularly on the Works of Ernest Theodore William Hoffmann", in Ioan Williams, ed., Sir Walter Scott on Novelists and Fiction. New York: Barnes & Noble, 1968.

Contains critical advice on the use of the supernatural -- brief, sparingly, obscure. A single employment is the most effective; ghosts should not speak; the reader's imagination should be excited but not gratified. Concludes that Hoffmann's tales "are not the visions of a poetical mind, they have scarcely even the seeming authenticity which the hallucinations of lunacy convey. . . ." Instead, "the inspirations of Hoffmann so often resemble the ideas produced by the immoderate use of opium, that we cannot help considering his case as one requiring the assistance of medicine rather than of criticism. . . ."

f.

Influence on Dickens

oolidge, Archibald C., Jr. "Charles Dickens and Mrs. Rad-   7/48
cliffe: A Farewell to Wilkie Collins", Dickensian,
LVIII (1962), 112-116.

Sees influence of Mrs. Radcliffe in Dickens' theme of a
heroine or child in danger, and in "the announced and pur-
poseful Gothic atmosphere, the announced and conscious
contrasts of scenery with mood, the announced and conscious concentration on Romantic scenery as scenery". Notes
Gothic influence in the Pickwick inserts, in Oliver Twist,
Nicholas Nickleby, Old Curiosity Shop, Barnaby Rudge.
"The Gothic elements in Dickens' first few books may have
been influenced by childhood memories, by the continued
lessening public interest in Gothic stories, and by contemporary crime novels which used some Gothic elements",
and also by Gothic melodramas. Notes that when Charles
Dickens had developed his suspense technique in BR in
1841, Collins was only seventeen.

irkpatrick, Larry. "The Gothic Flame of Charles Dickens",   7/49
VN, no. 31 (Spring, 1967), pp. 20-24.

Says that it is "immediately obvious that Bleak House and
Great Expectations owe a sizable debt to the Gothic tradition" and points out Gothicism in Old Curiosity Shop,
Little Dorrit, and Our Mutual Friend. Discusses the sur-
realistic aspects, the juxtapositioning, the chamber of
horrors, the grotesques, death as escape, and the theme
of imprisonment. Notes how CD used Gothic trappings, but
"tempered the genre by greater pathos and psychological
depth".

illips, Walter C. Dickens, Reade, and Collins, Sensational   7/50
Novelists: A Study in the Conditions and Theories of
Novel Writing in Victorian England [1919]. New York:
Russell & Russell, 1962.

Thesis is that Victorian sensationalism descends not from
Scott, but from Gothicism. The "direct connection" is
the picturesque ruffian who served as hero for Mrs. Radcliffe, Byron, and Bulwer Lytton".

131

Sucksmith, Harvey Peter. "The Secret of Immediacy: Dickens' 7/51
Debt to the Tale of Terror in Blackwood's", NCF, XXVI
(1971), 145-157.

Agrees that Dickens is a sensational novelist but says
Phillips (7/50) errs "in trying to trace the development
of Dickens exclusively from the Gothic tale through Byron
and Bulwer Lytton". Believes that this sensational strain
came from early tales in Blackwood's. The essential difference, he explains, is that "the Gothic tale generally
arouses a purely romantic terror through vague suggestion"
but the Blackwood's tale "creates a realistic terror
through precision of descriptive detail".

g.

Movie Monsters

Ackerman, Forrest J., ed. Boris Karloff: The Frankenscience 7/52
Monster. New York: Ace, 1969.

This anthology includes photos, lists of the departed master's movies, and about thirty articles by various hands
including Bloch, Bradbury, Dorothy Calhoun, Vincent Price,
Lon Chaney, Christopher Lee, and others. Topics range
from movies to comic books.

Amis, Kingsley, "Dracula, Frankenstein, Sons & Co.", in his 7/53
What Became of Jane Austen? and Other Questions. London:
Jonathan Cape, 1970.

A nostalgic recollection of the novelist's 35 years of
horror film watching. With an appreciation of the Hammer
revival.

Clarens, Carlos. An Illustrated History of the Horror Films. 7/54
New York: Putnam's, 1967.

A popular survey of the horror film with 170 pages of
text, 48 pages of photos, and a seventy-page appendix
which gives cast and credits of films mentioned in text.

)ouglas, Drake. Horror!. Toronto: Collier- Macmillan,1969. 7/55

Chapters include: "Vampire", "Werewolf", "Mummy", "Walking Dead", "Schizophrenic", "Phantom", "Creators of Horror". Treats each topic three ways -- in legend, in literature, in film. Final chapter deals with Poe, Lovecraft, and Machen. Illustrated; with bibliography and
list of films.

:verson, William K. The Bad Guys: A Pictorial History of   7/56
the Movie Villain [1964]. 4th ed. New York: Citadel,
1971.

Mainly pictures, from the Great Train Robbery through
sixty years of villains -- mustached Mexicans, grinning
Orientals, scar-faced Italians, black-hatted cowboys,
monacled Nazis, sword-wielding Japs, and pork-pie hatted
Commies. "The Monsters" offers fifty pictures from
Caligari to Christopher Lee.

uss, Roy and T.J. Ross, eds. Focus on the Horror Film.   7/57
Englewood Cliffs: Prentice-Hall, 1972.

Contains 25 essays ranging from the Frankenstein films of
the 1930's, through the atomic mutations, to Rosemary's
Baby. Contains a chronological list of notable films and
a valuable annotated bibliography.

irie, David. A Heritage of Horror: The English Gothic   7/58
Cinema 1946-1972. London: Gordon Fraser, 1973.

The English Gothic cinema is "in no way imitative of
American or European models" but instead derives "in
general from literary sources". Draws upon Varma (6/31)
and Praz (4/6), notes the literary backgrounds, discusses
surrealism and calls the horror film "the most popular
and frequently attempted cinematic form in England".
Looks at Terrence Fisher, Don Sharp, John Gilling, Ver-
non Sewell, Michael Reeves, Freddie Francis, and others.
With a "filmography" and many illustrations.

Willis, Donald C. Horror and Science Fiction Films: A   7/59
Checklist. Metuchen: Scarecrow, 1972.

Contains "about 4,400 titles in the main listing", a list
of titles announced for release in 1971-1972, and a bibliography. Entries give cast, production information,
a sentence or two on plot, and sometimes an extract from
a critic.

h.

Modern Thrillers

Barlow, Ron and Bhob Stewart, eds. Horror Comics of the   7/60
1950's. New York: Nostalgia, 1971.

Full color, full-size reprints of 23 EC horror comics
of the early 1950's. Prefatory essays by Stewart and
Larry Stark offer reminiscences of youthful reading in
that era, give details of artists, plots, etc., and
comment on the 1955 censorship ban which caused the demise of the horror comics.

Harper, Ralph. The World of the Thriller. Cleveland: Case   7/61
Western Reserve Univ. Press, 1969.

A brief but complex study of the thriller by a scholar
known mainly for his work on existentialism. Buchan,
Hammett, Fleming, Deighton, LeCarre, Chandler, Ambler,
and Greene are the main subjects of study, yet the book
provides many enlightening comments and offers hints and
implications which can be used on the early Gothicists.
Discusses many topics including the reason for popularity,
the hero as "hero", the Freudian theme, sex and violence,
the hero as outlaw, detective vs. spy, and the theme of
deception.

Haycraft, Howard. Murder for Pleasure: The Life and Times   7/6
of the Detective Story. New York: Appleton-Century,
1941.

A handbook for lovers of detective stories, this work
covers the 100 years from "the first detective story",
Murders in the Rue Morgue (1841), to the sleuths of 1941.

134

Includes a bibliography of critical works, a "Who's Who in Detection", "A Comprehensive Detective Story Quiz", and photos of mystery writers of two centuries. Not concerned with Gothic roots.

"Heathcliffs, Cliff-Hangers", Newsweek, LXVII (April 4, 1966), 7/63
101-102.

In 1963 Ace Books issued their first Gothic paperback, and by 1966 claimed 150 titles in print, selling 1.5 million copies a month. Most neo-Gothic novels are written pseudonymously by women, are highly sterotyped, and are read by women, "women for whom the best sellers are too sexy".

Scott, Sutherland. Blood in Their Ink: The March of The 7/64
Modern Mystery Novel. Foreword by A. Beverly Baxter.
London: Stanley Paul, 1953.

Calls Otranto, Udolpho and Monk "the gory spring which has now become a blood-bespattered torrent" and regards the thriller as "a blood-relative of the mystery novel"; but the study, for all practical purposes, begins at 1918 and has little bearing on things Gothic. The mystery genre is regarded as escapist literature; suggestions are offered on do's and don't's, themes and techniques. Titles, settings and locales are examined, and the author, himself a physician, has a chapter on "Medicine and Murder". Doesn't treat supernatural or horror literature, only those of premeditated crime which the reader is invited to solve.

VIII

HORACE WALPOLE, 4TH EARL OF ORFORD
(1717-1797)

a.

Selected Texts

1. The Castle of Otranto (1764)

1907 - The Castle of Otranto. Preface by Caroline F.E. Spur- 8/1
geon. With Sir Walter Scott's introduction. The King's
Classics. London: Chatto & Windus, 1907.

1924 - The Castle of Otranto and the Mysterious Mother. 8/2
Edited, and with an introduction and notes by Montague
Summers. Edition limited to 550 copies. London: Con-
stable, 1924.

A collector's item. Cover and spine are engraved with
architectural features from Strawberry Hill. Has seven
colored plates from Jeffery's edition of 1796.

1929 - The Castle of Otranto. Edited, and with an introduc- 8/3
tion and notes by Oswald Doughty. London: Scholartis,
1929.

Text reprinted from first edition of 1765, "occasionally
corrected from the second edition".

1930 - The Castle of Otranto, in Shorter Novels: Eighteenth 8/4
Century [1930]. Edited, and with an introduction by
Philip Henderson. Everyman's. New York: Dutton, 1971.

Paperback. Bound with Vathek and Rasselas.

1931 - The Castle of Otranto, in Three Eighteenth Century   8/5
Romances [1931]. Introduction by Harrison R. Steeves.
New York: Scribner's, 1971.

An oversized paperback which also includes Vathek and
Romance of the Forest.

1963 - The Castle of Otranto [1963]. Introduction by Marvin   8/6
Mudrick.   With Sir Walter Scott's introduction. New
York: Macmillan, 1967.

Paperback. Contains the prefaces to the first and second
editions.

1963 - The Castle of Otranto, in Seven Masterpieces of Gothic   8/7
Horror [1963]. Edited, and with an introduction by
Robert Donald Spector. New York: Bantam, 1970.

Paperback. Includes also Old English Baron, "Mistrust",
"White Old Maid", 'Heir of Mondolpho", "House of Usher",
"Carmilla". Contains a general introduction, individual
introductions, footnotes, and bibliography.

963 - The Castle of Otranto, in "The Castle of Otranto" by   8/8
Horace Walpole; "The Mysteries of Udolpho" by Ann Radcliffe; "Northanger Abbey" by Jane Austen. Edited, and
with an introduction by Andrew Wright. New York: Holt,
Rinehart & Winston, 1963.

Paperback. Text of Otranto follows second edition of
1765.

964 - The Castle of Otranto [1964]. Edited, and with an in-   8/9
troduction by W.S. Lewis. Explanatory notes and a note
on the text by Joseph W. Reed, Jr. Oxford English Novels.
London: Oxford Univ. Press, 1969.

Follows the 1798 edition, the "last text of the novel
that the author prepared for the press".

1966 - <u>The Castle of Otranto</u>, in <u>Three Gothic Novels</u>. 8/10
Edited, and with an introduction by E.F. Bleiler. New
York: Dover, 1966.

Text follows the second edition, includes prefaces to
the first and second editions, Scott's introduction, and
a new one by Bleiler. A paperback volume, containing also
<u>Vathek</u> and "The Vampyre".

1968 - <u>The Castle of Otranto</u>, in <u>Three Gothic Novels</u>. Edited 8/11
by Peter Fairclough. Introduction by Mario Praz. Bal-
timore: Penguin, 1968.

A paperback which includes <u>Vathek</u> and <u>Frankenstein</u>. Text
of <u>Otranto</u> is of the 1798 <u>Works</u>.

2. The Mysterious Mother (1768)

1924 - <u>The Castle of Otranto and The Mysterious Mother</u>. 8/12
Edited, and with an introduction and notes by Montague
Summers. Edition limited to 550 copies. London: Con-
stable, 1924.

1971 - "Horace Walpole's <u>The Mysterious Mother</u>: A Critical 8/13
Edition". Edited by Janet A. Dolan. Unpublished doctoral dissertation, Univ. of Arizona, 1970.

Text follows "faithfully, without emendation", the edition
of 1770, "the last edition printed under Walpole's super-
vision", and is collated with editions of 1768, 1781,
1791 Dublin, 1791 London. Variants are included in the
text and again in an appendix. Summers' edition (8/12)
Dr. Dolan says, is "unsatisfactory for several reasons",
not collated as claimed, and has "unsatisfactory" explanatory and textual notes. Dissertation also includes
notes on various editions; a textual history, information
on the various printers at SH, and looks at Rev. Mason's
attempt at alteration.

3. An Essay on Modern Gardening (1780)

1931 - On Modern Gardening. Preface and bibliographical   8/14
notes by W.S. Lewis. Edition limited to 325 copies.
New York: Young, 1931.

Lewis says this is "the first time the Essay has appeared
without the accompanying Anecdotes or Nivernois' translation and confers upon it, after 160 years, an independent dignity". Text follows that of the 1798 edition.

943 - Chase, Isabel Wakelin Urban. Horace Walpole: Gar-   8/15
denist. An Edition of Walpole's "The History of the
Modern Taste in Gardening" with an "Estimate of Walpole's Contribution to Landscape Architecture". Princeton: Princeton Univ. Press, 1943.

Text of the Essay based on the 1782 edition.

4. Hieroglyphic Tales (1785)

926 - Hieroglyphic Tales. Edition limited to 250 copies.   8/16
London: Elkin Mathews & Marrot, 1926. (Reprinted, Folcroft: Folcroft, 1970.)

Text from the first edition of 1785. Says the 1798 edition by Miss Berry contains "alterations and excisions".
"Some notes, written by Horace Walpole in his copy of
the first sheets of the first edition, now in the British
Museum, have been added."

5. Letters

1857 - Cunningham, Peter, ed. The Letters of Horace Wal-   8/17
pole, Fourth Earl of Orford [1857-1859]. 9 vols.
Edinburgh: John Grant, 1906.

Offers "the entire correspondence of Walpole", 2665 letters, in a chronological order. Inaccurate letters,
inaccurate biographical sketch, but has important introductory matter.

1903 - Toynbee, Mrs. Paget, ed. The Letters of Horace Wal-   8/18
pole, Fourth Earl of Orford. 16 vols. Oxford: Claren-
don, 1903-1906.

Based on Cunningham's edition (8/17) but collated where
possible. Some suppressed passages have been restored,
yet others remain "quite unfit for publication". "Of
the 407 letters not included in Cunningham's edition,
111 are now printed for the first time." (Mr. Paget
Toynbee added three supplementary volumes, 1918-1925.)

1937 - Lewis W[ilmarth] S., ed. The Yale Edition of Horace   8/19
Walpole's Correspondence. New Haven: Yale Univ. Press,
1937 --.

Intended "to give a correct text, to include for the first
time the letters to him, and to annotate the whole with
the fullness that the most informative record of the time
deserves". Arrangement is "by correspondences and not
chronologically". When completed, will be the definitive
edition. WSL had hoped to bring out the fiftieth and
final volume in 1950, but by 1973, only 36 volumes have
appeared.

1973 - --------, ed. Selected Letters of Horace Walpole.   8/2(
New Haven: Yale Univ. Press, 1973.

A paperback collection intended for an introductory level.

6. Miscellaneous

1931 - <u>Fugitive Verses</u>. Edited by W[ilmarth] S. Lewis.   8/21
Edition limited to 500 copies. New York: Oxford Univ.
Press, 1931.

Includes those <u>Fugitive Verses</u> assembled by Walpole himself and all the others WSL could locate.

1923 - <u>Journal of the Printing Office at Strawberry Hill</u>.   8/22
<u>Now first printed from the MS of Horace Walpole</u>. With
notes by Paget Toynbee. Edition limited to 650 copies.
London: Constable, 1923.

Contains 149 pages, of which only 21 are formed from Walpole's notes. HW's diary-like entries list the editions
printed on his press.

b.

Bibliographies

llibone, S[amuel] Austin. <u>A Critical Dictionary of English</u>   8/23
<u>Literature and British and American Authors Living and</u>
<u>Deceased</u>. <u>From the Earliest Accounts to the Latter Half</u>
<u>of the Nineteenth Century</u>. 3 vols. Philadelphia:
Lippincott, 1871. (Reprinted, Detroit: Gale Research,
1965.)

azen, A[llen] T. <u>A Bibliography of Horace Walpole</u>. New   8/24
Haven: Yale Univ. Press, 1948.

Lists (1)books by Walpole, (2)books with editorial contributions by Walpole, (3)contributions to periodicals,
etc., (4)books dedicated to Walpole, apocrypha, unprinted
manuscripts.

141

Kunitz, Stanley J. and Howard Haycraft. British Authors Be-   8/25
    fore 1800. A Biographical Dictionary. New York: Wilson,
    1952.

Moulton, Charles Wells, ed. The Library of Literary Criti-   8/26
    cism of English and American Authors. 8 vols. Buffalo:
    Moulton, 1901-1905. (Reprinted, New York: P. Smith,
    1935.)

Moulton's Library of Literary Criticism of English and Ameri-   8/27
    can Authors Through the Beginning of the Twentieth Cen-
    tury. Abridged, revised, and with additions by Martin
    Tucker. 4 vols. New York: Ungar, 1966.

Patrick, David, and J. Liddell. Chamber's Cyclopaedia of   8/28
    English Literature. A History Critical and Biographical
    of Authors in the English Tongue from the Earliest Times
    till the Present Day, with Specimens of their Writings.
    3 vols. London: Chamber's, [1922-1938].

Tobin, James E. Eighteenth Century English Literature and   8/29
    its Cultural Background: A Bibliography. New York:
    Fordham Univ. Press, 1939.

Watson, George, ed. The New Cambridge Bibliography of Eng-   8/30
    lish Literature. 3 vols. Cambridge: Univ. Press,
    1969 --.

c.

Full-Length Studies

De Koven, Anna. Horace Walpole and Madame Du Deffand. New   8/31
    York: Appleton, 1928.

    Sees nothing odd about the relationship and views it as
    "selfless and spiritual".

Dobson, Austin. _Horace Walpole: A Memoir_. With an Appen-   8/32
dix of Books Printed at the Strawberry Hill Press [1890].
4th ed. Revised and enlarged by Paget Toynbee. London:
Oxford Univ. Press, 1927.

The first formal biography, written over eighty years
ago. Refrains from critical judgments.

Greenwood, Alice Drayton. _Horace Walpole's World: A Sketch_   8/33
of Whig Society Under George III. London: Bell, 1913.

A view of 18th-century society as recorded by Walpole.
The author regards HW as "a gentleman" who "had no interest in real history, only in its gossip". Emphasis
falls on England, not on Walpole.

Gwynn, Stephen. _The Life of Horace Walpole_. Boston: 8/34
Houghton Mifflin, 1937.

Gwynn says he will not attempt "any detailed study" of
Walpole's books since Stuart's work (8/47) "makes it un-
necessary", but asserts that he is mistaken in seeing
Otranto as the progenitor of Scott, Dumas, and others.
Biography does not differ much from Melville (8/44) or
Dobson (8/32). He labels Walpole the "worst kind of a
bad critic".

Harfst, Betsy Perteit. "Horace Walpole and the Unconscious: 8/35
An Experiment in Freudian Analysis". Unpublished doctoral
dissertation, Northern Illinois Univ., 1968.

A fascinating, highly complex and richly footnoted analysis of _Otranto_, _Mysterious Mother_, and _Hieroglyphics_.
The Oedipal fixation in Walpole was strong. Henry Conway,
his cousin, existed as a mother substitute and "the association between Walpole and Conway can be termed homosexual but it is a derivative of the old Oedipus complex".
Similarly Mme. du Deffand was a "mother" and a source of
guilt. _Otranto_, sparked by Conway's problems, gives Walpole success in parricide and incest. Guilt results;
Mysterious Mother represents self-punishment. _Hiero-
glyphics_, as the other two, deals in parricide, incest,
homosexuality and castration fears, but this time the
point of view is that of a child and regression makes
life "more pleasurable". The Freudian investigation of
Gothic machinery proves most interesting.

143

Havens, Munson Aldrich. Horace Walpole and the Strawberry   8/36
Hill Press, 1757-1789. Canton: Kirgate, 1901.

A 65-page essay together with a twelve-page chronological
listing of the output from Walpole's press, the second
private press in England. Discusses the editions and
printing problems; views Walpole as a hobbyist-printer
who seemed unaware of the dignity of labor and underpaid
his printer, Thomas Kirgate.

Hazen, Allen T. A Catalogue of Horace Walpole's Library.   8/37
With "Horace Walpole's Library" by Wilmarth Sheldon
Lewis. 3 vols. New Haven: Yale Univ. Press, 1969.

Hazen claims that this is "not a descriptive bibliography,
but a finding list arranged by presses and shelves". He
discusses how Walpole purchased, bound, read, annotated,
shelved, and catalogued his books. Notes strengths and
weakness of his holdings. Lewis covers the same topics
but offers additional information.

Honor, Hugh. Horace Walpole. Writers and their Work, No.   8/38
92. London: Longmans, Green, 1957.

A brief essay which touches on all aspects, finds Otranto
"ridiculous . . . stilted . . . preposterous", and the
Mysterious Mother "a distasteful little piece". Contains a bibliography and a list of Walpole's works.

Kallich, Martin. Horace Walpole. Twayne's English Author   8/39
Series. New York: Twayne, 1971.

In the Twayne style, a general study which synthesizes
previous scholarship. Kallich directed Harfst's dissertation (8/35), and here, he draws upon her for Otranto,
and Mysterious Mother. He notes that in Hieroglyphic
Tales, "some of the nonsense stories . . . , the first
four in particular, bring to mind the uncanny extravagances of surrealism, differing from Gothic supernaturalism and terror only in the lightness of the tone".

Ketton-Cremer, R[obert] W. Horace Walpole: A Biography   8/40
[1940]. 3rd ed. London: Methuen, 1964.

The best biography. Draws upon W.S. Lewis's extensive
Walpoliana and benefits from his guidance. Rights the
damage done by Macaulay (8/80) and presents an absorbing,
well-balanced picture. Criticism of Otranto and Mother
rather run-of-the-mill, but the life is excellent and
highly recommended.

Lewis, Wilmarth [Sheldon]. Collector's Progress. London: 8/41
Constable, 1952.

Sort of a detective story for the bibliophile, this work
recounts the adventures, trials, and tribulations in
collecting Walpoliana for the Yale edition of Letters.

--------. Horace Walpole. The A.W. Mellon Lectures in the   8/42
Fine Arts, 1960. New York: Pantheon, 1960.

Six lectures: "Family", "Friends", "Politics", "Strawberry Hill", "Works", "Letters". A pro-Walpole effort
which presents him as heterosexual, well-adjusted in his
relations with his parents, and of legitimate birth. Has
a good coverage of his political views, reproduces many
plates not seen elsewhere, and features many excellent
pictures of Strawberry Hill.

Mehrotra, K[ewal] K. Horace Walpole and the English Novel: 8/43
A Study of the Influence of "The Castle of Otranto",
1764-1820 [1934]. New York: Russell & Russell, 1970.

YWES (1/4) turned in a bad report on this study; Summers
(6/29) cites it as "a salient example" of the work of
"certain ill-equipped and superficial sophomores", and
now, forty years after publication, it seems still more
difficult to find anything of value. Mehrotra offers
much plot summary, quotes and cites contemporary reviews,
spews out obscure names and titles, but doesn't trace
Otranto's influence.

Melville, Lewis. Horace Walpole (1717-1797): A Biographical   8/44
Study. London: Hutchinson, 1930.

Draws heavily upon the Toynbee edition of Walpole's letters (8/18), and reads like an epistolary account. Avoids
critical judgments and sticks to biography.

Seeley, L[eonard] B. Horace Walpole and His World: Select   8/45
Passages From His Letters [1884]. New York: Scribner's,
[1895].

With the exception of the first chapter, this work is
little more than an anthology of Walpole's letters pieced
together with a minimum of editorial comment. The opening
chapter offers Seeley's general, laudatory view of HW,
and contends that Macaulay's attack resulted from political matters since Walpole was friendly with Conway who
"disobliged the Rockingham faction, from which the modern
Whigs deduce their origin".
    This book has also been published under the title
Horace Walpole and His World: An Autobiography, "Written
by Himself". Beaux and Belles of England Series. Edition
limited to 1000 copies. London: The Grolier Society,
[n.d.].

Smith, Warren Hunting, ed. Horace Walpole: Writer, Poli-   8/46
tician, and Connoisseur. Essays on the 250th Anniversary of Walpole's Birth. New Haven: Yale Univ.
Press, 1967.

Consists of nineteen essays by various hands. Divided
into three sections: "Politician & Political Commentator",
"Connoisseur & Antiquarian", and "Literary Figure". Only
one article, "The 'Theatre of George III'" by Charles
Beecher Hogan is devoted to HW's literary Gothicism, and
the thesis presented here is that Otranto, far more than
The Mysterious Mother or Nature Will Prevail, is dramatic
in form, theme, and characters. Hogan asserts also that
"the Gothic absurdities of The Castle of Otranto are
appendages. They are not really inside the story, but
are affixed, true gargoyles, on the outside of it."

Stuart, Dorothy Margaret. Horace Walpole. English Men of   8/47
Letters. New York: Macmillan, 1927.

For many years the standard biography but now rather out
of date. Sees Otranto as simply the forerunner of

Gothic -- and "in this case the interest may be extrinsic
rather than interest in 'the thing itself'". The reluc-
tance of critics to work with Mother, she sees as "ex-
cusable" since its theme is "so sombre and so revolting"
with "regrettable gruesomeness". No bibliography; no
footnotes.

Toynbee, Paget. Strawberry Hill Accounts: A Record of Ex-   8/48
penditure in Building, Furnishing, etc. Kept by Mr.
Horace Walpole From 1747 to 1795. Oxford: Clarendon,
1927.

Taken from HW's pocket book, the contents of which "consist of a continuous record of the expenditure on the
building and furnishing of the house, and on the laying
out of the grounds, at Strawberry Hill for nearly fifty
years, from the date of Walpole's first connexion with
it as tenant in 1747 down to the end of 1795, a little
more than a year before his death". Toynbee offers
extensive footnoting, has photo reproductions of the
original pages, points out Walpole's faulty arithmetic
and his inability to do mental calculations.

Welcher, Jeanne K. "The Literary Opinions of Horace Wal-   8/49
pole". Unpublished doctoral dissertation, Fordham Univ.,
1954.

Draws upon Walpole's published criticism, his letters and
marginalia and shows just how prolifically he read. HW's
opinions are evaluated in light of modern scholarship and
compared to those of his age, an era he found almost devoid
of genius. Walpole offered comments on poetry, prose,
drama, biography, history, etc., and all of these are discussed. Dr. Welcher points out that in prefatory material
to Otranto and Mother, HW scoffed at rules yet followed
them. She says, "while it was very grand to scorn rules
-- in principle and for other people -- he [HW] took any
and all defensive measure that he could to obviate harsh
criticism."

d.

Articles, Essays, and Introductions

Barbauld, Mrs. Anna Letitia. "Horace Walpole", in her An   8/50
Essay on the Origin and Progress of Novel Writing; and
Prefaces, Biographical and Critical from 'The British
Novelists'. London: Rivington, 1820. (On microfilm;
negative made by Library of Congress.)

Otranto "is much in the spirit of the tales of Count Hamilton. In one of those tales we meet with a vast leg of
a giant, which probably suggested the prodigy in the former." Mother "was much spoken of while it was handed about
with a certain air of secrecy, but sunk into neglect soon
after it was published". She calls the play "disgustingly
repulsive".

Bleiler, E[verett] F. Introduction to The Castle of Otranto,   8/51
in Three Gothic Novels. New York: Dover, 1966.

Offers biography of Walpole, notes his lack of understanding of the principles of Gothic architecture and his
influence on the Gothic revival. Believes "there is a
solid center of sincerity" within Otranto, and views it as
historically important but inferior to the works of Radcliffe and Lewis. Credits HW as "the founder of a school
of fiction", and asserts that his "strongest contribution
to the Gothic development lies in the inner dynamics of
his story".

Brandenburg, Alice Stayert. "The Theme of The Mysterious   8/52
Mother", MLQ, X (1949), 464-474.

Readers and theatregoers of the 18th century "enjoyed being shocked by a meretricious exploitation of unnatural
love if the sin was committed accidentally or was merely
imminent . . . but they were offended, without being
pleased, by an honest approach to the subject". Believes
HW "was attempting to treat incest as a tragic subject and
not merely as a device for achieving a cheap sensation".

C., R.W. "'The Castle of Otranto'", N&Q, CLXXX (1941), 209.   8/53

Asserts that Walpole's fictitious translator, "William
Marshall" may have been "suggested by Marshall's unsuccessful portrait of Milton". In his "Catalogue of
Engravers", 1763, HW refers to Marshall as "a coarse en-
graver".

Clarke, A.H.T. "Strawberry Hill", TLS (May 25, 1940), p.   8/54
255.

Explains that Rowlandson, Sir Joshua Reynolds' favourite
artist, painted a procession of monks or friars marching
to Strawberry Hill. This was to bring a romantic touch
to the picture and to emphasize the Gothic or medieval
spirit. As authority, Clarke cites Reynolds' directive
that if Alexander were a short man, he should nevertheless be depicted as tall to emphasize his renown.

Conant, Kenneth J. "Horace Walpole and the Gothic Revival",   8/55
Old Wedgwood, XII (1945), 62-69.

A brief, reportorial summary of a paper read at the Wedgwood Club "to commemorate Strawberry Hill". Emphasizes
Gothic survival, lists and gives dates for Gothic construc-
tions in the 16th, 17th, and early 18th centuries. "It
was Walpole," Conant says, "who gave the Gothic style
'aristocratic respectability' in his own time by taking
it from the cathedral and putting it into the home."
Notes some of the sources for Strawberry Hill; traces
Gothic into the 19th century; points out Gothic features
in Victorian furniture and dishes; looks at carpenter's
Gothic.

Constant Reader. "'The Castle of Otranto'", Literary   8/56
Review (Feb. 25, 1922), p. 451.

"Constant Reader" professes to be an admirer of Otranto
but says styles and idioms have changed so much, that
today, it seems "a summoner to supreme hilarity", "a
piece of supreme high comedy". He asserts that readers
and critics should now look at Otranto in perspective
and see it as "one of the world's humorous masterpieces".

Dobrée, Bonamy. "Horace Walpole", in Carroll Camden, ed.,   8/57
Restoration and Eighteenth-Century Literature. Essays
in Honor of Alan Dugald McKillop. Chicago: Univ. of
Chicago Press, 1963.

Claims to shed some light on Walpole the man. Deals
with romantic, picturesque, the Strawberry job, the
Otranto dream. Asserts Otranto "is saved from being ridiculous by a sense of situation", and suggests that
Mother sounds like something from Nat Lee, a playwright
whose work has been called Gothic.

Dobson, Austin. "A Day at Strawberry Hill", in his Eight-   8/58
eenth Century Vignettes. London: Chatto & Windus, 1892.

An imaginative recreation of what a visitor to Strawberry
Hill might see and do during a typical day.

--------. "Horace Walpole", in Leslie Stephen and Sidney   8/59
Lee, eds., Dictionary of National Biography. 63 vols.
London: Smith, Elder, 1885 --.

Mainly biographical, but notes editions and portraits.
Observes that "with the Castle of Otranto tentatively and
inexpertly, but unmistakably, began the modern romantic
revival".

Doughty, Oswald. Introduction to The Castle of Otranto.   8/60
London: Scholastics, 1929.

A long introduction which stresses biography and draws
heavily upon HW's letters. Little is said about the novel
itself, but it is regarded "aesthetically", as "a failure".

Esdaile, Mrs. "Walpole's Anecdotes of Painting", TLS (March   8/61
19, 1931), p. 224.

Basically, a history of the various editions of Anecdotes
with special attention to plates and woodcuts. Covers
prices, numbers, and problems Walpole encountered. Concludes by calling for a new edition, as A has remained
"unedited since 1849".

Fairfax, J.G. "Horace Walpole's Views on Literature", in   8/62
Eighteenth Century Literature: An Oxford Miscellany
[1909]. Essay Index Reprint Series. Freeport: Books
for Libraries, 1966.

A rebuttal to Macaulay's "insufferable essay" (8/80),
this piece presents extracts (unfortunately, unidentified)
from Walpole's letters in an attempt to vindicate his
character. Stresses that HW was "in advance of his age
in his appreciation of architecture, painting, and archaeology" and out of sympathy with much of the contemporary
literature. Extracts show Orford's opinions of Pope,
Fielding, Thomson, Swift, Addison, Sidney, Sterne, Ossian,
heroic poetry, Milton, Richardson, Johnson, Boswell, Gray,
Goldsmith, Fanny Burney, Gibbon, Arabian Nights.

Hartley, Lodwick. "A Late Augustan Circus: Macaulay on   8/63
Johnson, Boswell, and Walpole", SAQ, LXVII (1968),
513-526.

Concludes, "whether consciously or not, Macaulay used
Walpole against Boswell and in more subtle ways Boswell
against Walpole, Boswell against Johnson and Johnson
against Boswell, and each against himself -- around and
around." Sheds light on Macaulay's methods and motives.

Hazen, A.T. "Strawberry Hill Sale Catalogues, 1842", N&Q,   8/64
CXCII (1947), 33-35.

Lists, describes, and discusses the seven editions of
George Robins's auction catalogues. Mentions earlier
studies.

Henderson, Philip. Introduction to Shorter Novels: Eight-   8/65
eenth Century [1930]. Everyman's. New York: Dutton,
1971.

A general introduction, brief, but with a couple of
noteworthy points. "Walpole has a good claim to be considered the first surrealist novelist", he says, and
notes that Otranto "is particularly surrealist in its
dialogue, and the juxtaposition of the language and sentiments of the beau monde with Gothic violence".

Holzknecht, Karl J. "Horace Walpole as Dramatist", SAQ,   8/66
XXVIII (1929), 174-189.

Asserts that HW's literary talent was for drama; notes
that Otranto has dramatic features in structure and setting, and views Mother not as an obscene or eccentric work,
but one much in the main stream of drama. Discusses
sources for Mother, notes prevalence of incest theme on
stage, calls the play "a mixture of classic and romantic
notions", classic in unities and purpose of producing
pity and terror, romantic in its expression of Gothic.
Praises the structure, sees characterization superior to
that of Otranto, Gothic machinery better handled. "All of
the gothic machinery of Otranto is present; from the very
opening of the play the shadow of impending tragedy hangs
over the castle. The play has that totality of effect so
much talked about by Poe."

"Horace Walpole's Library", TLS (May 17, 1957), p. 312.   8/67

A brief article summarizing W.S. Lewis's three talks at
the 1957 Sandars Lectures.

Johnson, James William. "Horace Walpole and W.S. Lewis",   8/68
JBS, VI, no. 2 (1967), 64-75.

Notes the changing critical opinions on Walpole, praises
Lewis's efforts, and offers comments on both Lewis and
Walpole. Lewis, he says, bowed to pressure of the critics
and in 1948, changed the scope of his project so that "the
Yale Edition of the Correspondence became less a definitive
edition of Walpole's letters, or even a variorum edition,
than a synopticon of views connected solely by their form
and their addresse". Calls Lewis "the perfect interlocutor
between Walpole and 20th-century scholarship".

Kallich, Martin. "Houghton Hall: The House of the Walpoles", 8/69
PLL, IV (1968), 360-369.

Contends that Sir Robert's home exerted a strong aesthetic
influence on Horace and stimulated his interest in antiquarian researches. Suggests also that a relationship
exists between Houghton and Mysterious Mother. Both the
fictitious Edmund and the real Horry return home after
sixteen years, and Kallich sees the young Walpole unconsciously assuming the role of the father.

Ker, W[illiam] P. "Horace Walpole", in his Collected   8/70
Essays. Edited, and with an introduction by Charles
Whibley. London: Macmillan, 1925.

Essentially a defense of Walpole against Macaulay, but
with attention to his role as letter writer. Sympathetic;
sees him as bright, impatient with dullness, fond of new
experiences. Credits him as being the first of the scenery
hunters.

Lewis, Wilmarth Sheldon. "The Accords and Resemblances of   8/71
Johnson and Walpole", in W.H. Bond ed., Eighteenth Cen-
tury Studies in Honor of Donald F. Hyde. New York:
Grolier Club, 1970. (Previously published in BRMMLA,
XXII [1968], 7-12.)

An interesting short paper which points out the many, many
similarities between these men in politics, personality,
humanitarianism, canon, criticism, and care of the sick.

--------, ed. Horace Walpole's Fugitive Verses. New York: 8/72
Oxford Univ. Press, 1931.

WSL provides a brief introduction but supplies abundant
notes. "Much of Walpole's verse", he observes, "has
more biographical interest than poetic." Perhaps of
greatest interest are the notes to "Verses in Memory of
King Henry the Sixth, Founder of King's College, Cambridge",
a poem written in 1738. Lewis asserts that these verses
"establish the claim that Walpole's was the main influence
in the Gothic Revival. They are to poetry what Strawberry
Hill is to domestic architecture and what The Castle of
Otranto is to fiction."

-------. "The Genesis of Strawberry Hill", Metropolitan   8/73
Museum Studies, V, pt. 1 (1934), 57-92.

A full account of Strawberry Hill. Covers the pre-Walpole
buildings, HW's "Committee on Taste at SH", the sources of
the Gothic bits and pieces, alterations, floor plans, allusions and references in letters, the grafting of historical examples of Gothic art into a Georgian frame,
decorations, arms and armor, the library, the Chinese
building, the chapel, the printing house, the garden and
grounds, furniture, and finally, the resemblances of the
castle of Otranto to Strawberry Hill. Includes 38 plates,
a chronological summary of construction, and a bibliography.

153

Lewis, W[ilmarth] S.   "Horace Walpole", TLS (Jan. 24, 1935),   8/74
p. 48.

Walpole, in his "Short Notes of My Life", said he wrote
thirteen numbers of Old England and four of the Remem-
brancer but did not identify these anonymous publications.
Lewis has located the MSS, identifies the specific numbers, and says, despite what HW claimed, the published
versions do not display marked editing of the originals.

--------. "Horace Walpole's Correspondence", TLS (June 20,   8/75
1935), p. 399.

Lewis announces that he has completed the second year of
work on his edition of HW's letters and estimates that
fifty volumes may be produced, hopefully to be completed
by 1950.

--------. "A Library Dedicated to the Life and Works of   8/76
Horace Walpole", Colophon, I, pt. 3 (1930) [12 pgs.; un-
numbered].

Lewis briefly mentions his interest in Walpole and describes some of the holdings of his HW library. In the
section, "MSS and Letters", he writes: "The number of
Walpole's known letters is so large (nearly 3,500) and
they have been so admirably edited by the Toynbees that
I have made no effort to collect them and have only about
a dozen."

--------. "Walpole's Anecdotes", TLS (May 7, 1931), p. 367.   8/77

Tenderness towards Mrs. Hogarth caused Walpole to delay
publication of Anecdotes, IV which was completed in 1771.
WSL discovered an advertisement of 1773 which HW had prepared, but Walpole apparently changing his mind, sat on
A for seven more years, publishing it in 1780, nine years
before the demise of Mrs. H.

"Life Explores World's Finest Walpole Library", Life, XVII,   8/78
(Oct. 23, 1944), 116-120.

Photos of Walpole, his parents, Strawberry Hill, and some
of the books, file cards, and furniture. The collection
is, of course, that of W.S. Lewis.

Lucas, F[rank] L. The Art of Living: Four Eighteenth-Century 8/79
Minds: Hume, Horace Walpole, Burke, Benjamin Franklin.
London: Cassell, 1959.

The essay on Walpole, in tone and treatment, seems somewhat influenced by Ketton-Cremer (8/40), and presents a
noteworthy study both of the man and the artist. Otranto
and Mother "seem mainly remarkable as an instance of how
badly, sometimes, clever minds can write when they attempt
to create. Even Walpole's style, so admirable in his letters, here becomes almost illiterate."

Macaulay, Thomas Babington. "Horace Walpole", in his Critical 8/80
and Historical Essays, Contributed to "The Edinburgh Review" [1843]. 5th ed. London: Longman, 1848.

A devastating attack which appeared in 1833 and has caused
continual controversy. Walpole is accused of being im-
modest, trifling, stupid in matters political, insincere
in Whiggism, a gossiper, and a devotee of the odd and grotesque. He has "an unhealthy and disorganized mind", is
"the most eccentric, the most artificial, the most fas-
tidious, the most capricious of men". His prose is called
tiresome, distorted,and tainted with Gallicism; his literary criticism "false and absurd". His letters are his best
effort, since here "his faults are far less offensive".
But Macaulay has praise for Otranto. "There is little
skill in the delineation of the characters. . . . But the
story, whatever its value may be, never flags for a single
moment. There are no digressions, or unseasonable descriptions, or long speeches. Every sentence carries the
action forward. The excitement is constantly renewed.
Absurd as is the machinery, insipid as are the human
actors, no reader probably ever thought the book dull."

More, Paul Elmer. "The Letters of Horace Walpole", in his   8/81
Shelburne Essays [1906]. Fourth Series. Boston:
Houghton Mifflin, 1922.

Occasioned by the publication of Toynbee's edition of
Letters (8/18), which More criticizes for including "in-
significant scraps" and excluding "vital passages . . .
which might offend a prudish taste". Sees HW as a great
chronicler of his age; says he never was a republican, was
not Frenchified, and was "the most transparent of men",
not the "mask within mask" described by Macaulay (8/80).

Mudrick, Marvin. Introduction to The Castle of Otranto   8/82
[1963]. New York: Macmillan, 1967.

A brief piece by a man who doesn't seem a devotee of
Gothic. He doesn't like the plot or the characters,
thinks little of Manfred, and says that "it is the out-
rageous, the uncreditable, the aggressively miraculous --
the very claptrap of the chamber of horrors into which
Walpole was the first to stumble -- that saved his fable
for its special and minor immortality."

Pearson, Norman. "Some Neglected Aspects of Horace Walpole",   8/83
Fortnightly Review, NS, LXXXVI (1909), 482-494.

Intended as a counter-balance to Macaulay (8/80), this
essay presents some positive qualities. Says Walpole
had "some of a woman's failings" -- "caprice, . . . im-
pulsiveness . . . inconsistency, and . . . defective sense
of proportion", but he was unselfish, empathetic, fond of
children and animals, disliked cruelty to animals, hated
war, was pro-American, republican, anti-Catholic, chari-
table, and "strictly temperate in a society where de-
bauchery was rampant". "His character though full of
frailties, was not fundamentally false, and it contained
much that was lovable, much that was honest, much that
was almost great."

Perkinson, Richard H. "Walpole and the Biographia Dramatica", 8/84
RES, XV (1939), 204-206.

Mother was not cancelled in the 1782 edition of BD owing
to Steevens' personal opinions, but rather because HW
persuaded Reed to withdraw Steevens' notice when he found
out that they were to quote from his carefully suppressed
tragedy. Reed wrote a new article, the Dublin pirate pi-
rated it, and this article, mixed with the original article
obtained from the Censura Literaria appears in the 1812
edition of Biographia Dramatica , "a mélange of Reed and
Steevens, edited with some additions by Jones".

--------. "Walpole and a Dublin Pirate", PQ, XV (1936),   8/85
391-400.

The Strawberry Hill printing of Mother in 1768 "consisted
of but fifty copies, probably carefully distributed"; the
1781 Dodsley edition of the same number of copies was to
prevent a piracy; the Dublin piracy of 1791, however, was

not suppressed, nor was an attempt at suppression made by
HW. Indeed, Walpole gave his consent, thus solving his
dilemma of neo-classic decorum vs. romanticism. Times
had changed and HW became convinced that the public wanted
and was ready for his drama.

Prothero, Rowland E. "Horace Walpole and William Cowper", 8/86
Quarterly Review, CCII, no. 402 (1905), 35-60.

Considers two recent editions of letters -- Toynbee's
HW and Wright's Cowper; investigates claim of each man,
concludes that "to discuss the rival claims of Cowper and
Walpole to be considered the 'greatest of English letter-
writers' is wasted labour. The two authors are so essentially different in character, in subject matter, in style,
that they cannot be compared; they can only be contrasted."
Looks at politics, religion, personality, literary aims,
views of society, nature and sports, town and country,
readings.

Rose, Edward J. "'The Queenly Personality': Walpole, Mel- 8/87
ville, and Mother", Literature and Psychology [U. of
Mass.], XV (1965), 216-229.

Examines the themes of Mother and discusses the relationship of this play with the works of Melville, especially
Pierre. Mother is mentioned in White Jacket and Rose
points out that both authors share "the contrasted attitudes, pagan and Christian, towards sex and guilt; fate's
relentlessness, emphasized in thunderstorm scenes; the
ambiguity of father and mother; the banishment of the son
by the mother; the mother's love of her husband in the
image of his and her son; the daughter as a sister-wife;
the 'sovereign' mother's 'commanding sex' and the son's
desire to be obedient to his mother's power." Also, both
men employ phallic imagery. But "Walpole examines explic-
itly familial relationships which Melville only implies."
Asserts that Melville, in Walpole, Sophocles, and Shelley,
"saw confirmed his own deepest psychic experiences."
Urges that Mother be regarded as serious -- and great
literature.

Scott, Sir Walter. "Horace Walpole" [1823], in Ioan   8/88
Williams, ed., Sir Walter Scott on Novelists and Fiction.
London: Routledge & Kegan Paul, 1968.

Calls Otranto "the original and model of a peculiar species
of composition . . . [and] one of the standard works of our
lighter literature". Indicates a preference for this type
of Gothic rather than for that of the Radcliffe school, but
is not blind to defects. The supernatural appears "rather
too frequent, and presses too hard", has an "over degree
of distinctness and accuracy of outline" and the characters
are "rather generic than individual".

Seznec, Jean. "Madame du Deffand Loves Horace Walpole", Lis-   8/89
tener, LXXXII (1969), 825-826.

Asserts that "immediately after their first meeting, Madame
du Deffand had fallen in love with Horace Walpole". They
met only four times in the fourteen years of life remaining to her, yet a constant flow of correspondence ensued.
Orford, "alarmed at the idea that people might learn about
the old lady's infatuation . . . warned her again and
again, in the severest terms, to refrain from using any
sentimental expression". "The supreme interest of the
Du Deffand-Walpole correspondence remains", says Seznec,
"the psychological one."

Smith, Horatio E. "Horace Walpole Anticipates Victor Hugo",   8/90
MLN, XLI (1926), 458-461.

Hugo's "doctrine of the grotesque" was stated fifty years
earlier in the preface to the second edition of Otranto.
Even though Hugo follows these generalizations, Smith
does not claim that the Frenchman read Walpole.

Smith, Warren Hunting. "Strawberry Hill and Otranto", TLS   8/91
(May 23, 1936), p. 440.

Strawberry Hill is usually thought of as the model for
the castle in Otranto, but Smith in his Architecture in
English Fiction (6/28) demonstrated discrepancies. Now,
he points out that a letter from HW to Mme. du Deffand
clears up the matter. HW visited Cambridge the year before he wrote his romance, and Smith shows the similarities
in the school buildings and Otranto. The fictional castle
draws both on Cambridge and Strawberry Hill.

Spurgeon, Caroline F.E. Preface to The Castle of Otranto.   8/92
The King's Classics. London: Chatto & Windus, 1907.

Regards Otranto as important and influential -- but absurd. Calls it a "crude story, written as a half joke"
which no longer thrills. Nowadays, "it is almost impossible, on its intrinsic merits alone, to take the
Castle of Otranto seriously, or to do anything but laugh
at the portions of the gigantic Alphonso".

Stein, Jess M. "Horace Walpole and Shakespeare", SP, XXXI   8/93
(1934), 51-68.

Railo (6/26) had claimed a direct influence of Shakespeare on Walpole, but Stein denies this, saying that
while some of the bard's devices may contribute to the
whole of Castle of Otranto, "they are not the real es-
sence of the Gothic literary porduction. Constant terror
is the central quality of Gothic writings, and Walpole
did not get this effect from Shakespeare." Also, Stein
sees Mother as owing more to the Greek than Elizabethan
tradition. Concludes that "the influence was not as
thorough as Railo makes it; it was mainly incidental and
marginal."

Stephen, Leslie. "Horace Walpole", in his Hours in a Library. 8/94
New York: Putnam's, 1894.

Stephen admits "extreme cleverness" but can neither respect
nor find affection for Walpole. He credits him with being
the first Englishman to admire Gothic architecture, sees
his influence on Radcliffe and Scott, but calls Otranto's
machinery "simply babyish, unless we charitably assume
the whole to be intentionally burlesque".

Strachey, Lytton. Characters and Commentaries. London: 8/95
Chatto & Windus, 1933.

Includes three essays on Walpole. Two are laudatory reviews of Toynbee's edition of Letters and the Supplement
(8/18). The third, previously unpublished, deals with
HW's political views and regards him as a poor critic,
uninterested in literature, and interested in Gothic architecture "not because he thought it beautiful, but because he found it queer".

159

Summers, Montague. Introduction to The Castle of Otranto   8/96
and The Mysterious Mother. London: Constable, 1924.

Admits "a little crudity" exists in Otranto but contends
that it may "add to the strength and surprise of the narrative". Anyone who finds the walking portrait "too improper a prodigy must be singularly lacking in imagination
and fancy". Mother has "extraordinary merit" and "nervous and often beautiful" blank verse.

Vaughan, Herbert M. "Horace Walpole (1717-1797): Man of   8/97
Arts, Letters, and Fashion", in his From Anne to Victoria:
Fourteen Biographical Studies Between 1702 and 1901
[1931]. Port Washington: Kennikat, 1967.

Draws heavily on Dobson (8/32), and on HW's letters.
Mainly biographical and complimentary. Calls Walpole "the
founder of the historical romance", "undoubtedly the pioneer" of the Gothic revival, and "the king of British let-
ter-writers". Views him as "an admirable counterfoil" to
Dr. Johnson.

Whibley, Leonard. "The Foreign Tour of Gray and Walpole",   8/98
Blackwood's Magazine, CCXXVII (1930), 813-827.

A rather detailed account of the ramblings and sightsee-
ing of Gray and Walpole. Mentions the oft forgotten fact
that the travellers met the Abbé Prévost.

Whiteley, Emily Stone. "Horace Walpole -- Early American",   8/99
VQR, VII (1931), 212-224.

Based on HW's letters, this article shows his sympathy
with the American cause and his pain over civil war.

Whyte, S. "On the Plot of Lord Orford's Mysterious Mother", 8/100
Monthly Mirror, XI (1801), 187-191.

Presents extract from Walpole describing his source in
Archbishop Tillotson. Also, shows parallel in George
Faulkner's Eleanora, or a Tragic and True Case of Incest
(1751) and in Jeremy Taylor's Ductor Dubitantium, or the
Rule of Conscience, Etc. (ca. 1659).

Woolf, Virginia. "Two Antiquaries: Walpole and Cole", <u>YR</u>,   8/101
NS, XXVIII (1939), 530-539.

Begins as a review of W.S. Lewis's first two volumes of
HW's Letters but expands into the men themselves. Praises
the editor; sees contradictions in HW, "the most amusing,
the most intriguing -- the strangest mixture of ape and
Cupid that ever was".

                              e.

        Notices in General Works, Diaries, Etc.

Burney, Fanny. <u>Diary and Letters of Madame D'Arblay</u>.   8/102
Edited by Charlotte Barrett. 4 vols. London: Son-
nenschen, 1892.

"The opening of . . . [<u>The Mysterious Mother</u>] contains a
description of superstitious fear, extremely well, and
feelingly, and naturally depicted; it begins, too, in an
uncommon style, promising of interest and novelty," but,
"dreadful was the whole! truly dreadful!" Miss Burney
says that she "felt a sort of indignant aversion rise
fast and warm . . . against the wilful author of a story
so horrible" and hoped that the Queen "would never deign
to cast her eye upon it".

Byron, George Gordon, Lord. Preface to his "Marino Faliero,   8/103
Doge of Venice", in Thomas Moore, ed. <u>The Works of Lord</u>
<u>Byron. With His Letters and Journals. And His Life</u>.
17 vols. London: John Murray, 1833.

"It is the fashion to underrate Horace Walpole; firstly,
because he was a nobleman, and secondly, because he was
a gentleman; but, to say nothing of the composition of his
incomparable letters, and of the <u>Castle of Otranto</u>, he
is the 'Ultimus Romanorum', the author of the <u>Mysterious</u>
<u>Mother</u>, a tragedy of the highest order, and not a puling
love-play. He is the father of the first romance and of
the last tragedy in our language, and surely worthy of a
higher place than any living writer, be he who he may."

                              161

Coleridge, Samuel Taylor. The Table Talk and Omniana.   8/10
London: Oxford Univ. Press, 1917.

March 20, 1834: "Lord Byron, as quoted by Lord Dover,
says that the Mysterious Mother raises HW above every
author living in his, Lord Byron's, time. Upon which I
venture to remark, first, that I do not believe Lord B
spoke sincerely, for I suspect that he made a tacit exception in favour of himself at least; secondly, that it
is a miserable mode of comparison which does not rest on
difference of kind. It proceeds of envy and malice and
detraction to say that A is higher than B unless you show
that they are in pari materia; thirdly, that the MM is
the most disgusting, vile, detestable composition that
ever came from the hand of man. No one with a spark of
true manliness, of which HW had none, could have written
it. As to the blank verse, it is indeed better than
Rowe's and Thomson's, which was execrably bad: any approach, therefore, to the manner of the old dramatists
was of course an improvement; but the loosest lines in
Shirley are superior to Walpole's best."

Hazlitt, William. "On the English Novelists", in his Lec-   8/10
tures on the English Comic Writers and Fugitive Writings
[1819]. Everyman's. London: Dent, 1967.

"The Castle of Otranto . . . is, to my notion, dry,
meagre, and without effect. It is done upon false principles of taste. The great hand and arm which are thrust
into the court yard, and remain there all day long, are
the pasteboard machinery of a pantomime; they shock the
senses, and have no purchase upon the imagination. They
are a matter-of-fact impossibility; a fixture, and no
longer a phantom."

Thrale, Mrs. Hester Lynch. Thraliana: The Diary of Mrs.   8/10
Hester Lynch Thrale (Later Mrs. Piozzi) 1776-1809 [1942].
Edited by Katharine C. Balderston. 2 vols. 2nd ed.
Oxford: Clarendon, 1951.

18 Feb., 1794: "The Mysterious Mother is said by Lord
Orford, (then Horace Walpole) in his Preface, to be taken
from Tillotson, who received a confession of such crimes,
and bid the woman almost despair. It is not so; the
story is in Hall's Cases of Conscience, out of which the
Bishop related it to friends delighting more in anecdote
than truth, and they told it as having happened to him."

f.

Early Reviews

1. The Castle of Otranto (1764)

Critical Review, XIX (1765), 50-51.   8/107

Whether the translator "speaks seriously or ironically,
we neither know nor care. The publication of any work,
at this time, in England composed of such rotten materials,
is a phenomenon we cannot account for." So that "our
readers may form some idea of the absurdity of its contents", a brief summary is presented. The reviewer calls
the catastrophe "most wretched"; sees the helmet and portrait as "absurdities", but concedes that "the characters
are well marked, and the narrative kept up with surprising spirit and propriety".

Monthly Review, XXXII (1765), 97-99.   8/108

"Those who can digest the absurdities of Gothic fiction,
and bear with the machinery of ghosts and goblins, may
hope, at least, for considerable entertainment from the
performance before us: it is written with no common pen;
the language is accurate and elegant; the characters are
highly finished; and the disquisitions into human manners,
passions, and pursuits, indicate the keenest penetration,
and the most perfect knowledge of mankind." The reviewer
seems to disbelieve that C of O is a translation, and
cites as its "principal defect" the lack of a moral other
than that "very useless" one about sins being passed down.

Monthly Review, XXXII (1765), 394.   8/109

Review of the second edition, in which C of O becomes
identified as a new production. "While we considered
. . . [Otranto as a translation] we could readily excuse
its preposterous phenomena, and consider them as sacrifices to a gross and unenlightened age. -- But when, . . .
[it] is declared to be a modern performance, that indul-
gence we afforded to the foibles of a supposed antiquity,
we can by no means extend to the singularity of a false
taste in a cultivated period of learning. It is, indeed,
more than strange, that an Author, of a refined and pol-

ished genius, should be an advocate for re-establishing
the barbarous superstitions of Gothic devilism!"

Monthly Mirror, XVIII (1804), 246.   8/110

"This admirable production, the foundation of all the
subsequent romances of any merit published in England,
is too familiar to our readers to need description."

2. The Mysterious Mother (1768)

European Magazine, XII (1787), 191-193.   8/11

Written when MM was still unpublished. The editor received this account from an unidentified source but says
"it appears to have been intended as an article in The
Biographia Dramatica; but why it was suppressed, and an
inferior one, in every point of view, distributed in its
place, we are unable to give any information." Also, it
is suggested that Eleanora: or a Tragical but True Case
of Incest in Great Britain (1751), represents a source,
and parallels exist in the 1737, Innocence Distress'd,
or, The Royal Penitants. The account gives printing
details, notes it "is perhaps improper for the stage",
lists a few criticisms, but is mainly favorable.

Monthly Magazine, II (1796), 447.   8/11

"B" says that the story of MM may be found in Bishop Hall's
Resolutions and Decisions of Diverse Practical Cases of
Conscience, in Continual Use amongst Men, "of which the
second edition, dated 1650, is now lying before me. The
Bishop says he had it long ago from the relation of Mr.
Perkins, and since that, met with it in the report of
two several German authors." Also, the same story is
told by Julian de Medrano in his Common-Place Book, 1608.

Monthly Review, XXIII (1797), 248-254.   8/1

"The Mysterious Mother may fitly be compared with the
Oedipus Tyrannus of Sophocles, for unity and wholeness of
design in the fable, for dexterous conduct and ascending
interest of the plot, for crowded maxims of sublime in-

164

struction, and for the abominable horror of its petrifying event." Suggests that, in certain aspects, MM is superior. Concludes that MM "has attained an excellence nearly unimpeachable" and sees it as proper a stage production as Otway's Orphan.

Monthly Review, XXVI (1798), 323-327.   8/114

Reviews the 1798 Works. Says the language of MM "is more Shakespearian than that of any of his professed imitators; and so are the sentiments, -- except that Shakespeare was always a friend to religion, and treated its ministers with respect: but Mr. Walpole was a bitter foe to priests, without distinction". Great force, and admirable writing, appear in some of its scenes; but, in perusal, it excites more disgust and horror than pathos."

3. Adaptations

The Count of Narbonne, a Tragedy, by Robert Jephson. Reviewed in European Magazine, I (1782), 50-51.   8/115

A brief general account. Says the play is based on Otranto, a novel "which has always been considered as admirably calculated for the stage, if the magical part of it could be rendered subservient to the main design". Wonders, that even if virtue isn't always rewarded in real life, maybe it would be "advantageous to the interests of society" if it produced happiness in plays. Appends an account of Jephson.

IX

CLARA REEVE

(1729-1807)

a.

Selected Texts

1. The Old English Baron (1788)

1963 - The Old English Baron, in Seven Masterpieces of   9/1
Gothic Horror [1963]. Edited, and with an introduction
by Robert Donald Specter. New York: Bantam, 1970.

Paperback. Includes also Otranto, "Mistrust", "White Old
Maid", "Heir of Mondolpho", "House of Usher", "Carmilla".
Contains a general introduction, individual introductions,
footnotes, and bibliography.

1967 - The Old English Baron. Edited, and with an introduc-   9/2
tion by James Trainer. Oxford English Novels. London:
Oxford Univ. Press, 1967.

Text is of the revised second edition of 1778.

1969 - The Old English Baron. Microprint of the Philadel-   9/3
phia: Stewart & Cochran, 1797 ed. Early American Imprints. First Series 1639-1800. New York: Readex
Microprint, 1969.

See Shipton (1/37).

2. The Progress of Romance (1785)

1930 - The Progress of Romance and the History of Charoba,   9/4
Queen of Egypt. New York: Facsimile Text Society,
1930.

Reproduced from the Colchester edition of 1785.

1970 - The Progress of Romance through Times, Countries,   9/5
and Manners. New York: Garland, 1970.

Facsimile of 1785 edition; includes Charoba also.

b.

Bibliographies

Allibone, S[amuel] Austin. A Critical Dictionary of English   9/6
Literature and British and American Authors Living and
Deceased. From the Earliest Accounts to the Latter Half
of the Nineteenth Century. 3 vols. Philadelphia: Lippincott, 1871. (Reprinted, Detroit: Gale Research, 1965.)

Kunitz, Stanley J. and Howard Haycraft. British Authors   9/7
Before 1800. A Biographical Dictionary. New York:
Wilson, 1952.

Moulton, Charles Wells, ed. The Library of Literary Criti-   9/8
cism of English and American Authors. 8 vols. Buffalo:
Moulton, 1901-1905. (Reprinted, New York: P. Smith,
1935.)

Moulton's Library of Literary Criticism of English and Ameri-   9/9
can Authors Through the Beginning of the Twentieth Century. Abridged, revised, and with additions by Martin
Tucker. 4 vols. New York: Ungar, 1966.

Patrick, David, and J. Liddell. Chamber's Cyclopaedia of   9/10
English Literature. A History Critical and Biographical
of Authors in the English Tongue from the Earliest Times
till the Present Day, with Specimens of their Writings.
3 vols. London: Chamber's, [1922-1938].

Summers, Montague. A Gothic Bibliography [1941]. New York: 9/11
Russell & Russell, 1964.

Tobin, James E. Eighteenth Century English Literature and   9/12
its Cultural Background: A Bibliography. New York:
Fordham Univ. Press, 1939.

c.

Articles, Essays, and Introductions

Ashley-Montague, M.F. "'Imaginary Conversations'", TLS   9/13
(Jan. 27, 1940), p. 45.

Says that "it is generally known that Landor obtained the
idea for his first long poem, 'Gebir' (1798) from an
Arabic tale which he found in Clara Reeve's The Progress
of Romance", and contends that P of R, cast in dialogue
form, provided the idea for Imaginary Conversations.

Barbauld, Mrs. Anna Letitia. "Clara Reeve", in her An Essay   9/14
on the Origin and Progress of Novel Writing; and Prefaces,
Biographical and Critical from "the British Novelists".
London: Rivington, 1820. (On microfilm; negative made
by Library of Congress.)

"This work is something of a medium between the old romance
and the modern novel." "The story in simple and well connected. . . . The opening is striking. . . . The chief
fault of it is, that we foresee the conclusion before we
have read twenty pages." As to the toned-down supernatural, Mrs. Barbauld thinks it coincided with the beliefs
of Miss Reeve's readers, and for the "properly imbued,
the story will be striking."

Lee, Elizabeth. "Clara Reeve", in Leslie Stephen and Sid- 9/15
ney Lee, eds., Dictionary of National Biography. 63
vols. London: Smith, Elder, 1885 --.

Sees OEB as influence on Mrs. Radcliffe. Notes that it
was printed thirteen times between 1778 and 1886.

Reeves, John K. "The Mother of Fatherless Fanny", ELH, IX 9/16
(1942), 224-233.

FF, first published in 1819, was attributed on the title
page to the author of the OEB. Miss Reeve was then
twelve years dead. The 1741 edition was still attributed
to the author of the OEB, but this time the author is
named as "the Late Miss Taylor". A reference to Mannion,
a novel published the year after CR's death seems to indicate that this part is not by her, but it cannot be
stated that the entire novel is not her work, and there
seems evidence of two authors. "It is impossible to con-
clude with finality that the Irish ghost story in Fatherless Fanny represents Miss Reeve's last work, but the obvious differences in material and style between this section and the other parts of the book help to make this
conclusion a tempting one."

Roberts, W. "'Fatherless Fanny'", TLS (Jan. 17, 1935), p. 9/17
33.

In response to a question submitted to the TLS on 10
January, 1935 (p. 21) as to the author of FF, Roberts
writes that an 1835 edition identifies the author as
"the late Miss Taylor" and adds that the edition was
"edited and enlarged by Mrs. Sarah Green". Also, FF
has been attributed to T.P. Prest. Concludes: "It has
nothing to do with Clara Reeve, and is, I think, one of
the silliest of the 'mushy' type of romance which was so
widely read in the first two or three decades of the last
century."

Scott, Sir Walter. "Clara Reeve"[1823], in Ioan Williams, 9/18
ed., Sir Walter Scott on Novelists and Fiction. London:
Routledge & Kegan Paul, 1968.

Covers biography, family background, the missing
Castle Connor, and delves deeply into aesthetics of OEB.
Objects to imposition of limits on the supernatural;
sees the tale as "sometimes tame and tedious" but over-

looks the defects and lack of historicity concluding that OEB "has always produced as strong an effect as any story of the kind".

Trainer, James. Introduction to The Old English Baron.   9/19
Oxford English Novels. London: Oxford Univ. Press,
1967.

Points out CR's concern with toning down Walpole and shows similar attitudes towards propriety and decorum in characters and in strong didactic tendencies. Says "without her decisive intervention to make possible supernatural fiction which does not do violence to human reason the new direction taken by Ann Radcliffe would have been unthinkable."

Williams, Stanley T. "The Story of Gebir", PMLA, XXXVI   9/20
(1921), 615-631.

Says that Landor's epic poem Gebir (1798) has its source in Clara Reeve's History of Charoba, Queen of Egypt.

d.

Early Reviews

1. The Old English Baron (1778)

Critical Review, XLV (1778), 315-316.   9/21

"This is no common novel -- it may, in some respects, claim a place upon the same shelf with the Castle of Otranto, which has its faults as well as OEB -- . The Baron will probably live as long as the Castle stands but he should never forget that he was born in the Castle of Otranto."

Gentleman's Magazine, XLVIII (1778), 324-325.   9/22

The time of the novel is not Gothic -- "the title therefore seems a kind of contradiction in terms. The mis-
take seems to arise from the Gothic style in building,
which then prevailed." But, the book itself "is executed
in a pleasing interesting manner". Notes that Miss Reeve
criticizes Otranto for producing with the marvellous,
only laughter. "But, on the other hand, if this effect
be not in some degree excited, or, at least, if the circumstances be not self-evidently absurd, some weak minds,
perhaps, might be induced to think them true or possible,
and thereby be led into superstition."

Monthly Review, LVIII (1778), 85.   9/23

Complete review: "This writer has imitated with tolerable
success, the style and manner of ancient romance. The
story is enlivened with an agreeable variety of incidents;
the narrative is plain and simple; and the whole is adapted
to interest the feelings of the reader, -- providing he
has either faith, or fancy, enough to be interested in
the appearance of ghosts."

Monthly Review, LVIII (1778), 476.   9/24

The Champion of Virtue, reviewed earlier (9/23), "is revived and corrected, and more elegantly printed; and the
title is changed, as the Author tells us in her preface,
because the character of an Old English Baron is thought
to be the principal one in the story."

                    2. Miscellaneous

The Exiles. Reviewed in English Review, XII (1788), 465.   9/25

Reports that CR "has been unfortunate in the loss of a
very fine ghost story, which was sent to London by the
Ipswich blue coach; and which she tells us to print at
our peril. . . ."

Memoirs of Sir Roger de Clarendon. Reviewed in British
Critic, II (1793), 383-388.

"When the OEB made its appearance, every mouth was opened
in its praise; every line carried fascination along with
it. The younger branch of readers found their attention
absolutely rivetted to the story; and at its conclusion,
they have actually been seen to weep, in the spirit of
Alexander, because they had not another volume to peruse.
A more genuine and unaffected compliment was never paid to
any work of fancy." But, the reviewer finds this present
work "rather dull", objects to the prevailing and fashionable fault of blending truth with fable, a practice which
. . . is likely . . . to create in young minds a strange
confusion between truth and false, which subsequent study
may not easily clear away."

3. Adaptations

Edmund; Orphan of the Castle, a Tragedy, in Five Acts,
Founded on the "Old English Baron". Reviewed in British
Critic, XV (1800), 76.

"The romance on which this Tragedy is founded is well-
known for its good style and interesting conduct, and
has given deserved credit to the author, Clara Reeve.
Very different is the character which must be assigned to
the drama, which no one but a reviewer could, we think,
have laboured through."

X

CHARLOTTE (TURNER) SMITH

(1749-1806)

a.

Selected Texts

1. Emmeline, The Orphan of the Castle (1788)

971 - Emmeline, the Orphan of the Castle. Edited, and with   10/1
an introduction by Anne Henry Ehrenpreis. Oxford English
Novels. New York: Oxford Univ. Press, 1971.

Text is of the second edition.

2. The Old Manor House (1793)

969 - The Old Manor House. Edited, and with an introduction 10/2
by Anne Henry Ehrenpreis. Oxford English Novels. New
York: Oxford Univ. Press, 1969.

Text is of the first edition, collated with that of the
second.

3. Miscellaneous Works

ιe American Antiquarian Society (see 1/37) offers micro-   10/3
prints of the following texts:

D'Arcy. Philadelphia: Carey, 1796. (But, see Turner
    10/12.)

Elegiac Sonnets. Philadelphia: Dobson, 1787.
Elegiac Sonnets. 7th ed. Boston: Spotswood, 1795.
Elegiac Sonnets. 1st Worcester ed. Thomas, for Thomas
and Andrews, 1795.

Montalbert. Carlisle, Pa.: Kline for Carey, 1795.
Montalbert. Philadelphia: Snowden & McCorkle, 1800.

Romance of Real Life. Philadelphia: Carey, 1799.

Rural Walks. Philadelphia: Stevens, 1795.

b.

Bibliographies

Allibone, S[amuel] Austin. A Critical Dictionary of English   10/4
Literature and British and American Authors Living and
Deceased. From the Earliest Accounts to the Latter Half
of the Nineteenth Century. 3 vols. Philadelphia: Lippincott, 1871. (Reprinted, Detroit: Gale Research,
1965.)

Kunitz, Stanley J. and Howard Haycraft. British Authors   10/5
Before 1800. A Biographical Dictionary. New York:
Wilson, 1952.

Moulton, Charles Wells, ed. The Library of Literary Criti-   10/6
cism of English and American Authors. 8 vols. Buffalo:
Moulton, 1901-1905. (Reprinted, New York: P. Smith, 1935.)

Patrick, David, and J. Liddell. Chamber's Cyclopaedia of   10/7
English Literature. A History Critical and Biographical
of Authors in the English Tongue from the Earliest Times
till the Present Day, with Specimens of their Writings.
3 vols. London: Chamber's, [1922-1938].

Summers, Montague. A Gothic Bibliography [1941]. New York: 10/8
Russell & Russell, 1964.

Tobin, James E. Eighteenth Century English Literature and   10/9
its Cultural Background: A Bibliography. New York:
Fordham Univ. Press, 1939.

Watson, George, ed. The New Cambridge Bibliography of Eng-   10/10
lish Literature. 3 vols. Cambridge: Univ. Press,
1969 --.

c.

Full-Length Studies

Hilbish, Florence May Anna. Charlotte Smith, Poet and   10/11
Novelist (1749-1806). Printed for the Univ. of Philadelphia by Times and News Publishing, Gettysburg, 1941.

A 600 page doctoral dissertation printed and bound in
paper covers, this mammoth work is in two sections of
equal length, one devoted to biography, the other to criticism. Draws heavily on contemporary reviews and articles; includes much original research and offers some
new findings. The discussion of Gothicism forms but a
small part of the entire book, but in this field, Dr.
Hilbish tells us that "Mrs. Radcliffe owes more of her
success as a novelist to Charlotte Smith than the world
has been willing to acknowledge." Mrs. Smith used Gothic
suggestion earlier than Mrs. Radcliffe; AR borrowed "romantic description . . . ideas, characters, and situations"
from Mrs. S. "Mrs. S's use [of nature] was a permanent
contribution to literature; Mrs. R's was a short-lived
abnormality." Doesn't consider Mrs. S as a Gothic writer;
says she disliked the genre, used imaginary terror inci-
dentally, as did Smollett, but "The Story of Edourado"
is true Gothic. Traces Smith's influences and contributions; discusses her poetry, children's books, and
novels of purpose.

Turner, Rufus Paul. "Charlotte Smith (1749-1806): Some New   10/12
Light on Her Life and Literary Career". Unpublished
doctoral dissertation, Univ. of Southern California, 1966.

Draws upon 197 previously unexamined letters of CS and 64
letters and notes of her associates. Mainly biographical
and corrects, clarifies, and adjusts earlier efforts.

Shows that CS's life was "more laborious, problem laden,
and remarkable than her prior biographers have hinted".
She "disliked writing for a living, detested the novel"
and her "personal and family needs dictated and affected
her literary production and . . . life problems affected
her quality." Turner corrects her marriage date, veri-
fies the husband's name, discloses his infidelities,
gives new information on the children, her relations with
publishers, and lists locations in the U.S. of her
novels and letters. Says D'Arcy is not by CS. Although
the Gothic aspect is not studied, Emmeline, Ethelinde,
and Celestina are called "essentially novels of sentiment containing some Gothic elements", the Gothic elements in OMH are noted, and "Edourado" labeled "Gothic
to the fullest extent". Concludes that Mrs. Smith "held
the Gothic impulse in check and introduced sentimental
scenery -- the combined legacy that she passed on to Ann
Radcliffe".

d.

Articles, Essays, and Introductions

Barbauld, Mrs. Anna Letitia. "Mrs. Charlotte Smith", in her   10/13
An Essay on the Origin and Progress of Novel Writing;
and Prefaces, Biographical and Critical from "The British Novelists". London: Rivington, 1820. (On microfilm; negative made by Library of Congress.)

Says CS was one of the first to use scenery -- and used
it properly, "at judicious intervals, in compositions of
which variety rather than deep pathos, and elegance
rather than strength, are the characteristics". "The
situations and the scenery are often romantic; the characters and the conversations are from common life." But
"the asperity of invective and the querulousness of complaint too frequently cloud the happier exertions of her
imagination."

Brydges, Samuel Egerton. "Memoir of Mrs. Charlotte Smith",   10/14
in his Censura Literaria. 10 vols. London: Longman,
1805-1809.

A rather general memoir which discusses family background,
marital problems, poverty as impetus to write, and mis-

176

fortunes of the children. Defends CS against charges of
"immorality" and "deficiency of religion"; notes that her
pro-French Revolution attitude caused prejudice against
her. "Of Mrs. Smith's poetry it is not easy to speak in
terms too high. There is so much unaffected elegance;
so much pathos and harmony in it; the images are so sooth-
ing, and so delightful, and the sentiments so touching, so
consonant to the best movements of the heart, that no
reader of pure taste can grow weary of perusing them."

Bushnell, Nelson S. "Artistic Economy in Jane Eyre: A Con-   10/15
trast with The Old Manor House", ELN, V (1968), 197-202.

Suggests that although no proof exists, Charlotte Brontë
may have drawn upon OMH. Notes parallels in theme and
points out how Mrs. Smith failed to take full advantage
of her materials.

"Mrs. Charlotte Smith", Lady's Monthly Museum, II (1799),   10/16
336-341.

Written during Mrs. Smith's lifetime, this account is
both general and flattering, but does not draw on an
interview nor use any personal information. Mentions her
works, her sadness, her indignation. Says "like all
original writers, her imitators have been numerous and
servile".

Foster, James R. "Charlotte Smith, Pre-Romantic Novelist",   10/17
PMLA, XLIII (1928), 463-475.

More of an introduction than an argument, this paper discusses the life, works and influence of Mrs. Smith. Foster places her in the school of the Richardsonian sentimental novel, and while her satirical thrusts   reveal
neo-classical tendencies, the exotic and poetic landscapes are romantic, and in fact, "she was the first in
England to give an appreciable attention to romantic
landscape description". In addition to landscape, CS
depicted Gothic gloom, ruins, and cemeteries. Mrs. Radcliffe borrowed from CS, but there was a back flow --
Romance of the Forest drew on Celestina, but Montalbert
took from Udolpho and gave to the Italian. Mrs. Radcliffe
"borrowed ideas and situations from Mrs. Smith, but the
chief indebtedness is on the score of description".

Howard, Edward G.   "An Unrecorded Baltimore Imprint from   10/18
Philadelphia", PBSA, LXI (1967), 121-123.

Charlotte Smith's Romance of Real Life was printed and
published in Philadelphia by James Carey in 1799, but
the University of Pennsylvania has acquired a copy bearing the imprint of Campbell, Conrad & Co., Baltimore,
rather than that of Carey. After a collation of texts,
Howard concludes that except for the title page they are
both of the Philadelphia run. Campbell, Conrad & Co.
were booksellers, not printers.

Hunt, Bishop C.   "Wordsworth and Charlotte Smith", WC, I   10/19
(1970), 85-103.

As an undergraduate, WW read and annotated his copy of
CS's Elegiac Sonnets. On his way to France in 1791 he
visited her, and the purpose may have been either poetical
or political. The Emigrants influenced "Tintern Abbey",
and possibly "The Old Cumberland Beggar", The Borderers,
and other poems. Notes that "both WW and CS set the out-
casts of society against the background of a desolate
landscape", and asserts that what distinguishes Mrs.
Smith's writing "from the usual 'terrible sublime', the
stagey, stock-in-trade horrifics of the Age of Sensibility
is that the events described are real".

Lee, Elizabeth.   "Charlotte Smith", in Leslie Stephen and   10/20
Sidney Lee, eds. Dictionary of National Biography.   63
vols. London: Smith, Elder, 1885 --.

General and unimportant.

McKillop, Alan Dugald.   "Charlotte Smith's Letters", HLQ,   10/21
XV (1952), 237-255.

Notes and comments on the 45 Smith letters held at the
Huntington Library. Says "Charlotte Smith was probably
the most popular contemporary novelist in the English-
speaking world of the early 1790's" and points out her
relations with the Lee sisters, Cowper, and Southey.
Comments on her dealings with publishers, her personal
misfortunes, and suggests that she includes much first-
hand information in her novels. "Erring husbands, haughty
aristocrats, difficult guardians, gentlefolk in distress
who deserve and require a mode of living suitable to their
rank -- such themes CS blended in various degrees with
the sentimental and the romantic."

Pollin, Burton R. "Keats, Charlotte Smith, and the Night-   10/22
ingale", N&Q, XII (1966), 180-181.

Presents text of Mrs. S's "On the Departure of the Nightingale", compares it with Keats' "To a Nightingale".
"The actual language used, the themes expressed, the
orientation of the poems, all made them highly significant
sources for Keats throughout his short life."

St. Cyres, Viscount. "The Sorrows of Mrs. Charlotte Smith",   10/23
Cornhill Magazine, NS, XV (1903), 683-696.

Points out a plagiarism from Pope; says CS "troubled
nothing at all about the external decencies of verse", and
argues that "quite an appreciable proportion of her tears
was due to purely literary requirements". Calls her the
"Laureate of the Lachrymose" and says she was "no sounder
than her brother-poet, William Wordsworth, on the subject
of the French Revolution". One of her few real merits, he
says, was her avoidance of picturesque descriptions for
"she forswore these abstract unrealities and honestly
tried to reproduce what her own eyes had shown her."

Scott, Sir Walter. "Charlotte Smith"[1827], in his The Lives   10/24
of the Novelists. Everyman's. London: Dent,[1910].

Praises her craftsmanship, her power of satire, character
portrayal and dialogue, yet finds several flaws. She is
too critical, too severe, too melancholy, and in Emmeline
has "a dangerous theme" -- sacrifices to passion. Includes
the lengthy biographical account written by CS's sister,
Mrs. Dorset.

Whiting, George W. "Charlotte Smith, Keats and the Nightin-   10/25
gale", KSJ, XII (1963), 4-8.

"I think it not improbable that he [Keats] owed something
to Charlotte Smith, particularly for the nightingale --
a small point apparently overlooked by Miss Hilbish[10/11]
in her exhaustive study. Why indeed should Keats not have
been influenced in some degree by Charlotte Smith, whose
Elegiac Sonnets was frequently republished and highly
esteemed?"

e.

Notices in General Works, Diaries, Etc.

Elwood, Mrs. [Anne]. Memoirs of the Literary Ladies of Eng-   10/26
land. 2 vols. London: Henry Colburn, 1843.

Contains a long essay on Mrs. Smith which draws on other
authors -- but does not identify sources. Biographical
and complimentary.

Heilman, Robert Bechtold. America in English Fiction 1760-   10/27
1800: The Influence of the American Revolution [1937].
New York: Octagon, 1968.

Consists mainly of a thematic investigation of the attitudes of several English novelists. Charlotte Smith is
given considerable attention since most of her works include American incidents, but the treatment is mainly a
cataloguing of ideas. No attention to literary skill or
techniques, and the Gothic aspect lies outside the scope
of this work.

Kavanagh, Julia. English Women of Letters: Biographical   10/28
Sketches. 2 vols. London: Hurst & Blackett, 1863.

Written 110 years ago by a critic now almost totally obscure, the two chapters on Charlotte Smith are perceptive
and well worth looking into. The first chapter deals
with biography and concludes that CS was of "a hasty
temper . . . irritable and resentful. . . . Her works
bear the traces of asperity. . . ." The next chapter
deals with her novels and concludes that "they remain
amongst the most remarkable but least read productions of
the time to which she belonged, stamped with the melancholy fiat -- above mediocrity, but below genius." CS
is praised for her truth -- truth in "a Cowper-like fi-
delity of description" of nature, antithetical to the
highly romanticized scenes of Mrs. AR. However, most
interestingly, Miss Kavanagh praises CS's truth in de-
lineating women -- in presenting "living and real" females. Before this, the masculine-dominated literature
saw "woman as mere woman -- as the embodiment of beauty,
often silly young creatures made to delight men, to amuse,
tease, and obey him."

Lascelles, Mary. Jane Austen and Her Art [1939]. London: 10/29
Oxford Univ. Press, 1970.

Contends that Northanger Abbey was written not with Mrs.
Radcliffe in mind, but rather with Mrs. Smith's Emmeline
(1788) as a model. Catherine is created as an inversion
of Emmeline, but Lascelles admits that all heroines of
that era display similarities.

Pilkington, Mrs. Memoirs of Celebrated Female Characters.   10/30
London: Albion Press, 1804.

The brief biographical sketch of Mrs. Smith puts emphasis
on her misfortunes, not her writings.

f.

Early Reviews

1. Emmeline, or the Orphan of the Castle (1788)

Analytical Review, I (1788), 327-333.   10/31

"M" laments that "the false expectations these wild scenes
excite, tend to debauch the mind, and throw an insipid
kind of uniformity over the moderate and rational pros-
pects of life, consequently adventures are sought for and
created, when duties are neglected, and content despised."
Notes that "some of the descriptions are . . . interesting
and beautiful."

English Review, XII (1788), 26-27.   10/32

"Charlotte Smith, after tripping not ungracefully among
the shrubbery of Parnassus, has attempted to tread the
more elevated and arduous paths of the mountain, and done
it, so far, with success. The story of her novel is interesting without perplexity; the characters are varied
without studied opposition, and marked without extravagance. She seems to aim at natural strokes of character,
not bizarre dashes of caricatura."

Calls the novel one "of real and unequivocal merit".
Says the author "made the interests of virtue her only
care", instructs and delights, presents "very just and
accurate observations upon life,and manners", has well-
drawn characters, but "now and then [has] appearances
of carelessness and inattention in the language".

2. Ethelinde, or, The Recluse of the Lake (1789)

Analytical Review, V (1789), 484-486.   10/34

Notes that Mrs. S "looks at nature with a poet's eye"
and offers "enchanting backgrounds to the historical
past", but asserts that "there is very little passion
in the tale".

European Magazine, XVII (1790), 270.   10/35

"Although the action of the novel . . . is less interesting than we expected . . . , yet the elegant descriptions
of the abounding scenery, and the correctly natural manners which are attributed to the respective characters,
make ample compensation. To use an expression from the
work itself, Mrs. Smith appears 'to view the face of
Nature with the taste of a painter and the enthusiasm of
a poet'."

Monthly Review , 2nd ser., II (1790), 161-165.   10/36

Says the novel represents "particular merit" and places
Mrs. S "considerably above the crowd of novelists who
have lately come under our Review". "We are so much
pleased . . . with the ruralities, with the pages descriptive of the more beautiful scenes in nature, that
we cannot but wish that the fair authoress had more
frequently indulged her talent in the same way. As her
imagination is really poetical, she sometimes considerably heightens our British scenery, and almost brings
the Thessalial Tempe to our view."

3. Celestina (1791)

Analytical Review, X (1791), 409-415.   10/37

"As a whole, Mrs. S's amusing production is certainly
very defective and unnatural; but many lucid parts are
scattered with negligent grace, and amidst the entangle-
ment of wearisome episodes, interesting scenes, and pros-
pects, seen with a poetic eye, start to relieve the
reader, who would turn, knowing something of the human
heart, with disgust from the romantic adventures, and
artificial passions, that novel reading has suggested to
the author."

Monthly Review, 2nd ser., VI (1791), 286-291.   10/38

"The modern Novel, well executed, possessing the essential
characters of poetry, perhaps even more perfectly than the
ancient Romance, certainly deserves a place among the
works of genius. . . ." Needless to say, Celestina belongs
to this class. These "essential characters" of poetry,
"we comprehend, with the first ancient critics, all those
literary productions, in which fancy collects, judgment
combines, and taste expresses in suitable language, images
furnished by nature; whether the expression be, or be not,
subjected to the artificial restrictions of metre."

4. Desmond (1792)

Analytical Review, XIII (1792), 428-435.   10/39

"The subordinate characters are sketched with that peculiar dexterity which shoots folly as it flies; and the
tale, not encumbered with episodes, is a more interesting,
as well as a more finished production than any of her
former ones."

European Magazine, XXII (1792), 21-23.   10/40

   "Our Authoress has certainly vindicated the cause of
   French liberty with much acuteness. She has thought
   proper, however, to apologize for the introduction of
   political matter. . . ." Praises the novel; sees it as
   "not less useful than entertaining".

Monthly Review, 2nd ser., IX (1792), 406-413.   10/41

   "Novels, which were formerly little more than simple
   tales of love, are gradually taking a higher and more
   masculine tone, and are becoming the vehicles of useful instruction". Notes that Mrs. S has "ventured beyond the beaten track, so far as to interweave with her
   narrative many political discussions".

            5. The Emigrants: A Poem (1793)

British Critic, I (1793), 403-406.   10/42

   Compares the works of Mrs. S with those of Cowper. Asserts that "descriptive poetry, like landscape painting,
   becomes doubly interesting when into the picture is introduced any human figure."

            6. The Old Manor House (1793)

British Critic, I (1793), 148-150.   10/4

   "We have not often been more interested by the fictions
   of invention, and the sensibilities excited by the perusal of the work are in general such as are favourable
   to virtue." Praises the characterization, the swift
   incidents, the poetic descriptions, but judges "censurable"
   the introduction of political reflections.

Critical Review, 2nd ser., VIII (1793), 44-55.   10/44

Praises the genre of the novel, praises Mrs. S, but dis-
likes OMH. "We are afraid we can say little of plot,
for there seems to be none but the concealment of a will,
and still less of the denouement, which, in our opinion,
is 'most lame and impotent'." Praises CS's "powers in
exciting emotions of terror"; admits "she certainly possesses in no inferior degree the power to arrest and command attention, by a happy description of circumstances
and objects awful, terrific, and sublime . . . ," but
asserts OMH is too tedious and too drawn out.

English Review, XXI (1793), 264-270.   10/45

"The OMH is one of those novels that must receive general
applause, inasmuch as it is adapted to the level of domestic life. There are no noble personages whose dis-
tresses we pity a moment and then forget, because we cannot assimilate them to any scenes in which we have been,
are, or can be engaged."

Monthly Review, XI (1793), 150-153.   10/46

Praises the "many very successful imitations of the ordinary language of people in different classes of the
inferior ranks". Objects that the novel is not always
"guided by probability". Thinks OMH not superior to the
earlier novels "yet it discovers, in a considerable degree, facility of invention, knowledge of life, and command of language".

XI

ANN (WARD) RADCLIFFE

(1764-1823)

a.

Selected Texts

1. Collected Works

1971 - The Novels; Gaston de Blondeville; A Journey Made in   11/1
the Summer of 1794. Anglistica & Americana. Hildesheim:
Georg Olms, 1971.

Facsimile reprints. Novels is the 1824 Ballantyne's
Novelist's Library edition of Sicilian Romance, Udolpho,
Italian, and Athlin and Dunbayne. Gaston is of the 1826
issue, Journey a copy of the 1795 release.

2. The Castles of Athlin and Dunbayne (1789)

1970 - The Castles of Athlin and Dunbayne. New York: John-   11/2
son Reprint, 1970.

Facsimile reprint of the 1796 edition. No new introduction. Author listed as "Anne Rattcliffe".

1972 - The Castles of Athlin and Dunbayne. Edited by De-   11/3
vendra P. Varma. Foreword by Frederick Shroyer. New
York: Arno, 1972.

Facsimile reprint of 1821 edition.

3. A Sicilian Romance (1790)

1971 - A Sicilian Romance. Edited by Robert Donald Spector   11/4
and Martin Tucker. Belles Lettres in English Series.
2 vols. New York: Johnson Reprint, 1971.

Facsimile reprint of the first edition of 1790.

1972 - A Sicilian Romance. Edited, and with an introduction   11/5
by Devendra P. Varma. Foreword by Howard Mumford Jones.
New York: Arno, 1972.

Facsimile reprint of "a new edition" of 1821.

4. The Romance of the Forest (1791)

1931 - The Romance of the Forest, in Three Eighteenth Century   11/6
Romances [1931]. Introduction by Harrison R. Steeves.
New York: Scribner's, 1971.

Abridged. Otranto and Vathek are also in this paperback.

1970 - The Romance of the Forest. 3 vols. New York: John-   11/7
son Reprint, 1970.

Facsimile reprint of the fourth edition of 1794.

1974 - The Romance of the Forest. Edited, and with an intro-   11/8
duction by Devendra P. Varma. Foreword by Frederick
Garber. 3 vols. New York: Arno, 1974.

Facsimile reprint of the 1824 edition.

5. The Mysteries of Udolpho (1794)

1931 - The Mysteries of Udolpho [1931]. Introduction by R.   11/9
Austin Freeman. Everyman's. 2 vols. New York: Dutton,
1965.

1960 - The Mysteries of Udolpho. Vol. III of The Classics of   11/10
Mystery. Edited by Michael Eenhoorn. Forge Village:
Murray, [1960].

Abridged.

1963 - The Mysteries of Udolpho, in "The Castle of Otranto" by 11/11
Horace Walpole; "The Mysteries of Udolpho" by Ann Radcliffe; "Northanger Abbey" by Jane Austen. Edited, and
with an introduction by Andrew Wright. New York: Holt,
Rinehart & Winston, 1963.

Text is an abridgment of the first edition of 1794.

1966 - The Mysteries of Udolpho. Edited, and with an intro-   11/12
duction by Bonamy Dobrée. Oxford English Novels. London:
Oxford Univ. Press, 1966.

Text follows the first edition of 1794.

6. The Italian; Or,
The Confessional of the Black Penitents (1797)

1956 - The Confessional of the Black Penitents. With wood-   11/13
engravings by Philip Ross. London: Folio, 1956.

1968 - The Italian; or, The Confessional of the Black Peni-   11/14
tents. Edited, and with an introduction by Frederick
Garber. Oxford English Novels. London: Oxford Univ.
Press, 1968.

Text follows that of the first edition of 1797, "the
only one with any certain authority".

1968 - The Italian; or, the Confessional of the Black Peni-   11/15
tents. Edited, and with an introduction by Devendra P.
Varma. 2 vols. New York: Russell& Russell, 1968.

Facsimile reproduction of the 1828 edition.

7. Gaston de Blondeville: Or,
The Court of Henry III Keeping Festival in Ardenne;
A Romance (1826)

1972 - Gaston de Blondeville; or, The Court of Henry III   11/16
Keeping Festival in Ardenne: A Romance. Edited, and
with an introduction by Devendra P. Varma. 2 vols. New
York: Arno, 1972.

Facsimile copy of the first edition of 1826. Contains
the anonymous "Memoir of the Author".

7. Miscellaneous

The American Antiquarian Society (see 1/37) offers micro-   11/17
prints of the following texts:

Athlin and Dunbayne. Philadelphia: Bradford, 1796.
Athlin and Dunbayne. Boston: West, 1797.

Italian. Boston: Etheridge, 1797.
Italian. Mount Pleasant, N.J.: Durell for Magill, 1797.
Italian. New York: Greenleaf, 1797.
Italian. Philadelphia: Carey, 1797.
Italian. Philadelphia: Folwell for Rices & Campbell,
1797.

189

Udolpho. Boston: Etheridge for White, Spotswood, Thomas
& Andrews, etc., 1795.
Udolpho. Philadelphia: Rices, 1800.

Romance of the Forest. Boston: Etheridge for Larkin,
Spotswood, Thomas & Andrews, etc., 1795.
Romance of the Forest. Philadelphia: Bradford, 1795.

Sicilian Romance. Philadelphia: For H&P Rice, and for
J. Rice, 1795.

b.

Bibliographies

Allibone, S[amuel] Austin. A Critical Dictionary of English   11/18
Literature and British and American Authors Living and
Deceased. From the Earliest Accounts to the Latter Half
of the Nineteenth Century. 3 vols. Philadelphia: Lippincott, 1871. (Reprinted, Detroit: Gale Research,
1965.)

Kunitz, Stanley J. and Howard Haycraft. British Authors   11/19
Before 1800. A Biographical Dictionary. New York:
Wilson, 1952.

Moulton, Charles Wells, ed. The Library of Literary Criti-   11/20
cism of English and American Authors. 8 vols. Buffalo:
Moulton, 1901-1905. (Reprinted, New York: P. Smith,
1935.)

Moulton's Library of Literary Criticism of English and Ameri- 11/21
can Authors through the Beginning of the Twentieth Century. Abridged, revised, and with additions by Martin
Tucker. 4 vols. New York: Ungar, 1966.

Patrick, David, and J. Liddell. Chamber's Cyclopaedia of   11/22
English Literature. A History Critical and Biographi-
cal of Authors in the English Tongue from the Earliest
Times till the Present Day, with Specimens of their
Writings. 3 vols. London: Chamber's, [1922-1938].

Summers, Montague. A Gothic Bibliography [1941]. New York: 11/23
Russell & Russell, 1964.

Contains a list of Mrs. R's works, abridgments, adaptations,
spurious attributions, and translations.

Tobin, James E. Eighteenth Century English Literature and   11/24
its Cultural Background: A Bibliography. New York:
Fordham Univ. Press, 1939.

Watson, George, ed. The New Cambridge Bibliography of Eng-   11/25
lish Literature. 3 vols. Cambridge: Univ. Press,
1969 --.

c.

Full-Length Studies

Grant, Aline. Ann Radcliffe: A Biography. Denver: Alan   11/26
Swallow, 1951.

Draws on the scant information and fills out the pages
with historical happenings, weather reports, and much of
what must be speculation or pure conjecture. Abounds in
asides and irrelevant material and, since not a single
footnote appears, there is no way or separating fact from
imaginative-supplementary-biography.

Keebler, Lee E. "Ann Radcliffe: A Study in Achievement".   11/27
Unpublished doctoral dissertation, Univ. of Wisconsin,
1967.

Not a study of sources or influences, and not a study of
Gothic -- but rather an investigation of Mrs. R's artistic development. Looks at structure, characterization,
setting, buildings, supernaturalism, and atmosphere.
Shows how plot emphasis moves from action to mystery, how
villains grow darker and more mysterious, how buildings
increase their solemnity and gloom, and how landscape
description grew but finally came under control. Says
that heroes and heroines are sterotypes but suggests that
the primary purpose of the heroine is "to pass on to the

reader all the terror resulting from her situation and
trembling imagination".

McIntyre, Clara Frances. Ann Radcliffe in Relation to Her   11/28
Time [1920]. [Hamden]: Archon, 1970.

This slim volume predates the major works on the Gothic
novel and was intended to show what Mrs. Radcliffe's
contemporaries thought of her and to determine what was
original and what was derived. Relates biography, offers
extracts from about forty contemporary reviews and looks
at translations and stage adaptations. Says Mrs. R's "distinctive and important" contribution was in the structure
of the novel. Valuable for its list of early reviews.

Murray, E[ugene] B. Ann Radcliffe. Twayne's English Author   11/29
Series. New York: Twayne, 1972.

Consists of eight chapters: "Life and Times", "The Gothic
Background", "Athlin and Dunbayne", "Sicilian Romance",
"Romance of the Forest", "Udolpho", "Italian", "Evaluation
and Influence". Gaston does not receive any attention
and the poetry is similarly neglected as "neither important nor relevant". Competent, though introductory, and
unlike many works on Mrs. R, pays special attention to
the novels themselves. The development of the lady's art
becomes skillfully traced and emphasis falls on the moral
attributes -- the disinterestedness and selfishness of
heroine and villain.

Pound, Edward Fox. "The Influence of Burke and the Psycho-   11/30
logical Critics on the Novels of Ann Radcliffe". Unpublished doctoral dissertation, Univ. of Washington, 1963.

Walpole originated the Gothic novel by looking backward
into literary history; Reeve continued in this vein, but
Mrs. Radcliffe introduced contemporary aesthetic theory
into the romance. In fact, claims Pound, "in Udolpho
Radcliffe has ceased to produce romance in the old way
and is writing a psychological novel". Mrs. R drew upon
Hume, Burke, Gerard, Blair, Beattie, and Alison and this
study points out how she used their ideas on association
psychology and taste theory and shows that she and Burke
are not in agreement on several points. Says the Radcliffian villain may be a product of these aestheticians
rather than a warmed-over Elizabethan villain; believes

her character portraits are unsatisfactory and depend upon
the reader's awareness of certain theories. "Particularly
in character", he concludes, "Radcliffe's fiction becomes
a monument to the improper use of psychology."

Ronald, Margaret Ann. "Functions of Setting in the Novel: 11/31
From Mrs. Radcliffe to Charles Dickens". Unpublished
doctoral dissertation, Northwestern Univ., 1970.

Begins with an analysis of AR's use of setting and then
investigates how Scott, Charlotte Brontë and Dickens use
these same techniques. "Mrs. Radcliffe's use of setting
to evoke atmosphere is studied and extensive, while she
makes only very rare use of setting to supplement the
characterization, to aid the plot, or to convey meaning."
Notes how she follows Burke, uses vague outlines, blends
Salvator and Claude. Comments on her use of aesthetic
terms and notes how she stations her characters. AR's
influence is found in Scott but he combines Gothic con-
stituents with more concretely visual images, names his
images, and employs specific images as symbols, thus adding
a new dimension to his novels. "Miss Brontë's utilization
of setting as symbol, to add meaning and import to her
novel, takes her far beyond the limitations of Mrs. R and
Scott." But Dickens makes "setting so important to the
structure of his novel that it not only functions simul-
taneously in each of its roles, but also functions in the
roles of each of the other elements found in fiction --
that is, as character, as plot, as meaning."

Smith, Nelson Charles. "The Art of Gothic: Ann Radcliffe's   11/32
Major Novels". Unpublished doctoral dissertation, Univ.
of Washington, 1967.

Demonstrates that the old division of "the school of Mrs.
Radcliffe" fails to consider the progress that this
writer made. "Radcliffe" does not equal "explained supernatural"; there is much more than this. Smith dissects
Otranto and OEB, discusses the conventions and machinery:
the hero, heroine, villain, castle, the didacticism, and
says that Mrs. R's first two novels are "completely conventional" Gothic romances, but then subjects her later
works to a careful analysis. All of the conventions and
machines are given a special twist -- and something new
develops. The novelist moves away from didacticism, reverses the roles of the characters, introduces "the vac-
illating character", gives sympathy to a villain, does
not adhere to strict poetic justice, gives vengeance to

193

the establishment, experiments in narrative techniques,
focuses on the hero-villain, and moves the setting closer
to contemporary times. Mrs. R, like Jane Austen two
decades later, was not an advocate of sensibility, but
rather showed its weaknesses and flaws. "The Gothic novel
was a perfect vehicle to show the extreme effects of sensibility."

Swigart, Ford Harris. "A Study of the Imagery in the Gothic   11/33
Romances of Ann Radcliffe". Unpublished doctoral dissertation, Univ. of Pittsburgh, 1967.

Exemplifies, classifies, and analyzes AR's images according to their major qualities and functions. The
first category is that of the picturesque and the visual.
Here, "imagery of painting, veil, and light contributes
to that quality by presenting, respectively, the color
and form of a surface, the covering of a surface, and
the brightening of a surface. The resultant emphasis is
visual." The second group of images are those of mutation
and sensibility.. Unlike the first group, there exists
here little originality. Images employed are those of
"conflict, liquid, music, and the qualities of softness,
swelling, and warmth", and they render "an almost constant
awareness of the changeable world of an AR romance". The
final main category contains those images of the mysterious
and the supernatural -- "of magic and enchantment, religion,
ghosts, evil spirits, and death; those images help rein-
force the qualities of mystery and the supernatural".
These images are "usually conventional and generalized".
Concludes: "Besides contributing to the major qualities
of the romances, her images serve varied functions in her
work: they characterize, create atmosphere, describe,
express theme, emphasize plot conflicts, and decorate her
prose."

Tompkins, J[oyce] M.S. "The Work of Mrs. Radcliffe and its   11/34
Influence on Later Writers." Unpublished master's
thesis, Univ. of London, 1921. (Publication pending; introduction by D.P. Varma, foreword by M. Lévy.)

A very detailed and richly documented study of sources,
debts and influences. The opening chapter treats life and
character; Ch. II investigates debts to HW and the Lees;
Ch. III, on landscape, tracks down traces of Ossian.
Charlotte Smith, Claude, Salvator, and Raymond de Carbonnières. In Ch. IV, the German influence is seen as mini-
mal -- with a probable influence from Herman of Unna,

Horrid Mysteries, and possibly, the _Ghost-Seer_. The
final two chapters discuss the influence on later Gothic
writers and the influence upon literature in general.

Ware, Malcolm. _Sublimity in the Novels of Ann Radcliffe: A_   11/35
Study of the Influence upon her Craft of Edmund Burke's
"Enquiry into the Origin or our Ideas of the Sublime and
Beautiful". Essays and Studies on English Language and
Literature, XXV. English Institute, Upsala University.
Upsala: Lundequistska, 1963.

A sixty-page work which incorporates extensive quotation.
Ware acknowledges that his study is not original in approach but he hopes for new depths. He discusses Burke's
seven points, does a novel-by-novel, extract-by-extract
analysis of AR's work and concludes that (1)she does indeed follow Burke very closely, (2)her pre and post-tour
prose styles are exactly the same, and (3)she is not a
"radical innovator in the art of fiction".

Wieten, Alida Alberdina Sibbellina. _Mrs. Radcliffe; Her Re-_   11/36
lation Towards Romanticism. With an Appendix on the
Novels Falsely Ascribed to Her. Amsterdam: H.J. Paris,
1926.

In her political outlook, AR was conservative. "We receive the impression of a peasantry, living on fruit and
cream, dancing in the sweet moonlight. . . . They are not
a discontented class." But she loved nature and animals,
portrayed sensual villains and sentimental lovers, saw
the city as bad, the country as good, admired Shakespeare
and Milton, and has certain similarities in imagery with
Shelley and Byron. Concludes that "in prose as well as
in poetry. . . . [AR] gave an unmistakable impulse to the
romantic movement, and may therefore be considered one
of its first exponents".

d.

Articles, Essays, and Introductions

Allen, M.L. "The Black Veil: Three Versions of a Symbol",   11/37
ES, XLVII (1966), 286-289.

In Udolpho, the black veil "is central to the design of
the novel" and stands in its own right as "a simple but
effective symbol of 'mystery' itself". Dickens and Hawthorne read MU and they themselves wrote black veil stories. Hawthorne's "The Minister's Black Veil" uses the
veil to "explore the ambiguous relationship of the abstract . . . and the psychological". Dickens's "The
Black Veil" is "less profoundly obsessed with these aspects of experience, but brings its symbolism directly
to bear on a social situation".

"Anecdote of Mrs. Radcliffe", Godey's Magazine and Lady's   11/38
Book, XLV (1852), 225-227.

A curious story presented as truth. In 1795, AR was ar-
rested entering France from Switzerland. She had no
passport, "her knowledge of French was limited to a few
mispronounced words", and she stated her purpose was to
visit the chateau "where the barbarous Sieur de Fayel had
made Gabrielle de Vergy eat the heart of her lover".
Jailed as a spy, Mrs. R was cast into a dripping dungeon,
but undismayed, said: "Never did a grander inspiration
overflow my spirit. I will to work." Mme. Tallon recognized and freed the writer, and at the Tallon home it
was observed that at midnight, Mrs. R saw and conversed
with an apparition named Henry. The anonymous author of
the article notes that there was no ghost: The lady suffered "a partial disarrangement of the nervous system".
Her novels were once popular, he adds, but "now they appear nothing more than the efflux of a morbid imagination,
full of hallucinations and absurdities, and insufferably
tedious."

Barbauld, Mrs. Anna Letitia. "Mrs. Radcliffe", in her An   11/39
   Essay on the Origin and Progress of Novel Writing; and
   Prefaces, Biographical and Critical from "The British
   Novelists". London: Rivington, 1820. (On microfilm;
   negative made by Library of Congress.)

   AR's works "exhibit a genius of no common stamp". She
   seems to scorn to move those passions which form the
   interest of common novels: she alarms the soul with
   terror; agitates it with suspense, prolonged and wrought
   up to the most intense feeling, by mysterious hints and
   obscure intimations of unseen danger." AR's scenes are
   compared to those of Salvator Rosa; Mrs. B observes
   that "her living characters correspond to the scenery:
   -- their wicked projects are dark, singular, atrocious".
   Natural explanations are criticized as they render "a
   sort of disappointment and shame" when we see we have
   been tricked. "The interest is painfully strong while
   we read, and when once we have read it, it is nothing;
   we are ashamed of our feelings, and do not wish to recall them."

Beaty, Frederick L. "Mrs. Radcliffe's Fading Gleam", PQ,   11/40
   XLII (1963), 126-129.

   Suggests Udolpho provides the philosophy of "the fading
   gleam" which appears later in Coleridge's "Mad Monk"
   and Wordsworth's "Ode: Intimations of Immortality".
   Also, "Intimations" derives from Udolpho "the compen-
   sating remembrance of the fugitive inspiration, the
   'questionings of sense' that convince the poet of the
   soul's immortality, the humanitarian sympathies, and
   even a diminished enjoyment of nature's wonders -- that
   Mrs. R had already suggested less impressively." Finally,
   Coleridge's "Monk" draws on the character of Schedoni.

Bernard, Kenneth. "Charles Brockden Brown and the Sublime",   11/41
   Person, XLV (1964), 235-249.

   Brown's nature descriptions are rare and derive not from
   the American countryside, but from Mrs. Radcliffe, Burke,
   and Gilpin. But, while Mrs. R used scenery "as a decor-
   ous backdrop to heighten her drama", Brown utilized it
   as symbol, made it functional and "such functional uses
   of scene were not the province of Radcliffe".

Brown, Charles Brockden. "On a Taste for the Picturesque",   11/42
Literary Magazine and American Register, II, no. 9 (1804),
163-165.

"Ann Radcliffe is, without doubt, the most illustrious
of the picturesque writers. Her Travels on the Rhine
and in Cumberland is, in this view, an inestimable performance. . . . Her two last romances, Udolpho and The
Italian are little else than a series of affecting pictures, connected by a pleasing narrative, and in which
human characters and figures are introduced on the same
principles that place them on the canvas, to give a moral
energy and purpose to the scene. This is the great and
lasting excellence of her works: and, to limit the attention, as is usually done, to her human figures, is no
less absurd than to look at nothing in a sea-view but
the features of the pilot, and to scrutinize, in a picture of Salvator, only the hooked nose of the sybil, the
sorry steed of the bandit, or the uncouth forms of the
imps that hovered around St. Anthony. Yet, Mrs. Radcliffe's narrative is beautiful and interesting."

Christensen, Merton A. "Udolpho, Horrid Mysteries, and   11/4?
Coleridge's Machinery of the Imagination", WC, II
(1971), 153-159.

Discusses Coleridge's critical theories and applies them
to Udolpho and Horrid Mysteries. Finds MU lacks organic
unity; says the Gothic "drapery" misleads. "We do not
sense inevitably that relation to the Idea governing the
Epos, and it may be just as forcibly argued that the
crowd of Gothic incidents is so great that the governing
Idea appears only occasionally among them as almost something of an afterthought." HM, unlike MU, lacks a clear
"leading Idea of the Imagination" even though it "seems
to have a center". The Ancient Mariner is contrasted
with these novels to show "Coleridge's successful use of
the Gothic".

Dobrée, Bonamy. Introduction to The Mysteries of Udolpho.   11/4
Oxford English Novels. London: Oxford Univ. Press,
1966.

Covers biography and influence; notes distinction between
"terror" and "horror". Asserts popularity of MU stemmed
from its dual nature: "horror novel" and "novel of sentiment". Praises Mrs. R's character portrayals and the
structure of her works. Says "there is a great deal of
the novel proper mingled with the pure romance".

Ellis, S[tewart] M. "Ann Radcliffe and Her Literary Influ-   11/45
ence", Contemporary Review [London], CXXIII (1923),
188-197. (Reprinted in his Mainly Victorian [1925].
Essay Index Reprint Series. Freeport: Books for Libraries, 1969.)

Says this lady's "erroneous method of treating the supernatural is an indelible blot upon her artistry" but "no
feminine writer has exercised such a powerful and lasting
influence upon literature as Mrs. Radcliffe". Credits
her with the Byronic hero; finds her influence in Lewis,
Maturin, Oscar Wilde, Scott, Mary Shelley, Ainsworth,
G.P.R. James, Godwin, Bulwer Lytton, G.M.W. Reynolds,
Balzac, Hugo, Dumas, Sue, Charlotte Brontë, R.L. Stevenson, and Le Fanu. Discloses that her exact burial spot
has been lost. During the First War, Ellis visited the
cemetery only to find it a field of cabbages and potatoes.
AR's gravestone was leaning against the fence.

Epstein, Lynne. "Mrs. Radcliffe's Landscapes: The Influence   11/46
of Three Landscape Painters on her Nature Descriptions",
HSL, I (1969), 107-120.

Points out some specific parallels between Mrs. R's nature descriptions and the landscapes of Claude, Salvator,
and Poussin. From these men, AR drew her melancholy evening landscapes, sunrises and sunsets on water, distant
mountains, storm scenes, enthusiasm for the sea, inter-
play of light and darkness, forest scenes, and mountain
scenes of terror. Notes how her characters respond to
Nature but says her characters are intended as types
since "it is Nature who is the real protagonist".

"Extricating Emily", Time, LXXXVII (April 22, 1966), 88.   11/47

Features a full-page review of Udolpho. Its influence
and popularity are sketched, and the reviewer treats it
as camp, calling it "unintentionally . . . one of the
funniest books ever written" and laughs at the swooning,
weeping heroine, the saccharine hero, and the not-so-
terrible villain. Includes a sketch of Mrs. R.

Farrand, Margaret L. "Udolpho and Childe Harold", MLN, XLV   11/48
(1930), 220-221.

Asserts that Mrs. Radcliffe "is responsible for the description in the fourth canto of Childe Harold which is
one of the most satisfactory pictures of Venice in English
literature". Says that even though AR had never seen
Venice, she "gave Byron his point of view and even the
phrases in which to praise the city when he visited it in
the flesh".

Foster, James R. "The Abbé Prévost and the English Novel",   11/49
PMLA, XLII (1927), 443-464.

Objects to classifying Mrs. Radcliffe's novels with the
Schauerroman. The Radcliffian novel is one of sensibility
and a descendant of a line which runs from Prévost and
D'Arnaud, to the Lees, to Clara Reeve, to Charlotte Smith.
Notes that unacknowledged traces of Mrs. Smith appear in
AR's novels and points out that AR and Sophia Lee were
close friends.

Freeman, R[ichard] Austin. Introduction to The Mysteries of   11/50
Udolpho [1931]. Everyman's. 2 vols. New York: Dutton,
1965.

Notes the surplus of scenery, lack of historicity, the
inaccuracies in describing monastic life, but in general
gives a good report. In fact, some of his praises are
open to question. He claims MU's story is good enough to
stand on its own merits", and "in spite of its bulk,
there is a total absence of any tendence to 'padding'".
He contends also that Mrs. R's explanations are "satisfying and conclusive" and "the reader closes the book
with the feeling that he has been honestly dealt with".

Garber, Frederick. Foreword to The Romance of the Forest.   11/51
New York: Arno, 1974.

Looks at RF as a specific stage of development and pays
close attention to character of La Motte. Says the
novel "has value not only as an interim study but, in
itself, as an examination of certain kinds of mid-eight-
eenth century moral conflicts associated with feeling,
and sensibility".

Garber, Frederick.   Introduction to The Italian.   Oxford   11/52
English Novels.   London: Oxford Univ. Press, 1968.

Sees both strengths and weaknesses.   Looks at affinities
with the Bildungsroman and the novel of sentiment.   Notes
the degree of sentiment in the hero and in the villain.
Defends the unrealistic domain -- in character, landscape, morality, and decorum.   Suggests that "perhaps
the closest generic analogy appears in the fairy tale".
Sees The Italian as "something more than a Gothic thriller" as it "has within it the elements of tragedy".

Garnett, Richard.   "Ann Radcliffe", in Leslie Stephen and   11/53
Sidney Lee, eds., Dictionary of National Biography.
63 vols.   London: Smith, Elder, 1885 --.

Says that "Mrs. Radcliffe's novels may not be much read,
either now [1896] or in the future" but credits her as
being the founder and most eminent representative of a
school.   Praises plot ingenuity, romantic spell, landscape; asserts that "the general conventionality of her
personages disentitles her to rank among great novelists
[but] she cannot be excluded from a place among the
great romancers".

Harrison, Lucy.   "Ann Radcliffe -- Novelist", in her A Lover   11/54
of Books: The Life and Literary Papers of Lucy Harrison.
Written and arranged by Amy Greener.   New York: Dutton,
1916.

Admires and praises Ann Radcliffe; says that she was "the
first to introduce into the novel studied descriptions
of Nature and architecture", but admits that her explanations of mysteries "are sometimes disappointing, if
not ludicrous".

Havens, Raymond D.   "Ann Radcliffe's Nature Descriptions",   11/55
MLN, LXVI (1951), 251-255.

Looks at nature descriptions in Mrs. R's novels and in
her journals.   Sees three stages of descriptions: (1)
Those written on the spot for her own pleasure; (2) those
written on the spot and later revised with publication
in mind; (3) those written for her novels.   Concludes
that she not only delighted in nature but could describe
in clear detail.   "Clearly a mistaken conception of literature permeated almost every aspect of her novels,
giving them a melodramatic effectiveness but robbing

them of reality, simplicity, and that sensitiveness to
the natural world which was distinctive of their author."

J.J. "London Chit-Chat", Blackwood's, XI (1822), 331.   11/56

Passes on the rumor that Mrs. Radcliffe "is about to re-
sume her exertions, after a long interval". "Whoever
has tasted the melancholy sweetness and mystery of her
writings, (for her helpless commonplace and prosing sink
in the memory of the reader, leaving nothing behind but
mingled impressions of moonlight festivals, and convent-
chaunts heard over still waters, and Italian skies, and
love-lorn girls, and dim forests, and dusky chambers in
old forsaken castles,) will be uneasy at hearing she is
about again to essay these things, and to vex the charm
which has wrapped itself, I hope for ever, round her name."

Lang, Andrew. "Mrs. Radcliffe's Novels", Cornhill Magazine,   11/57
NS, IX, no. 49 (1900), 23-34.

In a single day, "with breathless haste", Lang once read
Sicilian Romance and Romance of the Forest. Athlin and
Dunbayne he found "unreadable", Udolpho and Italian very
good, but he preferred RF, which is, he says, "infinitely
the most thrilling of modern English works of fiction".
Mrs. R's verse, he believes, was skipped over even by
her contemporaries.

McIntyre, Clara F. "The Later Career of the Elizabethan   11/58
Villain-Hero", PMLA, XL (1925), 874-880.

Discusses the characters of Mrs. R; says she "was the
person really responsible for the revival of the Elizabethan villain". Examines these men against the characteristics of Machiavellian villainy enumerated by Boyer
(6/6): "egotistical, cruel, faithless, remorseless,
murderous, and a poisoner".

--------. "Were the 'Gothic Novels' Gothic?", PMLA, XXXVI   11/59
(1921), 644-667.

Says if Gothic = medieval, then Gothic novel is a mis-
nomer. Takes Mrs. R as a typical Gothic novelist and
asserts that her works draw not upon the Middle Ages,
but rather on the Elizabethans' interpretations of the
Renaissance. Sees Elizabethan influence in theme, dramatic structure, attitudes to death and supernatural,

use of terror, villain-hero, poison, revenge motive.
Notes that the rise of the Gothic novel coincides with
a revival of interest in Elizabethan drama; points out
Mrs. R's admiration of Shakespeare and traces some direct
influences of the poet.

McKillop, Alan D. "Mrs. Radcliffe on the Supernatural in   11/60
Poetry", JEGP, XXXI (1932), 352-359.

Examines AR's "On the Supernatural in Poetry" (11/63),
highlights her main points and clarifies where necessary.
Notes that in 1802, when this essay was written, it
"would have interested Wordsworth and Coleridge" but
when it appeared in 1826 it was a "historical relic".
Concludes by noting that the evidence of Mrs. R's "minute
knowledge of Shakespeare both in the library and on the
stage is worth having, and her development of a general
theory of Gothic aesthetics under the influence of Burke
has considerable significance."

Mayo, Robert D. "Ann Radcliffe and Ducray-Duminil", MLR,   11/61
XXXVI (1941), 501-505.

Suggests as a source for Romance of the Forest, the
French romance Alexis, ou la Maisonnette dans les bois
(1789) by François-Guillaume Ducray-Duminil. Points out
specific plot parallels and suggests a similarity in
titles. Notes that "there are more horrors in the Gothic
vein in Alexis than in any single work of his predecessors in France." Believes Mrs. R may have read it in
French; says that if indeed it is an actual source, then
it represents "an additional link between the French and
English traditions of horror".

Memoirs of Mrs. Ann Radcliffe". Prefixed to The Mysteries   11/62
of Udolpho. London: J. Limbird, 1826.

A three page account which lists AR's works, tells us
she received Ƀ500 for MU and Ƀ800 for Italian, suffered
from asthma, "was low in stature, and of a slender form,
but exquisitely proportioned; her countenance was beautiful and expressive". Calls her characters "original
and well-drawn", her poems "elegant and fanciful". Says
she "shook the soul by the awe of superstition, and the
terrors of guilt".

"On the Supernatural in Poetry". By the Late Mrs. Radcliffe.   11/63
New Monthly Magazine, XVI, pt. 1 (1826), 145-152.

"Terror and horror are so far opposite, that the first
expands the soul, and awakens the faculties to a high degree of life; the other contracts, freezes, and nearly
annihilates them. . . . Neither Shakespeare nor Milton
by their fictions, nor Mr. Burke by his reasoning, any-
where looked to positive horror as a source of the sublime, though they all agree that terror is a very high
one; and where lies the great difference between horror
and terror, but in the uncertainty and obscurity that accompany the first, respecting the dreaded evil?" Obscurity becomes distinguished from "confusion", and AR
adds that objects of terror are most striking when introduced into scenes of gaiety and splendor.

Peck, Walter E. "Keats, Shelley, and Mrs. Radcliffe", MLN,   11/64
XXXIX (1924), 251-252.

Professor Shackford's article (11/70) pointing out that
Keats' "Eve of St. Agnes" draws on Mrs. Radcliffe caused
Peck to reread Udolpho, and he now suggests that Keats
also displays parallels in "Ode to a Nightingale".
Shelley, Peck asserts, similarly drew on Udolpho for names
of characters in Zastrozzi and St. Irvyne and for the
poisoned goblet incident.

"Mrs. Radcliffe". Obituary notice in New Monthly Magazine,   11/65
IX (1823), 232.

Lists works. Says ₺1000 paid for MU; ₺1500 for Italian.
Comments on editions and translations. Notes "the dé-
nouement is not considered by many persons as a justification of the high colouring of the previous narrative;
but it was Mrs. R's object to show superstitious feelings
could feed on circumstances easily explained by the ordinary course of nature. This object she attained, though
it disappoints the votaries of superstition, and in some
degree, irritates the expectations of philosophy." Says
"the anonymous criticisms . . . the imitations of her
style and manner by various literary adventurers, the publication of some other novels under a name slightly
varied for the purpose of imposing on the public, and the
flippant use of the term 'Radcliffe school', by scrib-
blers of all classes, tended altogether to disgust her
with the world, and create a depression of spirits, which
led her for many years, in a considerable degree, to se-
clude herself from society." Claims that she "had written

204

other works" which are unpublished. Says her health
broke down, there came a "gradual decay of her mental
and bodily powers", and she died, aged 62.

Ruff, William. "Ann Radcliffe, or, the Hand of Taste", in   11/66
The Age of Johnson. Essays Presented to Chauncey Brewster
Tinker. New Haven: Yale Univ. Press, 1944.

Calls AR a "lucky novelist" who "certainly wrote trash",
lacked the sufficient degree of suspense, blood, and
terror, and produced poor prose and poetry. But she
stands as a link between Richardson and Jane Austen.
"The novel of taste . . . is Ann Radcliffe's contribution
to English literature, for in three novels she has combined adventure with the most high principled characters
in fiction."

Ruland, Richard E. "A View from Back Home: Kafka's Amerika", 11/67
AQ, XIII (1961), 33-42.

A discussion of the "fact and fancy", the "dreamlike blur",
the picture "neither realistic portrayal nor fictious
illusion", of Amerika. In describing Pollunder's castle-
like country home, Kafka draws an infinitely high edifice.
"The candlelight, replacing the disconnected electricity,
sends long eerie shadows toward the countless closed
doors of the endless corridors; it is an American country
house only in name, for it is another of Kafka's castles
with a total effect too reminiscent of Ann Radcliffe."

Sadleir, Michael. "Poems by Ann Radcliffe", TLS (March 29,   11/68
1928), p. 242.

In 1816 appeared "The Poems of Mrs. Ann Radcliffe" with
a preface suggesting posthumous publication, but AR did
not die until 1823. The 1826 Posthumous Works of Mrs.
Radcliffe contain miscellaneous poems -- but none included in the 1816 booklet. Sadleir speculates that the
1816 booklet could be a forgery, but there is no record
of a protest; or, on the other hand, the poems could be
genuine and issued in anticipation of the author's death.
"Is it possible that AR really was mentally afflicted;
at one time seemed so ill that her death might momentarily
be expected, or, at any rate, that no hope of recovery
was entertained?" Suggests that the booklet may have
been issued, then hastily withdrawn on news of recovery.

Scott, Sir Walter. "Ann Radcliffe", in Ioan Williams, ed.,   11/69
Sir Walter Scott on Novelists and Fiction. New York:
Barnes & Nobel, 1968.

A long essay which treats each of AR's works, discusses
her techniques, points out strengths and weaknesses, and
offers some insight into the entire Gothic movement. Says
that the Radcliffe romance is to the novel as the melodrama is to the proper drama. Thus, AR attains interest
by arousing fear and presents characters who lack indi-
viduality. Compares her use of landscape with that of
Mrs. Smith.

Shackford, Martha Hale.   "The Eve of St. Agnes and The Mys-   11/70
teries of Udolpho", PMLA, XXXVI (1921), 104-118.

Asserts that Keats drew upon MU for his poem and borrowed
for setting, plot, and character. Offers extensive quotations for comparison. Concludes that Keats was not
"slavishly imitative, but rather, intensely original" in
the way he handled the materials.

Steeves, Harrison R.   Introduction to The Romance of the   11/71
Forest, in Three Eighteenth Century Romances [1931].
New York: Scribner's, 1971.

Says all of Mrs. R's romances are alike in design: the
plots loose, the story meaningless, the poetry "hopelessly
pedestrian", the prose "impoverished", details redundant,
inconsistent and anachronistic, and with "insular, and
even childish" political views. But she "has done in-
disputable service for imaginative vigor and romantic
beauty in prose fiction".

Summers, Montague. "A Great Mistress of Romance: Ann Rad-   11/72
cliffe, 1764-1823", in his Essays in Petto [1928].
Freeport: Books for Libraries, 1967.

This 27-page survey of the literature of terror and horror
devotes about eight pages to Mrs. Radcliffe. Longsword,
not Otranto, Summers says is the "first English romantic
novel". Otranto he prefers "to enjoy rather than to defend"; OEB he finds "cold and commonplace"; Mrs. R he
idolizes -- but notes her explanations frequently constitute "a serious blemish". Gives details on the Northanger Seven; offers remarks on Maturin, Godwin, the Shel-
leys, Ainsworth, C.B. Brown, G.W.M. Reynolds, Mary Anne
Radcliffe, Sade, and others. Concludes that influence of
Mrs. R is "a landmark and a power in English literature".

Swigart, Ford H., Jr. "Ann Radcliffe's Veil Imagery",   11/73
Studies in the Humanities, I (1969), 55-59.

Points out that in her writing, Mrs. R strove for a visual
effect and nearly one-third of her imagery comes from the
categories of veil, art, and light. "Veils", he says,
consist of "veils themselves, facial expressions that
mask and hide a person's true feelings, and clouds, vapors
and light tints that soften outlines and obscure vision".
He discusses these categories, offers examples, concludes
that AR's use of veil imagery is "rather conventional and
generalized" but "its importance is primarily functional
as it emphasizes her interest in visual effects that focus
on picturing and seeing".

Sypher, Wylie. "Social Ambiguity in a Gothic Novel", PR, XII   11/74
(1945), 50-60.

Sees in AR's novels an ambiguity between aesthetic values
and moral values. The moral values are conservative or
bourgeois values; the aesthetic values are "romantic",
and "in a limited sense 'revolutionary'". Suggests that
this attitude was unconscious, but the result is "an implied priggishness . . . set against an implied bohemian-
ism: caution/incaution, selfishness/generosity, purity/
impurity, etc." Concludes that Radcliffe's "fiction is
meaningful because it so inadequately conceals the naked
contradictions intrinsic in bourgeois romanticism, a revolt so radically inhibited that it failed to be in a deep
social sense creative".

[Talfourd, Sergeant]. "Memoir of the Life and Writings of   11/75
Mrs. Radcliffe". Prefixed to Gaston de Blondeville
[1826]. New York: Arno, 1972.

Slightly over 50% of this 130 page essay consists of extracts from Mrs. R's journals. The remainder covers biography, notes style, and renders criticism of each of
her romances. Discusses her long retirement, rumors of
death and insanity, mentions her evening composition,
shuddering husband, family background, marriage, and details of demise. Speculates that retirement came, since
"in Romance, she probably felt that she had done enough;
and feeling it impossible to surpass her MU and her Italian,
declined again to subject herself to criticism by publication". Says she invented a new style of romance in
"that middle region between the mighty dreams of the
heroic ages and the realities of our own". Praises her
terror and her descriptions but notes that the former is

marred by "a succession of mockeries" and "impotent conclusions", and in MU, "the description of external scenery
may occur too often". Notes that her people are "figures
rather than characters" but adds that "to develop characters was not within the scope of Mrs. R's plan, nor com-
patible with her style".

Thomas, Donald. "The First Poetess of Romantic Fiction: Ann   11/76
Radcliffe, 1764-1823", English, XV (1964), 91-95.

Covers AR's background, the circulating libraries, the
growing reading public, and gives thumbnail sketches of
her novels. Sees two basic plots in romantic fiction:
(1)Girl aspires for and finally weds her superior; (2)
young lovers suffer from interference from a parent or
outsider. The second plot has an "obvious appeal to an
established middle class". "To disregard the fancy
dress and the carnival settings of AR's novels is to be
left with this stock romantic plot which has a domestic
rather than a social ambience." Scott dubbed AR "the
first poetess of romantic fiction" because of her "ability
to give depth and significance to the unremarkable and
commonplace".

Thompson, L.F. "Ann Radcliffe's Knowledge of German", MLR,   11/77
XX (1925), 190-191.

Miss McIntyre (11/28) pointed out that the Geisterseher
might have provided a source for Montoni and the description of a trip on the Bretna, but Udolpho was published in 1794, no English translation appeared till
1795, and it was not known if AR could read German.
Thompson looks at the 1794 Journal and shows either the
lady or her husband could read German, so either directly
or through her spouse, "she could have known Der Geisterseher previous to the publication of MU".

Tompkins, J.M.S. "Raymond de Carbonnières, Grosley and Mrs.   11/78
Radcliffe", RES, V (1929), 294-301.

Mrs. R drew upon Raymond de Carbonnières' Observations
faites dans les Pyrenees (1789) and Pierre Jear Grosley's
New Observations on Italy and its Inhabitants (1769).
From Raymond, AR obtained the Pyrenees scenes of Udolpho,
and if it could be proved that she read Raymond "before
her style reached maturity in Romance of the Forest (1791)
one would credit him with a decisive influence on it"

since he interspersed into his narrative, scenes of
lyrical description and sentiment. From Grosley Mrs. R
derives Emily's journey to Italy and most important -- the
wax replica of a worm infested corpse.

Varma, Devendra P. Introduction to The Italian. New York: 11/79
Russell & Russell, 1968.

Offers a thumbnail biography, a suggestion for the source
of Schedoni, a discussion of AR's terror technique and
an investigation of her relationship to the cult of the
picturesque. Includes also a note on publication history,
editions, translations, and influence on the 19th-century
novel.

--------. Introduction to Romance of the Forest. New York: 11/80
Arno, 1974.

Delivers a long treatment of the Gothic villain in his
three manifestations: "First, Walpole's Manfred of
Otranto, moody, irascible, ambitious and sensual; second,
the Victim of Destiny, passionate and disillusioned . . .
third, the gothic superman. . . ." Tracks down the appearances and notes the changes in these types. Devotes
special attention to the influence on the Romantic poets.

--------. Introduction to A Sicilian Romance. New York: 11/81
Arno, 1972.

Relates Radcliffe's works to Burke's aesthetics and theory
of the sublime. Notes Mrs. R's own theories and techniques and comments briefly on content and style of her
various novels.

Ware, Malcolm. "Mrs. Radcliffe's 'Picturesque Embellish-   11/82
ment'", TSL, V (1960), 67-71.

Draws on Nathan Drake (3/11) to explain Mrs. R's "frequency, length, and sameness of . . . tedious descriptions of . . . sublime scenery". Asserts she understood
better than Burke the distinction between terror and horror and used picturesque description to keep terror from
descending into horror. Thus, her defect is due to "a
sturdy if rigid adherehce to an aesthetic theory in
which she firmly believed".

209

Whitt, Celia. "Poe and the Mysteries of Udolpho", Univ. of   11/83
Texas Studies in English, XVII (1937), 124-131.

Poe's "The Assignation", first published as "The Visionary"
in Godey's Lady's Book in 1843 shows some specific borrowings from Udolpho. In both name and character, Poe's
Mentoni resembles AR's Montoni; Poe's unnamed young hero
and his heroine resemble those of Mrs. R, and "in addition
the novel contains a surprising number of details that are
similar to the story, including the very unusual one of
Venetian glass that is sensitive to poison". Also, it is
suggested that Montresor in "The Cask of Amontillado" represents a later version of Montoni. Finally, since Poe,
in "The Oval Portrait" refers to Mrs. Radcliffe, it seems
certain that he was familiar with her work.

Wright, Eugene P. "A Divine Analysis of The Romance of the   11/84
Forest", Discourse, XIII (1970), 379-387.

The University of Texas has a manuscript of 28 lines of
prose and 208 lines of rimed couplets written by Joanna
Southcott as a divine analysis of RF. God inspired Mrs.
R to write this work and gave Miss Southcott the correct
interpretation. Wright says that this new reading is not
"worth much as literary criticism", but does reflect how
many people viewed the novel. Thus, far from being trash
the sensational novel continued its didactic role and
could be "a handbook to life itself". The 100,000 South-
cottians shunned the works of Byron, Shelley, and Keats
"as worldly and therefore un-Godly", but held in high esteem what many moderns deplore.

                          e.

         Notices in General Works, Diaries, Etc.

Byron, George Gordon, Lord. Childe Harold's Pilgrimage, IV   11/85
[1818], in Russell Noyes, ed., English Romantic Poetry
and Prose. New York: Oxford Univ. Press, 1956.

In Canto IV, verse xviii, Byron writes of Venice:

    "I loved her from my boyhood; she to me
    Was as a fairy city of the heart,
    Rising like water-columns from the sea,

                         210

Of joy the sojourn, and of wealth the mart;
And Otway, Radcliffe, Schiller, Shakespeare's art,
Had stamp'd her image in me. . . ."

Coleridge, Samuel Taylor. Collected Letters of Samuel Taylor 11/86
Coleridge. Edited by Earl Leslie Griggs. 4 vols. Oxford: Clarendon, 1959.

October, 1810: "I amused myself a day or two ago on reading a romance in Mrs. Radcliffe's style with making out
a scheme, which was to serve for all romances a priori --
only varying the proportions -- A Baron or Baroness ig-
norant of their birth, and in some dependent situation --
Castle-on a rock -- a sepulchre -- at some distance from
the rock -- deserted rooms -- underground passages --
pictures -- a ghost, so believed -- or -- a written record -- blood on it! -- a wonderful cut throat -- etc.,
etc., etc."

Hazlitt, William. "On the English Novelists", in his Lec- 11/87
tures on the English Comic Writers and Fugitive Writing
[1819]. Everyman's. London: Dent, 1967.

Mrs. Radcliffe's "descriptions of scenery, indeed, are
vague and wordy to the last degree; they are neither like
Salvator nor Claude, nor nature nor art, and she dwells
on the effects of moonlight till we are sometimes weary
of them; her characters are insipid, the shadows of a
shade, continued on, under different names, through all
her novels; her story comes to nothing. But in harrowing
up the soul with imaginary horrors, and making the flesh
creep, and the nerves thrill with fond hopes and fears,
she is unrivalled among her fair country-women."

[Hogg, James]. "Noctes Ambrosianae, No. XXVII", Blackwood's, 11/88
XX (1826), 90-109.

"Tickler" questions "Shepherd" (Hogg) about Mrs. Radcliffe.
Hogg calls her "a true genius", defends her decision not
to use a real ghost and says: "I hae nae doubt . . .
that had I read Udolpho, and her ither romances in my
boyish days, that my hair would hae stood on end like that
o' ither folk. . . ."

211

Howells, W[illiam] D[ean]. _Heroines of Fiction_. 2 vols.   11/89
New York: Harper, 1901.

Contains a highly laudatory essay on Mrs. R, whose romances are "distinctly not despicable" as is _Otranto_.
Sees her characters as "inadequate and partial" but not
false. Praises the decorum of her ladies. Her technique
of suspense brings disappointments and appears as the
sole flaw.

Hunt, Leigh. _A Book for a Corner_. New York: Derby, 1861.   11/90

Hunt anthologizes "Ludovico in the Haunted Chamber" from
Udolpho and prefaces the selection with a perceptive two
page introduction covering both Walpole and Radcliffe.
Praises Walpole's genius, says that _Otranto_ has "real
merit . . . even grandeur of imagination, yet the conversion of dreams into gross daylight palpabilities . . .
turns the sublime into the ridiculous". Mrs. R "understood to perfection" the use of Gothic effects and "possessed also the eye of a painter as well as the feeling
of a poetess". Concedes that Hazlitt (11/87) is perhaps
correct in asserting that for AR, background is more important than character, but defends this by saying "that
Nature herself deals in precisely such effects, leaving
men to be operated upon by them passively, and not to
play the chief parts in the process by means of their
characters".

Kavanagh, Julia. _English Women of Letters; Biographical_   11/91
Sketches. 2 vols. London: Hurst & Blackett, 1863.

Thinks _Romance of the Forest_ "not the best" but "the least
defective" of AR's works; _Udolpho_ is a "remarkable book"
but features "bad taste, bad grammar, characters weakly
drawn, deep terrors that resolve into commonplace incidents, strange and horrible adventures that lead to nothing"; _The Italian_ is "better constructed and told . . .
than _MU_" and "has less of the false supernatural". Sees
her defects the result of a society which refused to
offer equal opportunities to women for education. By the
time Mrs. R learned to write, when "perfect knowledge
came, imagination had poured out her stories".

Marshall, Roderick. Italy in English Literature, 1755-1815:   11/92
Origins of the Romantic Interest in Italy. Columbia
University Studies in English and Comparative Literature.
New York: Columbia Univ. Press, 1934.

Chronicles and clarifies the growing interest in things
Italian: painters, poets, history, sublime landscapes.
Investigates "The Vicious Italian of the Tale of Terror:
1764-1815". Contends that Mrs. R drew upon Beckford's
Dreams for the description of Venice in Udolpho.

[Mathias, Thomas James]. The Pursuits of Literature: A   11/93
Satirical Poem in Dialogue. With Notes. 2nd ed. Revised. London: J. Owen, 1797.

Note to line 100, Dialogue I: "Mrs. Charlotte Smith,
Mrs. Inchbald, Mrs. Mary Robinson, Mrs. etc. etc., though
all of them are ingenious ladies, yet they are too frequently whining or frisking in novels, till our girls'
heads turn wild with impossible adventures, and now and
then they are tainted with democracy -- Not so the mighty
magician of The Mysteries of Udolpho, bred and nourished
by the Florentine Muses in their sacred solitary caverns,
amid the paler shrines of Gothic superstition, and in all
the dreariness of enchantment: a poetess whom Aristo
would with rapture have acknowledged, as 'La nudrita
Damigella Trivulzia al sacro speco'."

Moorman, Mary. William Wordsworth: A Biography. 2 vols.   11/94
Oxford: Clarendon, 1957.

Asserts that Romance of the Forest was an influence on
Wordsworth's The Borderers. "Wordsworth owes as much to
Mrs. Radcliffe and Schiller as he does to Godwin. Indeed
The Romance of the Forest seems to have been lying beside
him as he wrote."

Robinson, Henry Crabb. Henry Crabb Robinson on Books and   11/95
their Writers. Edited by Edith J. Morley. 3 vols.
London: Dent, 1938.

In 1798 HCR "re-perused The Mysteries of Udolpho with delight". In 1815 he thought Waverley "overpraised", as
Scott's "sense of the romantic and picturesque in nature
is not so delicate nor is his execution so powerful as
in Mrs. Radcliffe. But his paintings of men and manners
are more valuable." However, in Guy Mannering "there are
some scenes of terror hardly inferior to Mrs. Radcliffe".

Finally, in 1829, HCR read MU once again. "But not so strongly as in youth, this romance even now is capable of diverting my attention from objects that would seem to be irresistible in their demands. . . . But, after all, the interest is merely that of the worry of finding out a riddle. The poetry and much of the description I skipped. Yet thirty years ago these were much admired."

Seward, Anna. _Letters of Anna Seward: Written Between the Years 1784 and 1807._ 6 vols. Edinburgh: George Ramsey, 1811.   11/96

Comments on four separate occasions from 1794 to 1799. Calls the novels of the era "trash" but cites AR as one of the better writers. MU contains too much landscape description and wearies the reader; the vestiges of Mary Stewart at Hardwick influenced the Marchiness's apartment in MU; the _Italian_ has incidents which are "confused, improbable, and ill-accounted for in the _denouement_". Finally, she says: "One has heard of a labouring mountain bringing forth a mouse: In Mrs. R's writings mice bring forth mountains."

Talfourd, T[homas] Noon. _Critical and Miscellaneous Writings,_ in _Talfourd and Stephen._ The Modern British Essayists, VII. Philadelphia: Hart, 1853.   11/97

"There is always majesty in . . . [AR's] terrors. She produces more effect by whispers and slender hints than ever was attained by the most vivid display of horrors. Her conclusions are tame and impotent almost without example. But when her spells actually operate, her power is truly magical."

Thrale, Mrs. Hester Lynch. _Thraliana: The Diary of Mrs. Hester Lynch Thrale (Later Mrs. Piozzi) 1776-1809 [1942]._ Edited by Katherine C. Balderston. 2 vols. 2nd ed. Oxford: Clarendon, 1951.   11/98

September 1, 1794: "We have all been reading the _Mysteries of Udolpho_; 'tis very horrible indeed says one, very like _Macbeth_ says another: Yes truly replied H: L: P. as like Pepper-Mint Water is to good Brandy."

f.

Early Reviews

1. The Castles of Athlin and Dunbayne (1789)

Critical Review, LXVIII (1789), 251.   11/99

Complete item: "There is some fancy and much romantic
imagery in the conduct of this story; but our pleasure
would have been more unmixed had our author preserved
better the manners and costume of the Highlands. He
seems to be unacquainted with both."

Monthly Review, LXXXI (1789), 563.   11/100

Complete review: "To those who are delighted with the
marvellous, whom wonders, and wonders only, can charm,
the present production will afford a considerable degree
of amusement. This kind of entertainment, however can be
little relished but by the young and unformed mind. To
men who have passed, or even attained, the meridian of
life, a series of events, which seem not to have their
foundation in nature, will ever be insipid, if not dis-
gustful. The author of this performance appears to have
written on the principle of Mr. Bayes, to elevate and surprise. By means of trapdoors, false panels, subterranean
passages, etc, etc, this purpose is effected: and all
this, as was before intimated, will possibly have its admirers. But though we are not of the number of such
readers, we must honestly confess, that this little work
is to be commended for its moral; as also for the good
sentiments and reflections which occasionally occur in
it."

Scots Magazine, LI (1789), 645.   11/101

"To be commended for its moral; as also for the good sentiments and reflections which occasionally occur in it."

215

2. A Sicilian Romance (1790)

Monthly Review, 2nd ser., III (1790), 91.   11/102

Complete item: "In this tale, we meet with something
more than the alternate tears and rapture of tender lovers.
The writer possesses a happy vein of invention and a correctness of taste, which enables her to rise above the
level of mediocrity. Romantic scenes, and surprizing
events, are exhibited in elegant and animated language."

Scots Magazine, LII (1790), 438.   11/10

Complete review: "Exhibits romantic scenes, and surprizing events in elegant and animated language."

Critical Review, 2nd ser., I (1791), 350.   11/10

Complete item: "This very interesting novel engages the
attention, in defiance of numerous improbabilities and
'hair-breadth escapes' too often repeated. Perhaps, on
a second reading, these might be still more disgusting;
but it is an experience that we can scarcely venture to
try but with modern novels of the first class. We found
the tale, we have said, very entertaining and involved
with art, developed with skill, and the event concealed
with great dexterity. If our author again engages in
this task, we would advise her not to introduce so many
caverns with such peculiar concealments or so many
spring-locks which open only on one side."

3. The Romance of the Forest (1791)

Critical Review, 2nd ser., IV (1792), 458-460.   11/10

"The novel . . . engages the attention strongly, and interests the feelings very powerfully: the general style
of the whole, as well as the reflections, deserve also
commendation. The greater part of the work resembles, in
manner, the Old English Baron, formed on the model of the
Castle of Otranto." The props "are managed . . . with

skill, and do not disgust by their improbability: everything is consistent, and within the verge of rational belief: the attention is uninterruptedly fixed, till the veil is designedly withdrawn."

English Review, XX (1792), 352-353.   11/106

"Of modern novels, The Romance of the Forest must certainly be allowed to rank among the first class. The design and the executions are new; and we cannot accuse the fair author of the slightest tendency to the crime of plagiarism." "The characters are drawn with a bold and vigorous pencil -- the incidents, always interesting, o'erstep not the modesty of nature, and the reader is properly prepared for those transitions which occur in the progress of the work."

Monthly Review, 2nd ser., VIII (1792), 82-84.   11/107

A long review, full of praise. "Adeline, is a highly interesting character, whom the writer conducts through a series of alarming situations, and hair-breadth escapes, in which she has very skilfully contrived to hold the reader's curiosity continually in suspense, and at the same time to keep his feelings in a state of perpetual agitation." "Several characters, marked with different degrees of folly or criminality, are drawn with bold and decisive strokes; and these are contrasted with others, whose amiable qualities relieve the horrors of the scene. . . ."

Scots Magazine, LIV (1792), 292.   11/108

Complete review: "We have seldom met with a fiction which has more forcibly fixed the attention, or more agreeably interested the feelings, throughout the whole narrative."

4. The Mysteries of Udolpho (1794)

Analytical Review, XIX (1794), 140-145.   11/10

"A.Y." writes that it is not enough to say "that MU is
a pretty, or an agreeable romance. The design has ingenuity and contrivance; the style is correct and elegant;
the descriptions are chaste and magnificent; and the
whole work is calculated to give the author a distinguished
place among fine writers." Also, he finds the verse worthy
of praise.

British Critic, IV (1794), 110-121.   11/11

Calls MU "one of the best and most interesting" of Mrs.
R's works. Offers an extremely long plot outline and
concludes by pointing out weaknesses. Believes Mrs. R
should publish her verse separately; says her descriptions
are excessive and the language "is too poetic a prose".
There exists "too much of the terrific: the sensibility
is sometimes jaded, and curiosity in a manner worn out.
The endeavours to explain supernatural appearances and incidents, by plain and simple facts, is not always happy."

Critical Review, 2nd ser., XI (1794), 361-372. (Attributed   11/1?
    to Coleridge. Reprinted in Garland Greever, A Wiltshire
    Parson and His Friends, London: Constable, 1926; Thomas
    M. Raysor, ed., Coleridge's Miscellaneous Criticism,
    Cambridge: Harvard, 1936; Ioan Williams, ed., Novel and
    Romance, London: Routledge & Kegan Paul, 1970. But see
    7/32.)

    Begins by praising AR's suspense -- then turns against it.
    "Four volumes cannot depend entirely on terrific incidents
    and intricacy of story. They require character, unity of
    design, a delineation of the scenes of real life, and the
    variety of well supported contrast." Asserts that "cur-
    iosity is raised oftener than it is gratified; or rather,
    it is raised so high that no adequate gratification can
    be given it; the interest is completely dissolved when
    once the adventure is finished, and the reader, when he
    is got to the end of the work, looks about in vain for
    the spell which had bound him so strongly to it." Notes
    lack of accuracy in portrayal of ancient manners, comments
    on "sameness" of descriptions and is not impressed by

218

her characters. Says the character of Annette, "a talk-
ative waiting-maid, is much worn, and that of the aunt,
Madame Cheron, is too low and selfish to excite any degree of interest, or justify the dangers her niece exposes herself to for her sake".

European Magazine, XXV (1794), 433-440.   11/112

Eight pages of extracts and two short paragraphs of observations. Says "though Mrs. Radcliffe be correct and
faithful to the truth of geography and natural history,
yet is the often, nay, for the most part, minute even to
tedious prolixity in her local descriptions; a weight
which would have hung with a deadening power about the
neck of a composition not animated by the utmost vigour
of imagination."

Gentleman's Magazine, LXIV, pt. 2 (1794), 834.   11/113

"We trust . . . we shall not be thought unkind or severe
if we object to the too great frequency of landscape-
painting; which, though it shows the extensiveness of her
observations and invention, wearies the reader with re-
petitions. The plot is admirably kept up; but perhaps the
reader is held too long in suspense, and the development
brought on too hastily in the concluding volume."

Monthly Review, 2nd ser., XV (1794), 278-283. (Attributed 11/114
     to William Enfield. Reprinted in Ioan Williams, ed.,
     Novel and Romance, London: Routledge & Kegan Paul, 1970.)

A most complimentary and enthusiastic review which praises
sentiment, style, invention, variety, ingenuity, use of
suspense, character portrayal, plot, poetic justice,
scenery, and poetry. Four full pages of observations.

     5. Journey Made in the Summer of 1794 (1795)

Analytical Review, XXII (1795), 349-350.   11/115

"In the present work, though Mrs. R is not inattentive to
style, she is very properly contented with a less laboured

                            219

and artificial diction than is found in many parts of her
novels." Laments that she followed the beaten trail and
so has little room for novelty of detail" but on the whole,
the work is "amusing and interesting".

<u>Critical Review</u>, 2nd ser., XIV (1795), 241-255.   11/11

"The repeated instances of . . . [landscape description]
in <u>Mysteries of Udolpho</u>, where the objects are fanciful,
and the descriptions consequently arbitrary, and sometimes redundant, excited a public wish that she might
engage in a work where the same talent should be necessarily employed to delineate the grandeur, beauty, or sublimity of real scenery, and where the recurrence of description, following only the exhibitions of nature, should
not be oppressive. Such a work is now before us, and we
have not been disappointed in the expectations we were
taught to form."

<u>English Review</u>, XXVI (1795), 1-5, 89-90, 173-178.   11/11

"Mrs. R, in her <u>MU</u>, as well as in her other romances, discovers a strong turn and taste for landscape, or the description of the external face of nature. This may be said,
in a language now very generally adopted, to be her forte;
although in those writings she has indulged it to a length
wholly disproportionate to the narrative which it was intended only to relieve and variegate. The same taste and
turn of mind runs throughout the whole of the volume before us." But, "in her romances she paints fancy-pieces;
here she draws from nature". Concludes that Mrs. R "possesses very happy talents for narration and description,
both moral and physical". "To those readers who take delight in such descriptions, even though minute, and we
understand there are such readers, this volume will afford a great deal of various entertainment. For our own
part, it seems to us that it is a very faint outline, a
very glimmering and unsteady prospect of the face of
nature that can be exhibited by writing; and the ideas
we form of objects so complex and various, are not so
much real images of those objects as confused combina-
tions and analogies drawn from others that had previously
come within the sphere of our own perceptions."

European Magazine, XXVIII (1795), 98-103, 257-261.   11/118

Sees travel literature as a genre "in which instruction
and amusement are happily blended" and believes critical
criteria include "the novelty of the information, the
habit of observation, or the power of description". "In
picturesque description Mrs. R is confessedly allowed to
excel; she is peculiarly happy in her selection of images,
and her powers of communication are so copious as to form
in the mind of the reader a lively and distinct picture of
the objects, and, in fact, to accomplish that by the pen
which has always been considered as belonging necessarily
to the province of the pencil."

Monthly Review, XVIII (1795), 241-246.   11/119

"The ingenious author of this tour has carefully avoided,
in the present work, every kind of decoration which might
give her narrative the air of fiction. Her admirers will,
indeed, still find her employing her powers of description,
but evidently with the closeness of a copyist, rather
than with the freedom of an original inventor."

6. The Italian (1797)

Analytical Review, XXV (1797), 516-520.   11/120

Praises AR's "uncommon talent for exhibiting, with the
picturesque touches of genius, the vague and horrid
shapes which imagination bodies forth". Notes that "her
mode . . . of accounting in a natural manner for supernatural appearances, now the secret has gotten vent,
lessens the effect, and the interest of the story is in-
terrupted by the reader's attention to guard against the
delusions of the imaginations which he knows to be glis-
tening bubbles, blown up in air, only to evaporate more
conspicuously; leaving the aching sight searching after
the splendid nothing."

British Critic, X (1797), 266-270.   11/121

Praises landscapes; thinks characters of Vivaldi, Ellena,
the Marchessa, and Schedoni "are drawn with much ability".

"After a perusal of the volumes before us, we are inclined
to think that our authoress has failed in this attempt,
not so much from want of power to astonish, as from another
cause. It was impossible to raise curiosity and expectation
to a higher pitch than she has done in her MU; yet these
mysteries she accounted for in a natural manner. The reader of the Italian now before us sets down with this con-
viction. As children who have been frightened, by an ideal
bugbear, and afterwards convinced that there was nothing
in it, will cry 'No, no! we know what it is: you cannot
frighten us again;' so, we acknowledge, does the perusal
of the present romance affect us. It is a complication of
horrors without interest and reminds us of scenes and circumstances often gone over before in all her former productions. She still contrives to have a perfect command
over the sun, moon, and stars; which she produces much
more frequently than their natural course would allow.
The most beautiful imagery may be displayed too often, and
thereby lose its effect. This is the case with Mrs. R:
her pastoral scenes, which at first are relished as agreeable, at length become tiresome and languid until they are
passed over as repetitious, and disregarded."

"In this romance we do not think Mrs. Radcliffe has been
so successful as on some former occasions, though we admit it exhibits many of the same beauties, as well as the
defects of her former compositions. The same beautiful
descriptions of the scenery, some times extended to a
tedious length; the same terrific events, but extravagant
and improbable; and the same kind of characters, either
diabolically wicked, or unnaturally perfect, constitute
the present performance." Admits that "the wildness of
romance" allows much licence, but objects to the character of the monk and views the inquisition scenes as padding. Wishes Mrs. R would leave romance and become "engaged in the service of truth and nature".

In this work, Mrs. R has avoided some of her earlier
errors. "The reader of the Italian is not perpetually
harrassed with overcharged descriptions of the beauties
of nature, which, however interesting either the scenes
themselves, or a delineation of them in descriptive
poetry, may be, are impertinent in a work of narration,

inasmuch as they call off the reader's attention from
the principal objects, and interrupt the emotions which
the work is calculated to produce". Calls for a "unity
of emotions" and sees the insertion of sonnets an interruption. Regards Schedoni as "one of the best delineated portraits of a villain we have ever seen".

Monthly Review, XXII (1797), 282-284. (Attributed to Arthur   11/125
Aikin. Reprinted in Ioan Williams, ed., Novel and Romance,
London: Routledge & Kegan Paul, 1970.)

Discusses the distinction between novel and romance. Says
Italian shows "more unity and simplicity" than earlier romances. Approves the less abundant nature descriptions
which, "though truly beautiful in itself, palls by repetition on the pampered imagination".

Critical Review, XXIII (1798), 166-169. (Attributed to Cole-   11/126
ridge. Reprinted in Garland Greever, A Wiltshire Parson
and his Friends, London: Constable, 1926; Thomas M. Raysor, ed., Coleridge's Miscellaneous Criticism, Cambridge:
Harvard, 1936. But see 7/32.)

"The Mysteries of Udolpho fell short of the Romance of the
Forest, by the tedious protraction of events, and by a
redundancy of description; The Italian falls short of
the Mysteries of Udolpho, by reminding us of the same
characters and the same scenes; and, although the descriptive part is less prolix, the author has had recourse to
it in various instances, in which it has no natural connexion with the story."

7. Gaston de Blondeville (1826)

Ladies' Monthly Museum, XXIV (1826), 45-46.   11/127

"Posthumous works frequently disappoint the reader's expectations; for they are in general either unfinished productions, or pieces which their authors regarded as not
calculated to increase their fame. The present work is
of the latter description; and Mrs. Radcliffe seems to
have shewn her judgment in withholding it from publication. We meet with little in it to remind us of the
powerful enchantress who agitated and delighted us with
the Mysteries of Udolpho. Dulness pervades the narrative

in Gaston de Blondeville, the writer having copied the
style and manner of other novelists, instead of giving
the reins to her imagination, and treating us with the
flights of her own fancy, as on former occasions."

Scots Magazine, XVIII (1826), 703-704.   11/12

"B" says almost nothing about G de B, offers general
praise for Mrs. R and asserts that she improved her style
in the Italian by rejecting the use of poetry and cutting
down on "long particulars of rural scenery, and tedious
trackings of the agitated mind".

8. Miscellaneous

Poetical Works of Anne Radcliffe. Reviewed in Edinburgh Re-   11/12
view, LIX (1834), 327-341.

The supposedly new poems are pages from Gaston -- old
pagination, new covers. The review slips into a long
sketch of the Gothic movement from Walpole and Reeve to
the decline of the genre. Comments on the flood of
poor imitators.

9. Adaptations

Fontainville Forest, by James Boaden. Reviewed in Critical   11/13
Review, 2nd ser., XI (1794), 402-406.

"The RF received our warm commendations: it united interest with entertainment; kept the mind in suspense with
art, and gratified it without the violation of probability.
The rules of the opopèe were well observed, though the
fair authoress knew not, probably, of their existence,
but, as we had lately occasion to remark, doctrines founded in reason and common sense require no other qualifica-
tions to discover or follow them. It is singular, however, that our author, with a performance so truly dramatic before his eye, should have failed in this respect;
and that the novel should be more close to the laws of the
epopèe than the play."

224

The Italian Monk, by James Boaden. Reviewed in Monthly   11/131
    Mirror, IV (1797), 100-103.

A general piece covering both the playwright and actors
of the drama based on Mrs. Radcliffe's Italian.

Mysteries of the Castle, by M.P. Andrews. Reviewed in   11/132
    European Magazine, XXVII (1795), 124.

Notes that "a striking incident" is taken from The Sicilian
Romance and the name Montoni is used.

The Sicilian Romance; or the Apparition of the Cliffs, a   11/133
    drama, by H[enry] Siddons. Reviewed in European Magazine,
    XXV (1794), 467.

Complete review: "This Piece is taken from the well-
known Romance of Mrs. Radcliffe, with the same title. It
is marked with variety, and the succession of serious and
comic scenes are interesting and pleasing. It was received
with applause."

The Sicilian Romance: or, The Apparition of the Cliffs, an   11/134
    Opera, by Henry Siddons. Reviewed in Critical Review,
    2nd ser., XIII (1795), 338.

Complete item: "A very slight piece, in three acts,
with a very full dose of ghosts, plots, dungeons, iron
doors, and all the paraphernalia of the tragic muse."

XII

MATTHEW GREGORY LEWIS

(1775-1818)

a.

Selected Texts

1. The Monk (1796)

1906 - The Monk: A Romance. 3 vols. London: Gibbings,   12/1
1906.

Contains an anonymous introduction attributed to Francis
Reginald Stalham. Text is said to be from the first
edition "with all the additions, footnotes, etc. of the
fourth". Does not include the seven days of agony and
features the "Haughty Lady" passage.

1907 - The Monk: A Romance. Edited, and with an introduc-   12/2
tion by E.A. Baker. New York: Dutton, [1907].

Text is unidentified but excludes the seven days of suffering and offers the "Haughty Lady" passage.

1952 - The Monk [1952]. Edited by Louis F. Peck. Introduc-   12/3
tion by John Berryman. New York: Grove, 1959.

A paperback, based on the original edition. Contains the
death-agony passage and excludes the "Haughty Lady".
With variant readings and "A Note on the Text".

1973 - The Monk. Edited, and with an introduction by Howard   12/4
Anderson. Oxford Univ. Press, 1973.

"The text of this edition is the first since the original
(1796) to have been set from the author's manuscript,
which was recently found."

226

2. The Bravo of Venice (1805)

972 - The Bravo of Venice. Edited, and with an introduction   12/5
by Devendra P. Varma. New York: Arno, 1972.

A facsimile reprint of the 1805 edition.

3. "Mistrust, or Blanche and Osbright:
A Feudal Romance" (1808)

63 - "Mistrust, or Blanche and Osbright: A Feudal Romance", 12/6
in Seven Masterpieces of Gothic Horror [1963]. Edited,
and with an introduction by Robert Donald Spector. New
York: Bantam, 1970.

A selection from the 1808, Romantic Tales.

4. The Isle of Devils, A Historical Tale,
Founded on an Anecdote in the Annals of Portugal
(1827)

69 - The Isle of Devils. A Historical Tale, Founded on an   12/7
Anecdote in the Annals of Portugal. [Folcroft]: Folcroft, 1969.

"A faithful reprint of the rare edition of 1827."

5. Journal of a West India Proprietor (1834)

1929 - Journal of a West India Proprietor. Edited, and with   12/8
an introduction by Mona Wilson. London: Routledge, 1929.

The first unabridged reissue. The sole previous reprint,
that of 1845, is abridged.

1969 - Journal of a West India Proprietor. New York: Negro   12/9
Universities Press, [1969].

Reprint of the 1845 edition.

6. Miscellaneous Works

The American Antiquarian Society (see 1/37) offers micro-   12/1
prints of the following texts:

Ambrosio, or the Monk. Boston: Etheridge for Thomas and
Andrews, 1799.

Castle Spectre. Boston, 1798.
Castle Spectre. Salem, Macanulty, 1799.

Crazy Jane. Boston: Von Hagen for Gilfert, 1800.

The East Indian. New York: Davises for Caritot, 1800.

b.

Bibliographies

Allibone, S[amuel] Austin. A Criticial Dictionary of English   12/1
Literature and British and American Authors Living and
Deceased. From the Earliest Accounts to the Latter Half
of the Nineteenth Century. 3 vols. Philadelphia: Lippincott, 1871. (Reprinted, Detroit: Gale Research, 1965.)

228

Kunitz, Stanley J. and Howard Haycraft. British Authors of   12/12
the Nineteenth Century. New York: Wilson, 1936.

Moulton, Charles Wells, ed. The Library of Literary Criti-   12/13
cism of English and American Authors. 8 vols. Buffalo:
Moulton, 1901-1905. (Reprinted, New York: P. Smith,
1935.)

Moulton's Library of Literary Criticism of English and Ameri-   12/14
can Authors Through the Beginning of the Twentieth Century. Abridged, revised, and with additions by Martin
Tucker. 4 vols. New York: Ungar, 1966.

Patrick, David, and J. Liddell. Chamber's Cyclopaedia of   12/15
English Literature. A History Critical and Biographical
of Authors in the English Tongue from the Earliest Times
till the Present Day, with Specimens of their Writings.
3 vols. London: Chamber's, [1922-1938].

Summers, Montague. A Gothic Bibliography [1941]. New York: 12/16
Russell & Russell, 1964.

Lists works, adaptations, translations, and spurious attributions.

Tobin, James E. Eighteenth Century English Literature and   12/17
its Cultural Background: A Bibliography. New York:
Fordham Univ. Press, 1939.

Watson, George, ed. The New Cambridge Bibliography of Eng-   12/18
lish Literature. 3 vols. Cambridge: Univ. Press,
1969 --.

c.

Full-Length Studies

[Baron-Wilson, Margaret]. The Life and Correspondence of M.G. 12/19
Lewis, Author of "The Monk", "Castle Spectre", etc. With
Many Pieces in Prose and Verse, Never Before Published.
2 vols. London: Henry Colburn, 1839.

Lacks objectivity but remains invaluable for its inclusion
of poems and pieces not otherwise available. The work is
mainly biographical and splices in many of Lewis's letters
and some of his poems. Following the biographical account
are found further poems, pieces of prose, translations, a
bibliography of works by MGL, his last will and the codi-
cil.

Parreaux, André. The Publication of "The Monk": A Literary 12/2
Event, 1796-1798. Paris: Didier, 1960.

Sets out (1)to study the impact of The Monk on the British
public, (2)to investigate the symptoms of its success,
and (3)to offer a detailed examination of the attacks
upon it. Has a valuable annotated bibliography.

Peck, Louis F. A Life of Matthew G. Lewis. Cambridge: Har- 12/2
vard Univ. Press, 1961.

The definitive biography. Shows that Life & Corresp. (12/
19) is most unreliable; finds fault with accounts rendered by Stalham (12/63), Railo (6/26), and Summers (6/
29). Sees MGL's "chief role in literary history [as]
that of purveyor of German materials to the English Romantic movement". Includes a list of Lewis's works, a lengthy
bibliography, and about ninety pages of "selected letters",
some previously unpublished, and others badly distorted
by Margaret Baron-Wilson (12/19).

Wendel, John Richard. "E.T.A. Hoffmann's Die Elixiere Des   12/22
Teufels and its Dependence on Matthew G. Lewis' The Monk".
Unpublished doctoral dissertation, Univ. of Connecticut,
1966.

Examination of situations reveals that "Hoffmann was influenced by Lewis to a much greater degree than has here-
tofore been acknowledged". These men were of the same age,
were exposed to the same German influence, but in addition
to the general background and common influences, there
seems a direct link. Says Hoffmann is superior to the
Englishman in that MGL lacks "the deep psychological and
metaphysical aspects of Hoffmann's story".

d.

Articles, Essays, and Introductions

Anderson, Howard. "The Manuscript of M.G. Lewis's The Monk: 12/23
Some Preliminary Notes", PBSA, LXII (1968), 427-434.

Has located the MS from which the first edition of the
Monk was set. Says "it is certain that Lewis's original
version of The Monk is that in which the destruction of
the hero is described in dramatic detail." This MS is
on Dutch paper and might indicate that MGL finished his
fair copy before returning from the Hague in late Novem-
ber or December of 1794. "Its complete readiness for
printing at that time would tend to support the argument
that Todd [12/68] advances for the tradition that the
book was first published in 1795 though distributed with
new title pages on 12 March, 1796."

Baker, E[rnest] A. Introduction to The Monk. New York: 12/24
Dutton, [1906].

The Monk "has little claim to perpetuation on its own
merits". Of Lewis's "later works, poems, plays, tales,
translations and other effusions, very little need be
said". MGL, Baker says, "never had a brilliant idea in
his life", but "to write in complete defiance of the
literary canons requires cleverness of a sort; and this
is how The Monk is such a curiosity in the literary annals of that period."

Beattie, W. "'Tales of Terror'", _TLS_ (Jan. 14, 1939), p. 26. 12/2

Summarizes Johnson's findings (12/45; 12/46).

Berryman, John. Introduction to _The Monk_ [1952]. New York: 12/2
Grove, 1959.

Gives biography, printing history, and influences. Defends
The Monk while condemning the Gothic novel. Says "_The Monk_
is one of the authentic prodigies of English fiction, a
book in spite of various crudenesses so good that even
after a century and a half it is possible to consider it
unhistorically."

Bishop, Morchard. "A Terrible Tangle", _TLS_ (Oct. 19, 1967), 12/2
p. 989.

Traces the tangle over authorship of _Tales of Terror_.
Sees _T of T_ as a parody of Lewis but points out that it
was sold by Lewis's own publisher, was printed in a size
uniform with MGL's own work, and these books were adver-
tised together as companion pieces. Concludes: "My
guess, for what it is worth, is that these _Tales of Terror_
were a corporate effort done by able men not wholly ill-
disposed towards Lewis, and that possibly the book contains some of his own writing."

Brooks, Philip. "Notes on Rare Books", _New York Times Book_ 12/2
Review (Jan. 27, 1935), p. 21.

There was no 1795 edition of _The Monk_. The first edition
was released by Bell of London in 1796, reissued by Bell
in April of 1796 "with certain verbal changes, mere cor-
rection of misprints", and again by Bell in October, 1796
"in a so-called second edition". "The reputed third
edition appeared in 1797, but none of these editions contains changes in actual text." It was not till the fifth
edition (London, 1800), that MGL "thoroughly rewrote portions of his story". Also, the two-volume Waterford
edition of 1796 is a bogus edition with 1818 paper.

C., H.B. "'Tales of Terror'", _N&Q_, 3rd ser., X (1866), 508- 12/2
509.

Questions whether Lewis wrote _Tales of Terror, with an_
Introductory Dialogue, 2nd ed., London, 1808. Suggests
that he is not the author because, "in the _T of T_, Lewis

232

is sometimes laughed at. He might have done that himself
as a blind, but he was not addicted to mystification or
concealments of his good things. The cadence of the verse
is generally harsh, especially in the ballad meters.
Lewis's is always easy and flowing. He seldom has a
classical allusion. 'Smedley's Ghost' . . . abounds with
them. . . ."

Charon. "Shakespeare's Ghosts and Lewis's Specter!", Monthly 12/30
Mirror, V (1798), 110-113.

Argues that there is nothing Shakespearean in Lewis's use
of a ghost in Castle Spectre. "Our immortal bard has furnished no precedent, in his writings, for the employment
of supernatural agency, without a cause adequate to such
extraordinary means." With MGL, the ghost "is more con-
venient than needful. . . ; it has no positive control
over the action of the piece. It neither necessarily follows, nor necessarily conduces to any event."

Church, Elizabeth. "A Bibliographical Myth", MP, XIX (1922), 12/31
307-314.

MGL did not write Tales of Terror. In 1799, Ballantyne
at Kelso printed at Scott's request, twelve copies of
Apology for Tales of Terror. Of the nine pieces in this
work, five later appeared in Tales of Wonder, three by
Lewis, one by Scott, one by Southey. Tales of Wonder was
published twice in 1801 and between these two editions,
"some unknown person published T of T anonymously".
Apology, cited under the abbreviated title Tales of Terror
became confused with the second Tales of Terror. This
anonymous T of T, Church says, is the work of one man, and
"there is conclusive internal evidence that this author
was not M.G. Lewis".

Cook, Davidson. "Robert Burns Did Not Write 'The Hermit'", 12/32
Bookman, LXXXV (1934), 402-403.

Monk Lewis did. A Glasgow chapbook of 1798 attributed to
Burns, "An Inscription in an Hermitage"; an 1815 edition
of Burns' works followed suit; the Newcastle edition of
1815 included this poem; and finally, Hogg and Motherwell
in 1834 claimed they presented the first appearance of
this poem. But it appears in the 1839 Life and Correspondence (12/19) as an original by Lewis. Cook believes
that there was a 1795 edition of The Monk which he has

233

never seen, and says he doesn't know if this poem appeared
in the Monk "as published", but it certainly appears in
the second edition of 1796.

Cook, W.B. "The First Work of the Ballantyne Press", N&Q,   12/33
     5th ser., II (1874), 102-103.

     Says Minstrelsy not the first work from Ballantyne Press,
     An Apology for Tales of Terror was. Describes the 1799
     edition; says that of the six ballads "only three -- 'The
     Erl-King', 'The Chase', and 'William and Helen' -- are to
     be found in Scott's works. The other three are 'The Water
     King: A Danish Ballad' (quoere, who is the author?),
     'Lord William' and 'Poor Mary, the Maid of the Inn'." Says
     Southey is named as author of "Lord William" -- but he does
     not know who wrote the others.

Coykendall, Frederick. "Lewis's Monk", TLS (Apr. 25, 1935),   12/34
     p. 276.

     The Monk was first published in March of 1796 and reissued
     in April; a second edition appeared in October. The first
     issue ends with the quick death of Ambrosio, and below a
     short horizontal line has the "Haughty Lady" passage. The
     second issue adds the seven days of suffering and omits the
     "Haughty Lady". The second edition has the instant death
     and the "Haughty Lady" as in the original edition. "I
     have never seen a copy of the first issue with the length-
     ened ending or without the Haughty Lady paragraph, and I
     have never seen a copy of the second issue with the short
     ending or with the Haughty Lady paragraph."

--------. "A Note on The Monk", Colophon, NS, I (1935), 87-   12/35
     96.

     On dates and editions of The Monk. Earliest reference is
     in Monthly Magazine of March, 1796. London (Bell)
     editions as follows: first edition, March, 1796; second
     issue, with errors corrected, six days suffering added,
     and "Haughty Lady" omitted, April, 1796; second edition,
     October, 1796, with original ending restored; third edition,
     1797; fourth edition, 1798, with new title Ambrosio or The
     Monk "and with considerable additions and alterations;
     fifth edition, 1800, title and text of fourth edition.

Emerson, Oliver Farrar. "'Monk' Lewis and the Tales of Ter-   12/36
ror", MLN, XXXVIII (1923), 154-159.

Church (12/31) thought Morley (12/48) was incorrect in
assigning the date 1800 to Tales of Wonder, but Emerson
says that even though most of the volumes bore the date
1801, it is "possible that some copies of the Tales
were dated 1800" and released in that year. Offers additional information to bolster the view that Tales of Terror is a parody of Lewis.

Fairchild, Hoxie N. "Byron and Monk Lewis", TLS (May 11,   12/37
1946), p. 223.

Suggests that MGL's poem "The Exiles", from The Monk,
seems influential on Byron's Don Juan (II, 18-20). Lewis
"may have suggested not only the melancholy part of Juan's
speech but the seasickness which 'turns what was once romantic to burlesque'".

A Friend to Genius. "An Apology for the Monk", Monthly Mir-   12/38
ror, III (1797), 210-215.

The author of this letter to the editor says he is not acquainted with Mr. Lewis but acts on his part since "the
defence of genius is the common cause of all men of the
least pretensions to literature". He asserts that "this
beautiful romance is well calculated to support the cause
of virtue" and points out that the downfall of Ambrosio
is a strong lesson. As to the libidinous passages, "no
heart but one already depraved, could rise from them, if
the preceding part of the work had been perused, with
the least impurity."

Guthke, Karl S. "C.M. Wieland and M.G. Lewis", Neophil,   12/39
XL (1956), 231-233.

Says MGL's "chief literary importance rests on his position as an outstanding introducer of contemporary German
literature". For those who may believe that Lewis read
only German Schauerromanen, Guthke points out that he
met Wieland and translated Oberon and Hann und Gulpenhé.
Implies that Lewis's knowledge of German poetry was
passed, orally, to Byron, Shelley, Scott, Moore and his
English friends.

235

Guthke, Karl S. "Some Bibliographical Errors Concerning the   12/40
    Romantic Age", PBSA, LI (1957), 159-162.

    Lewis and Scott could not possibly have written Tales of
    Terror; The East Indian is not a translation of one of
    Von Kotzebue's plays; La Soirée d'Eté, attributed to the
    author of the Monk, is not from Lewis but shows his popu-
    larity in France; "through the author of the Monk sensa-
    tional 'German' literary materials must have enjoyed great
    popularity in France as well as in England". Also, Les
    Orphelines de Werdenberg is "a rather close translation"
    of Lewis's Feudal Tyrants which is itself a free transla-
    tion of Naubert's Elisabeth, Erbin von Toggenburg (1789).

--------. "Some Notes on the Significance of the Weimar   12/41
    Court Stage in Anglo-German Literary Relations", HLQ,
    XX (1957), 281-283.

    Suggests that L's The Twins is derived from J.F. Regnard's
    Les Menechmes; ou, Les Jumeaux. Thinks that MGL did not
    read the French edition, but instead, saw the German stage
    adaption by F.L. Schröder, Die Zwillingsbrüder, a play
    presented twice during his stay in Weimar in 1792-93. Un-
    fortunately, no copy of Die Z has been located for a com-
    parison. Suggests further traces of the Weimar stage in
    My Uncle's Garret Window and The Castle Spectre.

--------. "M.G. Lewis' The Twins", HLQ, XXV (1962), 189-223.   12/42

    Offers the hitherto unpublished The Twins; or, Is It He,
    or His Brother?. Guthke's introduction is mainly a rerun
    of his earlier article (12/41), but this time, he points
    out similarities and differences in the English and
    French versions.

--------. "F.L. Schröder, J.F. Regnard, and M.G. Lewis",   12/43
    HLQ, XXVII (1963), 79-82.

    In his earlier articles (12/41, 12/42), Guthke had been
    hampered by the lack of a copy of Schröder's Die Z. A
    copy has been located, a comparison made, and he now con-
    cludes that "while The Twins is independent to a consider-
    able extent, its similarities to Die Zwillingsbrüder
    suggests that Lewis was familiar with Schröder's play
    and was influenced by it". But he says that it is impos-
    sible to state with certainty whether MGL read or saw the
    play.

236

Guthke, Karl S. "Some Unpublished Letters of M.G. Lewis",   12/44
    N&Q, CCII (1957), 217-219.

    Prints three letters: one to Thomas Maurice, one to G.
    Roots, one to Sir Walter Scott.
       "A Friend of Accuracy" (N&Q, IV [1957], 389) corrects
    some "errors of identification and transcription" in the
    letter to Scott.

Johnston, George. "The First Book Printed by James Ballan-   12/45
    tyne: Being An Apology for Tales of Terror; With Notes
    on Tales of Wonder and Tales of Horror", Edinburgh Bib-
    liographical Society Publications, I, pt. 4 (1894), 1-
    15.

    Says that Ballantyne in 1799 printed twelve copies of An
    Apology for Tales of Terror. Two poems are by Scott, two
    by Southey, four by Lewis, and one by someone else. Mor-
    ley (12/48) "wrongly attribute[s] to Lewis what Lockhart
    [12/82] as wrongly attributes to Sir Walter Scott --
    namely, the sole authorship of its contents". Johnston
    credits MGL with the Bell, 1801, Tales of Wonder but de-
    nies that he wrote the Bell, 1801, Tales of Terror. This
    collection, J calls "the work of one hand; somewhat simi-
    lar in character to Lewis's own writings, only more hor-
    ribly gruesome and fantastic". Contains detailed bib-
    liographical information in appendix.

--------. "Note to a Paper Entitled The First Book Printed   12/46
    by James Ballantyne", Edinburgh Bibliographical Society
    Publications, IX, pt. 2 (1912), 90.

    One of the twelve copies printed at Kelso in 1799 bears
    the title Tales of Terror, not An Apology for Tales of
    Terror. "The copy . . . is in all respects, excepting
    the title, the same as the others: printed on the same
    paper, with the same water marks."

Monk Lewis", N&Q, 2nd ser., X (1860), 396-397.   12/47

    Answers a request in N&Q, 2nd ser., X (1860), 349, for
    "the pedigree" of MGL.

Morley, Henry. Introduction to Tales of Terror and Wonder,   12/48
    in Tales of Terror and Wonder; Confession of an English
    Opium Eater, Essays of Elia. London: Routledge, 1889.

    Lewis published at Kelso, in 1799, his Tales of Terror,
    followed them the next year with his Tales of Wonder and
    produced Tales of Wonder in London in 1801 with additional
    pieces collected from various sources. In this present
    volume (1889) the original books are reprinted, but four
    leaves missing from the Tales of Terror compelled the
    omission of one tale. Another copy could not be found --
    it is not in the British Museum, and the London Library
    contains only the 1801 edition of the Tales of Wonder.

Moss, Walter. "M.G. Lewis and Mme. de Stael", ES, XXXIV   12/49
    (1953), 109-112.

    Suggests that Baker (12/24) errs in viewing L's other works
    as of little importance. Thinks Leslie Stephen correct in
    seeing MGL as important for German literature (12/64), and
    disagrees with Stokoe (3/52) who sees L's works as "pesti-
    lent" for German letters. Stresses that Lewis was a rarity
    with his knowledge of German. Shows his aversion for Mme.
    de Stael who, in England, passed as an authority on Ger-
    many and German literature.

Peck, Louis F. "Act III of Lewis's Venoni", MLN, LVIII   12/50
    (1943), 265-268.

    When Venoni was first staged, the third act failed and MGL
    rewrote this section. Confusion has arisen over just what
    did constitute the original version, and Peck clarifies
    matters and suggests reasons for failure.

--------. "An Adaptation of Kleist's Die Familie Schroffen-   12/51
    stein", JEGP, XLIV (1945), 9-11.

    In his preface to "Mistrust, or Blanche and Osbright",
    Lewis acknowledged that he drew on a German tragedy but
    did not name it. Peck identifies it as Heinrich von
    Kleist's Die Familie Schroffenstein and shows how Lewis
    used the source to fashion "an interesting specimen of
    German Romantic literature reworked for the Gothic market
    in England".

Peck, Louis F. "An Early Copy of 'The Monk'", <u>PBSA</u>, LVII   12/52
(1963), 350-351.

As an addenda to Todd (12/68), Peck describes another early
edition. This copy, credited to J. Bell, and dated 1796,
"would appear to be a second issue of the third edition
. . . masquerading as a first edition" but a close examination reveals that "the book consists of ten sheets
from the first edition, 21 from the second, and six from
the third." Suggests that Bell "thriftily attempted to
clear his shelves before issuing the expurgated fourth
edition of <u>The Monk</u> in 1798; or that he practiced the
same economy soon after that edition was published, to
help satisfy a demand for the romance in its earlier,
more delectable form".

--------. "Lewis's <u>Monk</u>", <u>TLS</u> (March 4, 1935), p. 148.   12/53

Asserts that Brooks (12/28) errs when he claims that none
of the first three editions of the <u>Monk</u> contains changes in
text. In the first edition Ambrosio suffers for six days;
in the second edition Ambrosio's six days of suffering do
not appear, and Peck thinks that the "Haughty Lady" addition preceded this omission "and that it occurred during
the issue of the first edition, because in the second, as
has been said, the sufferings are already curtailed; yet
at least one reprint of <u>The Monk</u> (J. and H. Purkess, London, n.d. illus) contains the sufferings in full and also
the 'Haughty Lady' passage".
    E.G. Bayford (<u>TLS</u> [March 28, 1935], p. 216) says he too
has a copy of the Purkess <u>Monk</u>.

--------. "M.G. Lewis and the Larpent <u>Catalogue</u>", <u>HLQ</u>, V   12/54
(1942), 382-384.

The <u>Catalogue of the Larpent Plays in the Huntington Li-
brary</u> attributes sixteen items to Lewis. Peck asserts
that "six Larpent manuscripts included in the <u>Catalogue</u>
without attribution of authorship should be added to
Lewis's list". These include <u>The World</u>, a five-act comedy; <u>Quarter Day</u>, five-act comedy; <u>The Domestic Tyrant</u>,
a two-act farce; <u>The East Indian</u>, a three-act opera; a
poem, "Monody on the Death of Sir John Moore", and a
farewell address written for Mr. and Mrs. H. Johnson.

239

Peck, Louis F.   "The Monk and Le Diable Amoureux", MLN,   12/55
LXVIII (1953), 406-408.

The Monthly Review alleges that Lewis copied from Cazotte's
The Devil in Love. Railo (6/26) claims there are "passages that coincide almost word for word" but cites only
one. Peck now points out that Railo has reversed matters.
The French edition appeared in 1772, an English translation in 1793, the Monk in 1796, and in 1810 appeared
Biondetta, or the enamoured spirit, a second translation
of Devil, which to parody Lewis lifted the passage quoted
by Railo directly from the Monk. Apparently, Railo assumed that the 1810 translation was a later edition of
the 1793 translation.

--------.   "The Monk and Musäus' 'Die Entführung'", PQ,   12/56
XXXII (1953), 346-348.

MGL wrote that the Bleeding Nun episode was based on a
story which "was related to me". This, says Peck, suggests an oral version but critics including Scott have accused Lewis of plagiarizing directly from Musäus. Peck
quotes from an 1807 letter of Lewis to Scott which seems
to imply that he had not read "Die Entführung" until recently, so the contact must have been oral.

--------.   "New Poems by Matthew G. Lewis", Archiv, CCIII   12/57
(1967), 189-194.

Peck has acquired twenty pages, in Lewis's own hand, of
poems written for Lady Holland sometime between 1804 and
1808. Included among these eight poems are three previously unpublished works which are offered here. Peck
notes that L's reputation as a Gothic writer overshadows
his lighter side and suggests that "Lewis is entitled to
more attention than he has received as a song writer.
Coleridge admired his work in this genre, and many of his
songs were popular favorites of his day."

--------.   "On the Date of Tales of Wonder", ELN, II (1964), 12/58
25-27.

Summarizes the many articles arguing for/against an 1800/
1801 publication of Tales of Wonder and provides a new
piece of information. No edition dated 1800 has yet
turned up, but Cornell has a letter from John Wordsworth
(brother of William) dated and postmarked December 12,

240

1800, in which he notes: "I have seen Mr. Lewis' Tales of Wonder."

Peck, Louis F. "Southey and Tales of Wonder", MLN, L (1935), 513-514.   12/59

The first edition of Tales of Wonder contains eight of Southey's ballads but these do not reappear in the second edition. Lewis wrote a letter asking Southey to contribute; Scott records that he did. But a handwritten note by Alexander Dyce in his own copy of Tales says that Wordsworth told him (Dyce) that Southey said that Lewis used his (Southey's) ballads without his permission. Peck notes the possibility of a misquotation, points out that neither Wordsworth nor Southey liked Lewis, but still, the fact remains that the poems were later omitted. Concludes that Lewis "probably received no answer to his letter, and took Southey's silence for consent, or at least for indifference".

Pound, Louise. "'Monk' Lewis in Nebraska", SFQ, IX (1945), 107-110.   12/60

Mrs. Harriet Stevens Wert, born in Oswego, New York, in 1836, lived in Illinois, settled in Nebraska, and died there in 1927 at the age of 91. One of her children wrote down the seventeen stanza ballad which she used to sing, "The Lady and the Knight", and it is here identified as "Alonzo the Brave and the Fair Imogine" from The Monk. Miss Pound reproduces the ballad, notes that "there are only minor variations from the original", and although the route of transmission remains unknown, it seems undeniable that "Lewis's ballad must have had wide popular circulation at one time."

Roberts, W. "Lewis's Monk", TLS (March 14, 1935), p. 164.   12/61

Wonders whether the Purkess edition mentioned by Peck (12/53) might not be the penny weekly numbers issued "in the early forties" by G. Purkess of Soho.

Sadleir, Michael. "'Tales of Terror'", <u>TLS</u> (Jan. 7, 1939),   12/62
pp. 9-10.

Points out that Summers (6/29) errs when he attributes to
Lewis, <u>Tales of Terror</u> (Kelso, 1799), <u>Tales of Wonder</u>
(Bell, 1801) and <u>Tales of Terror</u> (Bell, 1801).   Refers to
an earlier article by G.P. Johnston (12/45).

[Stalham, Francis Reginald].   Introduction to <u>The Monk</u>. 3   12/63
vols. London: Gibbings, 1906.

This anonymous introduction calls the <u>Monk</u>'s moral "sound",
the plot "ingeniously worked out", the Raymond-Agnes episode "little connected with the whole story", but "exciting". Defends the novel; says it was "accepted on its
general merits, and not by reason of those scattered
phrases and passages which the author, from his masculine
point of view, thought might be justifiably inserted in
order to heighten the effect of the situations he described".

Stephen, Leslie. "Matthew Gregory Lewis", in Leslie Stephen   12/64
and Sidney Lee, eds. <u>Dictionary of National Biography</u>.
63 vols. London: Smith, Elder, 1885 --.

General and objective, but with errors. Says Lewis "ex-
punged the most objectionable passages" from the second
edition of the <u>Monk</u>. States, but has doubts, that <u>Tales
of Terror</u> was published at Kelso in 1799 and again in
1801 in London.

Summers, Montague. "'Santon Barsisa'", <u>N&Q</u>, CLXXV (1938),   12/65
174-175.

Offers a brief summary of the story that MGL claimed as
a source for <u>The Monk</u>. Traces the tale from its beginnings in Persia; notes 18th and 19th-century editions.

Taylor, Archer. "The Three Sins of the Hermit", <u>MP</u>, XX   12/66
(1922), 61-94.

Traces the Barsisa story which Lewis acknowledged as his
source. Concludes that the exemplum of the three sins is
a "distinct and readily recognizable story which has maintained itself in Europe for seven centuries" and can be
traced back to Levantine parallels, but the exact route of

242

the transmission of the legend from the East to Europe is
not entirely clear.

Thomas, William. "They Called Him 'Monk'", Person, XLVII   12/67
(1966), 81-90.

A general introduction which includes no new material.

Todd, William B. "The Early Editions and Issues of The   12/68
Monk, with a Bibliography", SB, II (1949), 3-24.

A few pre-publication copies of the M "were probably distributed" in 1795, but "the actual first published issue
was withheld for some reason until March, 1796, when it
officially appeared with new title leaves". Part of this
first printing was passed off as a second edition, but
the authentic second edition appeared in October, 1796.
This issue carried the name of the author and offered
the substitute "Haughty Lady" passage. After Mathias's
attack (12/77), the third edition was disguised as a
first and has been mistaken as the genuine first.

"Trollope on The Monk", NCF, IV (1949), 167.   12/69

Trollope's copy of the 1796 edition of the Monk has turned
up, and in his hand, at the end of the third volume, the
following annotation appears: "This is so bad, that nothing ever could have been worse; -- and yet the book had
a great success! There is no feeling of poetry in it.
Everything is pretended, made up, and cold. We are obliged
to suppose that its charm consisted in its indecency, --
which in itself would not have been much; but is enhanced
by being the indecency of a monk."

Wilson, Mona. Introduction to Journal of a West India Pro-   12/70
prietor 1815-17. London: George Routledge, 1929.

Draws heavily on Life & Correspondence (12/19), a work of
dubious reliability. Defends the morality of the Monk,
since "the wicked monk incurred no ambiguous damnation,
and the good gained peace either on earth or in heaven."

243

Young, A.B. "Shelley and M.G. Lewis", <u>MLR</u>, I (1906), 322-324. 12/71

Shelley's <u>Original Poems</u> contains "St. Edmund's Eve", "which is copied word for word from a poem entitled 'The Black Canon of Elmham or Saint Edmund's Eve' from Lewis' <u>Tales of Terror</u>, 1799 and 1808 editions". Also, "Ghasta" "is nothing more or less than a versification by Shelley of the tale of 'Don Raymond', 'The Bleeding Nun' and the 'Wandering Jew' as related in the <u>Monk</u> with some minor alterations". Shelley's "The Revenge" follows "Castle of Lindenberg", and "Alonzo the Brave" is from <u>Alonzo the Brave</u>. <u>Zastrozzi</u> is not from German originals but rather "nothing but a second version of certain portions of the <u>Monk</u>, with, however, great alterations".

e.

Notices in General Works, Diaries, Etc.

Bury, Lady Charlotte. <u>The Diary of a Lady-in-Waiting, Being</u>   12/72
<u>the Diary Illustrative of the Times of George the Fourth</u>
<u>Interspersed with Original Letters from the Late Queen</u>
<u>Caroline and From Other Distinguished Persons</u>. Edited,
and with an introduction by A. Francis Steuart. 2 vols.
New York: John Lane, 1908.

Includes nine of MGL's letters and some verse.

Byron, George Gordon, Lord. <u>The Works of Lord Byron</u>. <u>With</u>   12/73
<u>His Letters and Journals, and His Life</u>. 17 vols. London: John Murray, 1833.

Records in his journal for Dec. 6, 1813, that he looked "at the worst parts of the <u>Monk</u>. These descriptions ought to have been written by Tiberius at Caprea -- they are forced -- the <u>philtred</u> ideas of a jaded voluptuary. It is to me inconceivable how they could have been composed by a man of only twenty -- his age when he wrote them. They have no nature -- all the sour cream of cantharides."
    On MGL's death in 1818, Byron wrote: "Lewis was a good man, a clever man, but a bore. My only revenge or consolation used to be setting him by the ears with some vivacious person who hates bores especially, -- Madame de Staël or Hobhouse, for example. But I liked Lewis; he was the jewel of a man, had he been better set; -- I don't

mean personally, but less tiresome, for he was tedious,
as well as contradictory to every thing and every body."

Coleridge, Samuel Taylor. Collected Letters of Samuel Taylor   12/74
Coleridge. Edited by Earl Leslie Griggs. 6 vols. Ox-
ford: Clarendon, 1956-1971.

In a letter to Wordsworth, dated January 23, 1798, STC
severely criticizes Castle Spectre as defective in "1.
Language -- 2. Character. 3. Passion. 4. Sentiment.
5. Conduct", explains these charges, then concludes:
"The merit of the Castle Spectre consists wholly in its
situations. These are all borrowed, and all absolutely
pantomimical, but they are admirably managed for stage
effect. There is not much bustle, but situations for
ever. The whole plot, machinery, and incidents are borrowed -- the play is a mere patchwork of plagiarisms --
but they are well worked up, and for stage effect make
an excellent whole."

--------. The Table Talk and Omniana. London: Oxford Univ.   12/75
Press, 1917.

STC writes on March 20, 1834: "Lewis's Jamaica Journal
is delightful; it is almost the only unaffected book of
travels or touring I have read of late years. You have
the man himself, and not an inconsiderable man, -- certainly a much finer mind than I supposed before from the
perusal of his romances, etc. It is by far his best work,
and will live and be popular. Those verses on the Hours
are very pretty, but the Isle of Devils is, like his romances, a fever dream -- horrible, without point or terror."

Hazlitt, William. "On the English Novelists", in his Lec-   12/76
tures on the English Comic Writers and Fugitive Writings
[1819]. Everyman's. London: Dent, 1967.

"After Mrs. Radcliffe, Monk Lewis was the greatest master
of the art of freezing the blood. The robber scene in
the Monk is only inferior to that in Count Fathom, and
perfectly new in the circumstances and cast of characters.
Some of his descriptions are chargeable with unpardonable
grossness, but the pieces of poetry interspersed in this
far-fam'd novel, such as the 'Fight of Ronscevalles' and
'The Exile', in particular, have a romantic and delightful harmony, such as might be chanted by the moonlight
pilgrim, or might lull the dreaming mariner on summer seas."

245

[Mathias, Thomas James]. The Pursuits of Literature. A   12/77
Satirical Poem in Dialogue. With Notes. 2nd ed. Re-
vised. London: J. Owen, 1797.

In the fourth dialogue, July 4, 1797, the anonymous author, claiming "no private motive whatsoever", severely
denounces The Monk. "The publication of this novel by a
Member of Parliament is in itself so serious an offence
to the public, that I know not how the author can repair
this breach of public decency, but by suppressing it himself. Or Mr. Lewis might omit the indecent and blasphemous passages in another edition; there is neither
genius nor wit in them, and the work, as a composition,
would receive great advantage. I wish he may at least
take this advice."

Moore, Thomas. Memoirs, Journals, and Correspondence.   12/78
Edited by John Russell. 2 vols. New York: Appleton,
1858.

Moore writes in his diary on Oct. 7, 1818: "Talked of
poor Monk Lewis: his death was occasioned by taking
emetics for sea-sickness, in spite of the advice of those
about him. He died lying on the deck." Later, on May 3,
1819, he records the version of MGL's brother-in-law, Mr.
Sheddon: "Lewis died of the yellow fever, he said; very
unwilling to die; all the last days exclaiming every instant, 'The suspense! the suspense!' which the physician
who attended him was doubtful whether he meant to allude
to religious doubts, or the success of a medicine which
he had taken, and on whose operation his life depended."

Nicoll, Allardyce. A History of Late Eighteenth Century   12/79
Drama, 1750-1800. Cambridge: Univ. Press, 1927.

Calls Castle Spectre "a brilliant example of the more
thrilling type of melodrama". "The whole play, indeed, is
a tissue of spectacular 'romantic' episodes and devices,
confessedly gathered together, not for the sake of art
but for that of effect. To our eyes, the atmosphere is
ridiculous, with its conventionalised bombastic language
and lack of subtlety." "No doubt contemporary audiences
were duly thrilled and melted with soft pity, but we cannot today esteem Lewis any other than a mediocre dramatist
intent upon the cheapest of effects."

Nicoll, Allardyce. A History of Early Nineteenth Century   12/80
Drama 1800-1850. 2 vols. Cambridge: Univ. Press,
1930.

Treats Alfonso, "a blood-red drama of revenge, confessedly
unhistorical" and Adelmorn. Says Lewis "belongs more to
the popular than to the literary school, and one cannot
pretend -- he never pretended -- that he endeavoured to do
aught else than give the public what it wanted."

Scott, Sir Walter. "Essays on Imitations of the Ancient Bal-   12/81
lad", in T[homas] F. Henderson, ed., Sir Walter Scott's
Minstrelsy of the Scottish Border. New York: Scribner's,
1902.

Says The Monk was "published in 1795". It was extremely
popular, "but the public were chiefly captivated by the
poetry interspersed into the prose". Lewis, he says, "had
announced a collection, first intended to bear the title
of Tales of Terror and afterwards published under that of
Tales of Wonder." Scott contributed "Glenfinlas" and "The
Eve of Saint John" and one or two others. Southey added
"The Old Woman of Berkeley", "Lord William" and "several
other". Publication of T of W became "postponed till the
year 1801". Objections were raised to content, to Lewis's
attempts at comedy, at padded contents, and to the high
price. "A very clever parody was made on the style and
the person of the author, and the world laughed as willing-
ly as if it had never applauded."

--------, in J[ohn] G. Lockhart, The Life of Sir Walter   12/82
Scott, Bart. 1771-1832. London: Adam & Charles Black,
1893.

"Lewis was fonder of great people than he ought to have
been, either as a man of talent or as a man of fashion.
He had always dukes and duchesses in his mouth, and was
pathetically fond of any one that had a title.
    "Mat had queerish eyes -- they projected like those of
some insects, and were flattish on the orbit. His person
was extremely small and boyish.
    "He was a child, and a spoiled child, but a child of
high imagination; and so he wasted himself on ghost-stories
and German romances.
    "Matt, though a clever fellow, was a bore of the first
description. Moreover, he looked always like a schoolboy."

                              247

Seward, Anna. Letters of Anna Seward: Written Between the   12/83
    Years 1784 and 1807. 6 vols. Edinburgh: George Ramsey,
    1811.

    In a letter of Nov. 9, 1802, Miss Seward writes: "But in
    the midst of this, at least, partial dramatic impotence,
    where most we looked for strength, Lewis has given us what
    we failed to obtain from either of his superior rivals, a
    grand, interesting, and original tragedy, Alphonso of Cas-
    tile. The general style is not equal to that Jephson's
    truly noble dramas, nor yet, though considerably poetic,
    is it so poetic as Miss Baillie's . . . , but as to plot
    it is superior to any of theirs; busy, animated, and in-
    volved, without perplexity."

Thrale, Mrs. Hester Lynch. Thraliana: The Diary of Mrs.   12/84
    Hester Lynch Thrale (Later Mrs. Piozzi) 1776-1809 [1942].
    Edited by Katharine C. Balderston. 2nd ed. Oxford:
    Clarendon, 1951.

    On Sept. 1, 1797, Mrs. Thrale refers to Monk as one of those
    books which "come out every day to prove Depravity of Man-
    ners or Perversion of Talents so as to fright one from de-
    lighting in one's Humanity". But she says Lewis's "'Gipsy
    Verses' however, put all our Gipsy Lines to Flight: they
    are exquisitely pretty to be sure, -- the Incantation Scene
    is so sublimely Descriptive it amazes one; 'The ballads of
    Alonzo ye Brave' is very fine too, and the 'Stanzas in a
    Hermitage' exceedingly forcible. 'Tis a curst Book after
    all, full of every Thing yet should not be anywhere."

                              f.

                        Early Reviews

                    1. The Monk (1796)

Analytical Review, XXIV (1796), 403-404.   12/85

    Objects to the two plots as they are "not indispensably
    connected" and also, "two catastrophes have always a bad
    effect, splitting the interest". Notes that "the language
    and manners of the personages are not sufficiently gothic
    in their colouring, to agree with the superstitious

scenery, borrowed from those times. They want the sombre
cast of ignorance, which renders credulity probable;
still the author deserves praise for not attempting to
account for supernatural appearances in a natural way.
After being awakened to wonder by the rumbling of a
mountain, the reader has an unpleasant sensation of being
tricked, similar to the discovery of a slight of hand,
when he perceives only a mouse creep out."

British Critic, VII (1796), 677.   12/86

    Complete item: "Lust, murder, incest, and every atro-
    city that can disgrace human nature, brought together,
    without the apology of probability, or even possibility
    for their introduction. To make amends, the moral is
    general and very practical; it is, 'not to deal in witch-
    craft and magic because the devil will have you at last!!'
    We are sorry to observe that good talents have been mis-
    applied in the production of this monster."

Monthly Mirror, II (1796), 98.   12/87

    Complete item: "The author of this romance has amplified
    the character of the Santon Barsisa in the Guardian, in a
    most masterly and impressive manner. We really do not re-
    member to have read a more interesting production. The
    stronger passions are finely delineated and exemplified in
    the progress of artful temptation working on self-suffi-
    cient pride, superstition, and lasciviousness. The author
    has availed himself of a German tradition which furnishes
    an episodical incident, awful, but improbable. The whole
    is very skilfully managed, and reflects the highest credit
    on the judgment and imagination of the writer. Some beau-
    tiful little ballads are interspersed, which indicate no
    common poetical talents."

Monthly Mirror, II (1796), 323-328.   12/88

    Long extracts of prose and poetry, a portrait of MGL, and
    a brief introduction. Remarks that the recently elected
    M.P. is but 22 years old and says that the Monk "was
    written for the amusement of his leisure during his tra-
    vels".

Critical Review, XIX (1797), 194-200. (Attributed to Cole- 12/89
  ridge. Reprinted in Garland Greever, A Wiltshire Parson
  and His Friends, London: Constable, 1926; Thomas M. Raysor, ed., Coleridge's Miscellaneous Criticism, Cambridge:
  Harvard, 1936. But see 7/32.)

  Objects to the sexual indecency, irreligious air and lack
  of a moral. But The Monk, he calls, "the offspring of no
  common genius", and says that the underplot "is skilfully
  and closely connected with the main story". "Situations
  of torment, and images of naked horror, are easily conceived; and a writer in whose works they abound, deserves
  our gratitude almost equally with him who should drag us
  by way of sport through a military hospital, or force us
  to sit at the dissecting table of a natural philosopher."

European Magazine, XXXI (1797), 111-115.   12/90

  A long and rather severe denunciation. "This singular composition, which has neither originality, morals, nor probability to recommend it, has excited and will still continue to excite, the curiosity of the public." The reviewer notes the debt to Santon Barsisa, alleges plagiarization from The Knights of the Swan, complains that there
  exists "an oblique attack upon venerable establishments",
  admits "genius and talents in various parts", and praises
  the poetry, especially the imitations of the ancient ballad.

Monthly Review, XXIII (1797), 451.   12/91

  Cites as sources: Santon Barsisa, Devil in Love, Sorcerer,
  Ferdinand Count Fathom and Mrs. Radcliffe's works, but
  says that "all invention is but new combination. To in-
  vent well is to combine the impressive." Praises the
  verse but notes that "a vein of obsenity . . . pervades
  and deforms the whole . . . and . . . renders the work
  totally unfit for general circulation."

Monthly Mirror, V (1798), 157-158.   12/92

  Review of the Bell, 1798, "fourth edition, with considerable alterations and additions". "The clamour that has
  been raised against this novel on account of the warmth
  of colouring which the author had given to some of his
  descriptions, has induced Mr. Lewis either to omit or to
  soften the objectionable passages, and, by various judicious corrections and additions, to render it still more

250

deserving of the very extraordinary favour it has received
from the public." Welcomes the addition of "Erl-King's
Daughter"; objects to parody of "Alonzo".

2. The Controversy over the Monk

Pursuits of Literature, IV, [by Thomas J. Mathias]. Reviewed 12/93
in British Critic, X (1797), 303-306.

"We cannot too much commend this writer for his very severe, but most just castigation, of the Monk, and its
author. When we gave our critique upon it [12/86], what
we said was concise though strong, because we feared at-
tracting attention to a production so pernicious, even by
our censures. Attention has since been paid to it, infinitely more than enough, and whoever points out its tur-
pitude, and seductive tendency, pays a homage to virtue
and religion."

--------. Critical Review, 2nd ser., XXIV (1798), 418-423.   12/94

Thinks the censure of the Monk "most exaggerated" and
points out that "it is ungenerous and unjust, after ac-
cusing Mr. Lewis so bitterly for the improper passages
. . . not to mention that in the last edition of his book
they have been omitted."

Impartial Strictures on the Poem Called "The Pursuits of   12/95
Literature" and Particularly a Vindication of the Romance of "The Monk". Reviewed in British Critic, XII
(1798), 318-319.

Calls the "defence of that pernicious effusion of youthful
intemperence . . . sophistical and unsound". Offers two
"irrefragable" points: "1. That, in describing the progress of Vice, it is most vicious, and always utterly unnecessary, to give luscious and seducing descriptions of
the acts pretended to be censured [and] 2. that, in
speaking of a Sacred Book, no person who has a spark of
religion, or regard for it, will, or can, use such expressions as evidently tend to depreciate it, in any
respect, below the most trivial and contemptible works."

Epistle in Rhyme to M.G. Lewis, Esq. M.P. Reviewed in <u>Cri-</u> 12/96
   <u>tical Review</u>, 2nd ser., XXIV (1798), 110.

   "The author of this epistle undertakes to vindicate the
   morality of the <u>Monk</u>, and lavishes praise upon the <u>Castle</u>
   <u>Spectre</u>. To us Mr. Lewis's romance appears the vigorous
   production of a depraved imagination; and his play we
   deem excellent only in pantomimic stage effect.

--------. by _____ Soame. Reviewed in <u>Monthly Mirror</u>, 12/97
   X (1800), 384.

   "This epistle is altogether encomiastic, with respect to
   Mr. Lewis, who is commended, we presume, satirically, for
   adhering to <u>nature</u> and <u>probability</u>, in ushering his <u>Cas-</u>
   <u>tle Spectre</u> upon the stage, while his dramatic contemporaries are charged with exhibiting before the public, a
   <u>monstrous</u> <u>brood</u>, which they pretend to be <u>drawn</u> <u>from</u>
   <u>life</u>." "We have no decisive objection to the admission
   of praeternatural beings on the stage, if the machinery
   of the piece requires them, and any interesting effect is
   produced by their introduction."

3. The Minister (1797)

<u>British Critic</u>, X (1797), 551. 12/98

   "One thing, which surprises and offends us, is, that after
   the severe and most just reprehension he [MGL] has met
   with for his pernicious novel, he should choose to make
   himself known specifically by that book as a previous
   title to notice. [Author lists himself as M.G. Lewis,
   Esq. M.P., Author of <u>The Monk</u>.] Rather ought he to wish
   that all memory of so <u>disgraceful</u> a production should be
   completely obliterated!"

<u>Monthly Mirror</u>, III (1797), 356-358. 12/99

   Praises Schiller for the original and Lewis for the translation. "Mr. L has been very successful in his translation;
   he has never failed to give us the spirit and sense of his
   author, and seems well calculated, from his own genius, to
   convey the animated ideas of Schiller to the minds of English readers. He will, however, we are confident, pardon

us for wishing that he had adhered still more closely to
his author: though he has never failed to give us his
sense, yet he has, in several instances, dilated and spun
out his sentiments."

4. Castle Spectre (1798)

Monthly Mirror, IV (1797), 354-356.   12/100

Cites as "the principal objection" to Castle Spectre, "the
introduction of Africans . . . into a Gothic story . . .
[since] the simplicity of the romance is destroyed by it."
Also, "there is no necessity" for the use of a ghost and
MGL violates Horace's rule. "But if we pass over the necessity of the Spectre in this play, we must allow the
effect produced by her introduction, to be stronger than
any thing of the sort that has been hitherto attempted.
The ingenuity with which a point of so much delicacy is
managed, is admirable. . . . " Notes influence of German
literature and adds that "there has been . . . some attack upon the originality of Mr. Lewis's characters."

Analytical Review, XXVIII (1798), 179-191.   12/101

A long and highly critical examination. The reviewer admits the popularity of CS but views it as a disappointment. "For our parts, we cannot but regard the success of
this piece, and of others of a similar class, as truly
humiliating to the pride of our national taste. . . . "
Notes a strong influence of Mrs. R; objects to the use of
a ghost, says the fifth act drags and the prose is "rigid
and stilted".

British Critic, XI (1798), 436-437.   12/102

"The time will come", says the reviewer, "when Mr. Lewis
will wish to find some better distinction, than that of
author of a work, which degrades him in the mind of every
man who has one genuine feeling of morality or religion."
He regards CS as "a kind of nonsensical curiosity about
the grossest improbabilities", and "the spectre from which
it is named, instead of being necessary, contributes not
a little to the plot of the drama, and might be omitted
without any change, except the show."

<u>Critical Review</u>, 2nd ser., XXII (1798), 476-478.   12/103

"The <u>CS</u>, like the <u>Monk</u> . . . cannot obtain the approbation
of the critic, but it has secured, what Mr. Lewis perhaps
values more, the applause of the multitude." The reviewer
says "there is scarcely one original incident in the piece,
and yet the whole is wrought into a plot highly interesting and conducted with uncommon skill." Concludes: "We
should disapprove this drama, did we judge of it only in
the closet, but its effect in representation is admirable."

<u>European Magazine</u>, XXXIII (1798), 42.   12/104

"This Drama cannot be judged by common rules. It possesses
strong interest, but of a very improbable kind. The imagination rather than the judgment is influenced. In character or sentiment there is no novelty, but incident and
situation are produced with great effect. The introduction
of the aerial Being seems unnecessary; but it cannot be
denied but the silence and gestures of the Ghost operate
very forcibly on the audience. The tortures of guilt are
well displayed, and nothing in the Drama is to be found un-
favourable to morality."

<u>Monthly Mirror</u>, V (1798), 106-109.   12/105

<u>CS</u> "is not merely recommended to the town by <u>expensive
scenery</u>, <u>machinery</u>, <u>dresses</u>, <u>and</u> <u>decorations</u>". Notes that
it enjoys "extraordinary popularity" and attributes this
to "the happy management the author has exhibited in the
paraphernalia of his <u>spectre</u>, and to the air of romance
he has given to the <u>principal</u> situations".

<u>Monthly Review</u>, XXVI (1798), 96.   12/106

Complete item: "After having read this -- <u>What</u> <u>do</u> <u>you
call</u> <u>it</u>? -- a drama, it seems, it must be, <u>we</u> <u>cannot</u> but
<u>regret</u> that an author, whose talents seem designed for
better things, should condescend to make us stare at
<u>Groves</u>, and <u>Suits</u> <u>of</u> <u>Armour</u>, and <u>Pedestals</u> with <u>Names</u>,
and the <u>River</u> <u>Conway</u>, and in short, whatever presented
itself to his imagination. The whole, we found, depends
for success on the effect of the Castle Spectre; and
therefore all that we shall say is, that it seems ex-
tremely easy to <u>pen</u> <u>a</u> <u>ghost</u>, not indeed in <u>Shakespeare's</u>
manner, but of the silent kind, as in the play before us.
Mr. Lewis, we have no doubt, will draw after him a train

of imitators: but it is to be hoped that he himself will
retire from the regions of the marvellous."

5. The Love of Gain (1799)

ritical Review, 2nd ser., XXVII (1799), 231.   12/107

"If Mr. Lewis had published only his Monk, the world
would have given him credit for considerable, though mis-
applied, talents. That work attracted notice by its
faults; and the author was abused into popularity. But
he is now writing down his reputation; and, as this di-
luted satire (dilated is too weak a word) has neither the
high seasoning of the Monk, nor the stage effect of the
Castle Spectre to aid it, its naked dullness will find no
admirers."

6. Tales of Wonder (1800)

ales of Wonder. Written and Collected by M.G. Lewis. Bell,   12/108
   1800. Reviewed in British Critic, XVI (Dec., 1800), 681.

"We consider this production as a very daring imposition
on the public; nor can we forbear expressing our astonishment, that an individual in so distinguished a situation as a member of the British Parliament, should lend
his name to so palpable and mean a trick. A guinea is
charged for two thin volumes, which might, and which
ought, to have been comprised in one, and not a third of
the contents will be found to be original composition."
Lists some of the titles; calls "Grim White Woman" ."exceedingly stupid"; says "the best are those by Mr. Walter
Scott".

ales of Wonder. Written and Collected by M.G. Lewis. 2nd   12/109
   ed., Bell, 1801. Reviewed in Critical Review, 2nd ser.,
   XXXIV (Jan., 1802), 111-112.

"When Mr. Lewis sent his Monk into the world, we extracted
from it a beautiful elegy without a goblin; in the present
performance we are denied the power; there is nothing but

fiends and ghosts -- all is hideous -- all is disgusting."
"If the superstition, the filth and obscenity, . . . do
not curdle their [the readers'] blood, they will fare
better than we have done."

7. Tales of Terror,
with an Introductory Dialogue (1801)

British Critic, XVII (1801), 649.   12/11

"The reader will remember certain Tales of Wonder, which
we know not why, except for their eccentricity, caught
hold for a short time of public curiosity. Perhaps he may
not remember, but such there were; and these Tales of Terror appear, by their enormities, to be a well imagined and
well executed burlesque on the said Tales of Wonder." "As
to the Tales themselves, they are terrible indeed. . . . "

Critical Review, 2nd ser., XXXIV (1802), 112-113.   12/11

"We hardly know what opinion to form of the author of these
poems. Some of them are composed with so serious an air,
that we almost suspect them to be the progeny of the same
muse who sang, or rather screamed the Tales of Wonder;
whilst others are certainly written en badinant.   Be the
poet who he may, his church-yard tale is a most admirable
burlesque of Mr. Lewis's 'Cloud King'".

8. Adelmorn the Outlaw (1801)

British Critic, XVIII (1801), 545.   12/11

The author had been faced with the problem of making "a
change so sudden, in the mind of a guilty and hardened
culprit, understood by the audience. This Mr. Lewis obviated by his old expedient of a ghost; but his ghosts
are become to the public, what he seems to consider them
himself, rather ludicrous than terrible."

European Magazine, XXXIX (1801), 358-359.   12/113

"This piece is much in the style of The Castle Spectre by
the same Author; and ought to have been entitled More
Ghosts; for his Ghost, who in this play is a male, appeared three times during the performance. -- Without the
dialogue, which is wretched, Adelmorn would make a tolerable Ballet, or Pantomime; but as a Drama it is far below
criticism." Praises the music and scenery but reports
that the audience "hissed the dialogue almost from beginning to end". Some parts which MGL thought "witty and
humorous, were in reality absurd abortions". A revision
for the second performance has the ghost appearing but
once -- and then in a dream.

Monthly Mirror, XI (1801), 410-411.   12/114

"Mr. Lewis has presumed too much upon the favourable reception of his Castle Spectre. Though there was nothing
in the action of that drama to justify the appearance of
a supernatural visitant, there was a solemnity and good
management in its introduction, which made amends for the
breach of the Horation precept -- Nec Deus intersit, etc.
-- but the spectres in Adelmorn excite laughter instead of
awe."

Critical Review, 2nd ser., XXXIV (1802), 231-232.   12/115

"Mr. Lewis was not satisfied with success in the beaten
track; he introduces, as is usual with himself, praeternatural agents; what is worse, he introduces them uselessly
too -- and a useless ghost and vision have damned the Outlaw."

9. Alfonso, King of Castile (1801)

British Critic, XX (1802), 558.   12/116

"We have been so long used to meet with plays void of
originality, vigour, or any living spirit, that we hail
such an exception as this. . . . The catastrophe seems
to be faulty in both its forms; but so much dramatic
genius is displayed in the whole, that we doubt not that
the author will hereafter write a better Tragedy."

Critical Review, 2nd ser., XXXIV (1802), 355.   12/1

"The versification is in general bold and spirited, but
the thoughts are frequently too high-flown and over-
strained. The course of Mr. Lewis's reading may be traced
in this, as well as his other works; all his passions are expressed in ungovernable language; and the wild impetuosity
of Schiller and the German dramatists is visible in every
page. It appears as if the author were laying great violence on his inclinations in keeping the ghost off the
stage in the fourth and fifth acts, for he cannot forbear
making them visible to Ottilia and Amelrosa. We beg leave
to congratulate him on this victory over his prejudices;
and to remind him, that true fame consists in the approbation of the discerning few, not in the shouts of the
vulgar."

European Magazine, XLI (1802), 42-43.   12/1

"There is no striking novelty of character in this tragedy;
but many of its parts are sketched with ability and judgment, and there are scenes of considerable interest; yet,
if we were disposed to rigid criticism,we think that, as
a whole, there would be at least as much to condemn in it
as to praise." Views language and sentiments as "unequal";
alleges "great inconsistencies" in the plot.

Monthly Mirror, XIII (1802), 410-411.   12/1

Enthusiastic review of the second edition. "This edition
comprises all that was contained in the first (published
before the representation of the play), with the addition
of another preface, and the concluding scene as exhibited
on the stage. -- We are of opinion that this is the best
tragedy that has been produced in the theatres since Jephson's Count of Narbonne." Praises plot, characterization,
dramatic scenes. Notes that "suspense is one of the grand
attributes of tragedy, and here it is so well blended with
pity and terror, as to have the most powerful influence on
the feelings of the audience" but warns that the incidents
"are sometimes too nearly allied to horror".

10. The Captive (1803)

onthly Mirror, XV (1803), 266-267.   12/120

On stage, a madman attempts to seize the heroine. "This
effect was too strong for the feelings of the audience.
Two ladies fell into hysterics, the house was thrown into
confusion, some slight disapprobation was shown, and it
being the general sentiment that the piece was not a fit
subject for representation, the author immediately with-
drew it." Suggests that MGL "may have borrowed the idea
of his monodrama from Mrs. Wollstonecraft's Wrongs of
Woman".

11. Bravo of Venice (1805)

ritish Critic, XXV (1805), 201-203.   12/121

Though "the whole is attended with improbability, yet at
the same time it should not be forgotten, that . . . a
tale founded on the common events of domestic society is
but too apt to prove tedious and uninteresting." "The
language is bold and nervous, the tale not spun out to too
great a length, and the moral unexceptionable."

ritical Review, 3rd ser., V (1805), 252-256.   12/122

"Novels have commonly been divided into the pathetic, the
sentimental, and the humourous; but the writers of the
German school have introduced a new class, which may be
called the electric. Each chapter contains a shock; the
reader not only stares, but starts, at the close of every
paragraph; so that we cannot think the wit of a brother-
critic far fetched, when he compared that shelf in his library, on which the Tales of Wonder, the Venetian Bravo,
and other similar productions were piled, to a galvanic
battery." "Mr. Lewis possesses a fertile imagination and
considerable genius: we would therefore advise him to
quit the beaten track of imitation 'Ohe! jam satis est'.
We have had enough of ghostly visages, crawling worms,
death's heads and cross bones."

259

Review of the stage production. Says "the plot is from
a German novel, which has not only been translated in this
country, but even more than once dramatized. It was
dramatized on the French stage; the novel was translated
by Mr. Lewis; it was again dramatized at the Royal Circus;
and by Mr. Elliston, of Drury Lane, and also by an anonymous writer." Attributes most of its success to its
spectacle -- "The splendour of this part of the entertainment is beyond description. On the scenery, dresses, etc.,
immense sums must have been bestowed."

Monthly Mirror, XIX (1805), 177.   12/12

Complete item: "When we can, as we safely may, in the
present instance, affirm that Mr. Lewis's moral is liable
to no objection, we need use no further words to recommend
what he writes to all who love to be moved by the interest
of a well-told tale."

Rugantino, or the Bravo of Venice. 2nd ed. 1806. Reviewed   12/12
   in Critical Review, 3rd ser., VII (1806), 99.

"Walk in, ladies and gentlemen! Here are masks, coloured
lamps, musicians, conchs, cupids, and cockle-shells, Pan,
satyrs, and hamadryades, Neptune and Amphitrite, nereides,
tritons, artificial zephyrs, Pluto, Proserpine, and Lord
knows what. The dialogue of this piece is transcribed
nearly verbatim from the Bravo of Venice. . . ."

12. Feudal Tyrants (1806)

Critical Review, 3rd ser., XI (1807), 273-278.   12/12

Calls the Monk, "in some respects, considerably the best
of the works" of MGL. "It has more merit and less morality
than any of his other productions, though it has faults
enough even in a literary point of view." Here, in FT,
"sober reason is disgusted at the endless display of
ghosts, murders, conflagrations, and crimes. They are the
instruments with which children may be governed or
frightened, and by which grown people are liable to be affected exactly in proportion as they resemble children."

Complete item: "On seeing the name of Mr. Lewis, we hoped
that some taste had been exercised in the selection which
he has here made; but, on the contrary, never was heard
any thing so dismal as the direful croaking of this German raven!"

13. The Wood Daemon, or, The Clock Has Struck (1807)

"In point of splendour, variety, scenery, machinery, and
music, this afterpiece may rank with the most admired of
its species of entertainment: it also contains much interest of the terrific kind, arising from supernatural
agency. On its first performance, some very puerile dialogue disgraced it, and occasioned much disapprobation;
but the Author, with becoming deference to the public
opinion, pruned this part very considerably before the
second night. . . .   The plot appears to be founded on
the story of Lord Ronald, and the Grim White Woman, in Mr.
Lewis's Tales of Wonder."

14. Romantic Tales (1808)

A long coverage of each of the tales with a special eye to
sources. Praises MGL's genius but says "we confess he
would have met our wishes in a greater degree if, in his
former works, he had not indulged to so extravagant a
length in horrible pictures of human and supernatural de-
pravity; and yet, in expressing this slight disapprobation,
we would be understood to maintain, that we believe no
other living author is capable of producing pictures
equally awful, new, and sublime."

15. Adaptations, Imitations, Parodies, and Sources

Aurelio and Miranda, a play by James Boaden. Reviewed in   12/1
   Critical Review, 2nd ser., XXVI (1799), 112-115.

"This drama is founded upon the romance of the Monk; the
devil, however, is converted into a modest woman, and the
monk preserved from rape, incest, and damnation; incidents
which Mr. Boaden did not think altogether suitable for
dramatic representation. The play discovers not the
genius of the novel; nor, indeed, is it disgraced by its
faults."

--------. European Magazine, XXXV (1799), 41-42.   12/1

A long plot summary with the remark that "this piece is
avowedly formed on the celebrated novel of The Monk, by
Mr. Lewis, and the deviations from the original are such
as propriety points out, and requires. The effect, however, was not highly interesting, and there were improbabilities in the conduct of the performance that could
not escape the notice of the audience."

The Devil in Love. Translated from the French. Reviewed in   12/1
   British Critic, III (1794), 87-88.

Complete item: "This is a whimsical and not unamusing performance. We confess that the original never fell in our
way; and we have some reason to doubt whether it has
either appeared in Spanish or French. A noble Spaniard is
desirous of knowing necromancy; -- he is initiated, and
afterward followed by a lively, lovely sylph, who, becoming
enamoured of him, endeavours to mislead him, by flattering
his passions and sensuality; his virtue is at length tri-
umphant, and the Devil in Love confounded and defeated."
   The next month (III, 207), the reviewer identifies the
tale as from the French of M. Gazotte, recently translated
into English as Alvarez by Richardson. Notes "in Alvarez,
the hero becomes the dupe of the assumed virtues, which
the demon joins to the most alluring of personal charms;
and from this delusion, the opportunity arises of incul-
cating the necessity of not being imposed upon by the
appearance of virtue, for virtue itself."

The New Monk, a Romance, by R.S. Esq. Reviewed in <u>Critical</u>   12/133
    <u>Review</u>, 2nd ser., XXIV (1798), 356-357.

    "Vulgarity and indecency are frequently observable; and
    the description of the new monk's death is disgusting.
    The author's purpose would have been more successfully
    answered by a selection of certain passages.   The <u>whole</u>
    of the <u>Monk</u> cannot be injured by ridicule."

--------. Reviewed in the <u>Monthly Mirror</u>, VI (1798), 345.   12/134

    Complete item: "A parody, but not a successful one, upon
    Mr. Lewis's admirable romance.   The writing is bad; the
    humour is worse.   Even on the score of morality, R.S. has
    no advantage over the <u>old</u> monk: -- for his desire of bur-
    lesque has led him into indelicate descriptions of a very
    gross nature; and, with respect to <u>religion</u>, whether it is
    more injurious to her interests to expose the hypocrisy of
    a <u>methodist</u> <u>preacher</u>, or to represent the gradual effects
    of temptation upon a Roman Catholic friar, naturally
    haughty, vain, and sensual; and who regards only the super-
    stitious ceremonies of worship, so far as they minister
    to his pride and personal consequence?"

Rodolpho, A Poetical Romance, by James Atkinson.   Reviewed in   12/135
    <u>Monthly Review</u>, XXXVII (1802), 101-102.

    A satire of Lewis's verses "Alonzo. . . ." and "some Ger-
    man books of horror".   But, says the reviewer, MGL "had
    already burlesqued his own ingenious doggrel, in the bal-
    lad of 'Sally Green'".   "It seems to have been the ambi-
    tion of some late authors, to revive the terrors and super-
    stitions of the nursery; and it has been the momentary
    weakness of the public to lend some degree of attention to
    their efforts: but, in those circles which may be truly
    denominated literary, this vicious taste has never been
    admitted. . . ."

Tales of the Devil.   From the original Gibberish, by Pro-   12/136
    fessor Lumpwitz, S.U.S. and C.A.C. in the University of
    Snorinberg.   Reviewed in <u>British Critic</u>, XVII (1801),
    649-650.

    "These also [including 12/110] are a ridicule on the <u>Tales</u>
    <u>of Wonder</u>, and are ornamented with a very humourous front-
    ispiece. . . .   The name of Lumpwitz we recollect to be
    taken from certain burlesque lives of painters . . . at-

263

tributed to Mr. Beckford." "The tales seem to have been written rather for a frolic than with any ambition of poetic fame. . . ."

Tales of Superstition and Chivalry. Reviewed in British Critic, XXI (1803), 78.   12/1

"This beautiful little book belongs, as its title implies, to the family of Tales of Wonder. It is printed without a name; but, if we are not misinformed, it is the production of Miss Bannerman, already known for poetical talents. The Tales abound with fancy; but it is fancy perverted to the purpose of raising only horror, and raising it by preternatural agency."

The Three Monks. Translated from the French by H.J. Starrett. Reviewed in Critical Review, 2nd ser., XXXIX (1803), 235.   12/1

"It does not so properly belong to reviewers to take cognisance of this work, as it does to the society for the suppression of vice and immorality." "These volumes are preceded by a dedication to M.G. Lewis, esq. M.P. It is not the fault of that gentleman that an author should dedicate his ribaldry to him: yet we are convinced he must be sadly mortified at his former abuse of his respectable abilities, when it has given encouragement to this pretended translator to offer him, as a tribute of admiration, a contemptible jumble of absurdity and obscenity."

XIII

WILLIAM BECKFORD

(1760-1844)

a.

Selected Texts

. Biographical Memoirs of Extraordinary Painters (1780)

961 - Biographical Memoirs of Extraordinary Painters.   13/1
British Culture on Microcards. Ser. 2, no. 50. Louis-
ville: Lost Cause Press, 1961.

A microcard of the second edition of 1780 from Robson's
of London.

969 - Biographical Memoirs of Extraordinary Painters.   13/2
Edited, and with an introduction and notes by Robert J.
Gemmett. Rutherford: Fairleigh Dickinson Univ. Press,
1969.

The first reprint in 130 years.

   2. Dreams, Waking Thoughts and Incidents (1783)   13/3

928 - Dreams, Waking Thoughts and Incidents. Vol. 1 of The
Travel Diaries of William Beckford. Edited, and with an
introduction by Guy Chapman. 5 vols. Cambridge: Univ.
Press, 1928. (Reprinted, New York: Kraus, 1972.)

Reprinted from the suppressed edition of 1783. An appendix
notes textual variations between Dreams (1783) and Italy
(1834).

1971 - Dreams, Waking Thoughts and Incidents. Edited, and   13/4
       with an introduction and notes by Robert J. Gemmett.
       Rutherford: Fairleigh Dickinson Univ. Press, 1971.

       "Practically a verbatim reprint of the suppressed edition
       of 1783."

                        3. Vathek (1786)

1893 - Vathek. Introduction by Dr. [Richard] Garnett [1893].   13/5
       London: William Glaisher, 1924.

       Based on the third English edition of 1816.

1922 - Vathek. Introduction by R[eginald] Brimley Johnson.   13/6
       Abbey Classics. Boston: Small, Maynard, [1922].

1923 - Vathek. Introduction by J[ohn] G[ibson] L[ockhart].   13/7
       London: Allan, [1923].

1928 - Vathek. Introduction by Ben Ray Redman. Illustrated   13/8
       by Mahlon Blaine. New York: John Day, 1928.

1929 - Vathek. Translated by Herbert B. Grimsditch. Illus-   13/9
       trated by Marion V. Dorn.   Bloomsbury: Nonesuch, 1929.

       A new translation based on the revised third edition of
       1815. In England, 1,050 copies were offered by Nonesuch;
       in the U.S.A., 500 copies were distributed through Ran-
       dom House.

1929 - Vathek, with the Episodes of Vathek. Edited, and with   13/10
       an introduction and notes by Guy Chapman. 2 vols. Edition
       limited to 1000 copies. Cambridge: Constable, 1929.

       A reprint of the French language Paris edition of 1787
       into which Chapman has inserted the episodes. This addi-
       tion "has necessitated the alteration of a few words,
       but no more than to make the narrative consecutive".

930 - Vathek, in Shorter Novels: Eighteenth Century [1930]. 13/11
Edited, and with an introduction by Philip Henderson.
Everyman's. New York: Dutton, 1971.

Paperback. Bound with Otranto and Rasselas.

931 - Vathek, in Three Eighteenth Century Romances [1931]. 13/12
Introduction by Harrison R. Steeves. New York: Scribner's, 1971.

Paperback. Includes Otranto and Romance of the Forest.

958 - Vathek. Translated, and with an introduction by Her- 13/13
bert B. Grimsditch. Illustrated with lithographs by
Edward Bawden. London: Folio, 1958.

966 - Vathek, in Three Gothic Novels. Edited, and with an 13/14
introduction by E.F. Bleiler. New York: Dover, 1966.

Paperback. Text is that of the 1893 edition as edited by
Garnett (13/5).

968 - Vathek, in Three Gothic Novels. Edited by Peter Fair- 13/15
clough. Introduction by Mario Praz. Baltimore: Penguin, 1968.

Paperback. Text follows that of the fourth edition of
1823.

970 - Vathek. Edited, and with an introduction by Roger 13/16
Lonsdale. Oxford English Novels. New York: Oxford Univ.
Press, 1970.

Text is of the second issue of the 1816 edition.

971 - Vathek. Menston: Scolar, 1971. 13/17

Facsimile reprint of the first edition printed by J.
Johnson, London, 1786. Introduced with a new one-page
note.

1971 - The History of the Caliph Vathek, Including the "Epi- 13/18
    sodes of Vathek". Introduction by Lin Carter. Ballantine
    Adult Fantasy Series. New York: Ballantine, 1971.

    Paperback. Claims to include the original notes -- yet
    they are edited and pared down. "Never have the Episodes
    been inserted into any edition of Vathek ever published!
    That is, not until this one." Introduction contains addi-
    tional errors.

1972 - Vathek. The English Translation by Samuel Henley 13/19
    (1786) and the French Editions of Lausanne and Paris
    (1787). Introduction by Robert G. Gemmett. Delmar:
    Scholar's Facsimiles & Reprints, 1972.

    Facsimile reprints of the three editions.

                4. Modern Novel Writing (1796)
                          and
                   5. Azemia (1797)

1970 - Modern Novel Writing (1796) and Azemia (1797). Intro- 13/20
    diction by Herman Mittle Levy, Jr. Gainesville: Scho-
    lar's Facsimiles & Reprints, 1970.

    The publisher calls this edition "Four Volumes in One",
    and prints four facsimile pages on one 6" x 9" page.

                6. Episodes of Vathek (1912)

1912 - The Episodes of Vathek. Translated by Sir Frank T. 13/21
    Marzials. Introduction by Lewis Melville. London:
    Stephen Swift, 1912.

    The debut in English of the episodes. Includes the ori-
    ginal French version also.

1922 - The Episodes of Vathek. Translated by Sir Frank T.   13/22
       Marzials. Introduction by Lewis Melville. Abbey Clas-
       sics. London: Chapman & Dodd, [1922].

       As above (13/21), but without the French originals.

1960 - "The Third Episode of Vathek: The Story of Princess   13/23
       Zulkais and the Prince Kalilah", in Clark Ashton Smith,
       ed., The Abominations of Yondo. Sauk City: Arkham
       House, 1960.

       In a collection of seventeen tales, mainly from the pulps
       of the 1930's.

                        7. Miscellaneous

1928 - The Travel Diaries of William Beckford of Fonthill.   13/24
       With a memoir and notes by Guy Chapman. 2 vols. London:
       Constable, 1928.

       Contains: (I)Dreams, Waking Thoughts and Incidents, and
       (II)Sketches of Spain and Portugal; Recollections of an
       Excursion to the Monasteries of Alcobaça and Batalha.

1930 - The Vision and Liber Veritatis. Edited, and with an   13/25
       introduction and notes by Guy Chapman. Edition limited
       to 750 copies. London: Constable, 1930.

       Two previously unpublished items. Vision, written in
       1777, represents WB's earliest writing and contains
       Gothic touches.

1954 - The Journal of William Beckford in Portugal and Spain,   13/26
       1787-1788. Edited, and with an introduction and notes
       by Boyd Alexander. London: Rupert Hart-Davis, 1954.

       Pieced together from materials held by the Hamiltons.
       This journal was the basis for the 1834, Italy; With
       Sketches of Spain and Portugal.

                             269

1957 - Life at Fonthill, 1807-1822. With Interludes in Paris   13/27
and London. From the Correspondence of William Beckford.
Translated and edited by Boyd Alexander. London: Rupert
Hart-Davis, 1957.

A collection of hitherto unpublished letters, most of
which were written in Italian and directed to WB's close
friend Gregorio Fellipi Franchi. Alexander offers lavish
footnotes, a general introduction and separate introductions for each chronological group, but acts as censor
and deletes passages which are "too scabrous to quote".

1960 - Beckford's 1794 Journal. Edited, and with an intro-   13/28
duction by Boyd Alexander. In Howard B. Gotlieb, William
Beckford of Fonthill: Writer, Traveller, Collector,
Caliph, 1760-1844. New Haven: Yale Univ. Press, 1960.

                            b.

                       Bibliographies

Allibone, S[amuel] Austin. A Critical Dictionary of English   13/29
Literature and British and American Authors Living and
Deceased. From the Earliest Accounts to the Latter Half
of the Nineteenth Century. 3 vols. Philadelphia: Lippincott, 1871. (Reprinted, Detroit: Gale Research,
1965.)

Chapman, Guy, and John Hodgkin. A Bibliography of William   13/30
Beckford of Fonthill. Bibliographia: Studies in Book
History and Book Structure 1750-1900. London: Constable,
1930.

Includes: (1)published books, (2)attributed works, (3)un-
published prose writings (both original and translations),
(4)verses, (5)music, and (6)portraits of WB. With careful descriptions of the various editions of Vathek.

Gemmett, Robert J. "An Annotated Checklist of the Works of   13/31
William Beckford", PBSA, LXI (1967), 243-258.

"An enumerative bibliography of the various editions of
Beckford's works from 1780, the year his first book was

printed, to the present day." Includes foreign language
editions, offers brief notes on textual and publication
matters, etc.

Gemmett, Robert J. "William Beckford: Bibliographical Add-   13/32
enda", BB, XXV, no. 3 (1967), 62-64.

Praises Parreaux's study (A/59) and supplements and updates his bibliography by providing almost 100 entries
ranging from 18th-century articles to pieces published
after P's cutoff date.

Moulton, Charles Wells, ed. The Library of Literary Cri-   13/33
ticism of English and American Authors. 8 vols. Buffalo: Moulton, 1901-1905. (Reprinted, New York: P.
Smith, 1935.)

Patrick, David, and J. Liddell. Chamber's Cyclopaedia of   13/34
English Authors in the English Tongue from the Earliest
Times till the Present Day, with Specimens of their
Writings. 3 vols. London: Chamber's, [1922-1938].

Summers, Montague. A Gothic Bibliography [1941]. New York: 13/35
Russell & Russell, 1964.

Tobin, James E. Eighteenth Century English Literature and   13/36
its Cultural Background: A Bibliography. New York:
Fordham Univ. Press, 1939.

Watson, George, ed. The New Cambridge Bibliography of   13/37
English Literature. 3 vols. Cambridge: Univ. Press,
1969 --.

c.

Full-Length Studies

Alexander, Boyd. England's Wealthiest Son: A Study of   13/38
William Beckford. London: Centaur, 1962.

Presented not as a biography, but rather as a study which
draws on new source material and alters somewhat the standard view of WB. He was not England's wealthiest son, did
not possess the wealth generally attributed to him, and
although extravagant, lost capital through lawsuits, claims
from his father's illegitimate children, natural disasters,
and fluctuations in the price of sugar. Sees Vathek as
"clearly autobiographical"; claims WB probably innocent of
sodomy charge of 1784 and "wrote obsessively about sex because he was repressed and possibly impotent". Stresses
formative role of the father; notes that WB and Charlotte
Smith were the only radical novelists from the upper
classes; sees WB as an early Romantic, much maligned by
propaganda.

Brockman, H[arold] A.N. The Caliph of Fonthill. Introduc-   13/39
tion by Nikolaus Pevsner. London: Werner Laurie, 1956.

Surely the definitive work on Fonthill, this specialized
study by an architect treats WB as builder and landscaper,
investigates the relationship between the Caliph and
Wyatt, points out that neither knew much about the principles of Gothic, and shows that, in architecture, WB
was dominated more by emotion than by intellect. Pevsner
notes WB's "obsession with towers" and contends that
"Fonthill was the first neo-Gothic building to create sentiments of amazement, of shock, even of awe. The effects
of Strawberry Hill are playful, those of Fonthill sensational."

Chapman, Guy. Beckford [1937]. 2nd ed. London: Rupert   13/4C
Hart-Davis, 1952.

Contends that WB, with an eye towards posterity, took
great liberties with his letters and papers. Some items
are completely false, others revised, distorted, or re-
written at later dates. Doubt becomes cast on much ma-

terial upon which both Melville (13/48) and Oliver (13/49) drew. Also, Chapman admits that his own early essays on WB and his introduction to Travel Diaries, Vathek, and Vision contain errors. In the preface to the second edition of 1952, Chapman concedes that his earlier denial of WB's homosexuality was probably in error, as new evidence seems to indicate "homosexuality at a considerably later date". The 300 page text is almost exclusively biographical, avoids literary criticism, and does not dwell on physical aspects of Fonthill. Probably the "standard life" but should be supplemented with Alexander's work (13/38).

Gemmett, Robert James. "William Beckford with the Pictur-   13/41
esque: A Study of Fonthill". Unpublished doctoral dissertation, Syracuse Univ., 1967.

Modern criticism has often centered on Fonthill Abbey and neglected the grounds and landscaping. A common view is that the edifice represents the product of an overly-rich eccentric. Here, Gemmett shows that "not only was Fonthill received as one of the most enchanting landed estates in its day, it was also recognized by many as illustrative of the new style of informal landscape within which a magnificent Gothic building was successfully incorporated as an appropriate climax to the design." Fonthill was not conceived in imitation of scenes from Claude, Poussin, and Salvator, but is "an important example of the successful application of the technique of landscape painting to the field of landscape gardening". Also covers biography, looks in detail at the picturesque, discusses Fonthill as a picturesque composition, and points out the "observation of the surface of objects" and the "visual appeal" of Vathek, Vision, and Biographical Memoirs. Includes a bibliography of works by and on WB.

Gotlieb, Howard B. William Beckford of Fonthill: Writer,   13/42
Traveller, Collector, Caliph, 1760-1844. A Brief Narrative and Catalogue of An Exhibition to Mark the Two
Hundredth Anniversary of Beckford's Birth. With the Previously Unpublished Journal Kept by William Beckford in
1794. Edited by Boyd Alexander. New Haven: Yale Univ.
Press, 1960.

There are seven sections: (1)"WB Sr.", (2)"The Life and Works of WB", (3)"Books Attributed to WB", (4)"B as the Caliph of Fonthill Abbey", (5)"B the Collector" (6)"Books about WB", (7)"Appendices". Each section has a one or two page introduction and a list of items on display.

Gregory, W[illiam]. The Beckford Family: Reminiscences of   13/43
Fonthill Abbey and Lansdown Tower [1887]. 2nd. ed., revised and enlarged. Bath: The Bath Chronicle Offices,
1898.

A chatty book which abounds in all types of miscellanies.
Unfortunately, practically nothing is footnoted, and
there are many errors.

The Hamilton Palace Libraries. Catalogue of the First Por-   13/44
tion of the Beckford Library, Removed From Hamilton Palace
which will be Sold by Auction by Messrs. Sotheby, Wil-
kinson and Hodge, Auctioneers of Literary Property and
Works Illustrative of the Fine Arts, at their House, No.
13 Wellington Street, Strand, W.C. on Friday, the 30th
Day of June, 1882, and Eleven following Days, at One
o'clock Precisely. May be Viewed Three Days Prior, and
Catalogues Had. London: [1822].

The two page introduction notes the "splendid bindings",
the "quaint and often sarcastic notes written with a pencil on the fly leaves of almost the greater portion of his
books", and the great number of travel books, "including
many relating to America".

Lansdown, [Henry], Lord. Recollections of the Late William   13/45
Beckford of Fonthill, Wilts and Lansdown, Bath. [1893].
Facsimile reprint edition limited to 750 copies. Bath:
Kingsmead Reprints, [n.d.].

This brief work recounts visits to WB at Lansdown Crescent. The Caliph is seen as the gracious host, surrounded
by rare books, objects of art, and old masters. Gives a
description of his "natural" garden complete with artificial ruins and trees from all parts of the world and a
description of Fonthill in 1844.

Magnificent Effects at Fonthill Abbey, Wilts. To Be Sold   13/46
By Auction, by Mr. Christie, on the Premises, on Tues-
day, September 17, 1822, and Nine Following Days, (Sun-
day Excepted) Beginning Each Day Punctually at Twelve
"'Clock. [n.p., n.d.]

A 95 page sale catalogue which itemizes and briefly describes under the headings: "China", "Rich oriental
china", "Curious oriental porcelain", "Unique specimens
of Japan lacquer on wood", "Furniture", "Ornamental furniture", "Superb silver gilt plate", and "Pictures".

Mahmoud, Fatma Moussa, ed. William Beckford of Fonthill,   13/47
1760-1844. Bicentenary Essays [1960]. Port Washington:
Kennikat, 1972.

A collection of six essays (13/55, 13/64, 13/115, 13/117,
13/132, 13/148) together with a short note on the Yale
exhibition (13/42) and a supplement to its bibliography.

Melville, Lewis. The Life and Letters of William Beckford   13/48
of Fonthill (Author of "Vathek") [1910]. [Folcroft]:
Folcroft, 1970.

The second major work on Beckford, this study draws together earlier efforts and offers hitherto unpublished letters. The majority of the text is, in fact, composed of
letters and Meville has done a masterly job of arranging,
stringing together, and providing explanatory notes. The
result is a highly complimentary biography which suppresses,
denies, or glosses over unpleasantries.

Oliver, J[ohn] W. The Life of William Beckford. London: 13/49
Oxford Univ. Press, 1932.

Draws on Redding (13/50) and Melville (13/48), adds some
new materials, and is, Boyd Alexander (13/38) writes,
"fair and sympathetic". Emphasis falls on biography but
does not dwell on eccentricities nor does it deal with
literary criticism. Draws heavily on the letters and embodies a high percentage of direct quotation.

[Redding, Cyrus]. Memoirs of William Beckford of Fonthill,   13/50
Author of "Vathek". 2 vols. London: Skeet, 1859.

Published fifteen years after Beckford's death, this work
lacks objectivity and presents supposedly first-hand information which has since proven false. No mention of
eccentricities or homosexuality; WB seen as moral, proper,
and religious. Says WB told him in 1835 that Vathek was
written at a single sitting, three days and two nights.
Also the Caliph said: "The party who was the first translator of Vathek into English I never knew; it was tolerably
well done."

Sitwell, Sacheverell. Beckford and Beckfordism. Edition   13/51
limited to 265 copies. London: Duckworth, 1930.

This 32 page tract does a lot of philosophising, general-
izes about the Romantic era in Europe, but says very little about Beckford. He is credited as a pioneer of the
Gothic revival but Sitwell says that "his real contribution to literature is contained in the Letters from Spain
and Portugal and in the excursion to Alcobaca and Batalha".
Says WB's "whole lifework", in writing and building, "was
broken in two by the French Wars".

Summers, Peter. William Beckford: Some Notes on His Life in   13/52
Bath, 1822-1844. With a Catalogue of the Exhibition in
the Holburne of Menstrie Museum, 14 June to 3 July 1966,
compiled by Philippa Bishop. London: Curwen, 1966.

The ten pages of notes deal with WB's residences in Bath,
the Lansdown tower, the walk, grotto, and gardens. Proceeds of sale of booklet will be devoted to restoration
of the tower. Nine pages of advertisements offer more information. Examples: "Beckford's house wired throughout
with Fireproof Mineral Insulated Cables by _____"; "_____
are at present engaged on the installation of central heat-
ing at 19-20 Lansdown Crescent which includes the Beckford
Library".

d.

Articles, Essays, and Introductions

"Account of the Christmas Festivities at Fonthill", European   13/53
Magazine, XXXI (1797), 4-6.

"A correspondent who was present" describes the Twelfth
Day party at Fonthill. WB invited his construction crew
of 300 men, 700 neighborhood poor, and had roasted an ox,
and ten sheep. "Bread and strong beer" were provided for
the 10,000 spectators of the entertainment. The indigent
received money, blankets, and fuel.

"Account of the Works Now Executing at Fonthill", European   13/54
Magazine, XXXI (1797), 104-107.

Says that WB's construction was a plan "for the sake of
giving bread to the poor of an extensive neighbourhood,
destitute of manufactures and that through the laudable
medium of their own labour and industry". Discusses plant-
ing, reforestation, the garden, the wall, and the abbey.
Believes Fonthill is of a Gothic design since it represents a memorial tribute to WB's ancestors who first oc-
cupied that site.

Alexander, Boyd. "The Decay of Beckford's Genius", in Fatma   13/55
Moussa, ed., William Beckford of Fonthill, 1760-1844.
Bicentenary Essays [1960]. Port Washington: Kennikat,
1972.

Precocious and prolific, WB began writing at sixteen, but
his literary output declined in both quantity and quality.
Alexander probes and suggests some reasons -- bad luck,
early discouragement, boredom, bitterness, remorse, but
more than anything else, his internal struggle with homosexuality. Views Episodes as autobiographical; traces the
WB-Courtenay relationship; suggests that the youth may have
been the corrupter.

--------. "William Beckford of Fonthill", YULG, XXXV (1961),   13/56
161-169.

Notes WB's fondness for America, his republicanism, his
humanism, his turn against the French Revolution. Discusses Fonthill with special emphasis on the grounds "because they were unique and very much an expression of the
Romantic movement, and also because they were completely
his own work and conception".

--------. "William Beckford, Man of Taste", History Today,   13/57
X (1960), 686-694.

Defends WB against Hazlitt's attack on taste (13/103) and
asserts that "in at least two directions Beckford's taste
in pictures and objects d'art was well ahead of his time
-- in respect both of Primitives and of French 18th century furniture." Similarly, WB's interest in his contemporaries, Turner, West and the Cozens is noteworthy.

Armour, Richard W. "The Caliph of Fonthill", Reading and   13/58
Collecting, I (1937), 9-10.

An attempt to present a balanced picture of WB, not just
to look at eccentricities. Sees the builder of Fonthill
not as a man bent on achieving scenery, but rather as one
with a love of seclusion. Praises him as a collector;
calls Vathek his best work; asserts that its "delightful
humour, derived by way of extravagance and understatement"
is often overlooked.

Babb, James T. "William Beckford of Fonthill", YULG, XLI   13/59
(1966), 60-69.

Sees WB as a life-long homosexual, a friendless outcast,
an excellent linguist, good pianist, and art collector of
good taste. Calls the travel diaries "his best writing";
notes that "it is not generally known . . . that Beckford
must have seriously considered moving to the United States".
Comments on the Yale Beckford holdings.

Bell, C.F. "William Beckford", TLS (May 13, 1944), p. 235.   13/60

Contests an earlier article (13/69) which claimed that the
Caliph destroyed, defaced or falsified many of his papers.
Bell denies this saying that in 1922 he went through the
Beckford papers and suggests that he dug deeper and saw
things Melville (13/48) didn't. "There is now no good
reason for disinterring Beckford's own memoranda corrobo-
rating contemporary gossip -- but the material is there."
He thinks it "extraordinary" that WB's daughter did not
destroy these papers and believes that B's ."colossal
vanity" prevented him from doing so.
   A week later, in the May 20, 1944, issue, page 247, the
writer of the first article (13/69) refers Bell to Chapman's Beckford (13/40) where the "whole matter of the sup-
pressions and falsifications in the Beckford papers is
thoroughly discussed".

Belloc, Hilaire. "On Vathek", in his A Conversation With An   13/61
Angel and Other Essays. New York: Harper, 1929.

Calls Beckford "one of the vilest men of his time"; says
vice drove him "to something like madness". Finds Vathek
"one of the most profounding moral books of the world"
and implies that Providence had Beckford write it as a
warning to others.

Bloom, Margaret. "William Beckford's Vathek", University of   13/62
California Chronicle, XXXIII (1931), 424-431.

Covers WB's family backgrounds, his youthful studies, the
disgrace, the building of Fonthill, the treachery of Henley, the lost episodes reunited. Takes no special stand
and draws on previously published works.

Brown, Wallace Cable. "Prose Fiction and English Interest in   13/63
the Near East, 1775-1825", PMLA, LIII (1938), 827-836.

A general coverage which offers a few general remarks on
Vathek, "the best English imitation of a genuine eastern
tale". "At first", Brown says, "the story was generally
considered a typical 18th century moral tale", but later,
"interest in Vathek was shifted to the accuracy of its
picture of the Near East."

Bullough, Geoffrey. "Beckford's Early Travels and His Dream   13/64
of Delusion", in Fatma Moussa Mahmoud, ed., William Beckford of Fonthill, 1760-1844. Bicentenary Essays [1960].
Port Washington: Kennikat, 1972.

Discusses WB as a traveller and notes how his published accounts differ in tone over the years. Compares him with
Smollett, Shelley, Byron, Coleridge, and De Quincey. Sees
Dreams as the "fluent expression of a personality exploit-
ing its sensibility to the full".

Carter, John. "The Lausanne Edition of Beckford's Vathek",   13/65
Library, 4th ser., XVII (1937), 369-394.

Follows May's (A/44) suggestion that WB had Henley's translation retranslated to French. Suggests that the translator was the Rev. David Levade, professor of theology
and ecclesiastical history at Lausanne, a scholar who had
translated from English to French at least twelve works,
including Tristram Shandy.

--------. "Beckford and Vathek; Ged and Stereotype",   13/66
Library, 5th ser., XVIII (1963), 308-309.

Reverses his earlier stand (13/65). Admits that Parreaux
(A/59) demolishes "the May-Burdon-Muller-Carter theory".

279

Carter, John. "Two Beckford Collections", Colophon, NS, I 13/67
(1939), 67-74.

Discusses the collection of Rowland Burdon-Muller of Cambridge, Mass. and that of James T. Babb of New Haven,
Conn.

Chapman, Guy. "Beckford and Al Raoui", TLS (Oct. 31, 1936), 13/68
p. 887.

Adds four points to Oliver's (13/49) argument that Al
Raoui, a small English translation of 1799, might be by
Henley, but is not by Beckford.

[--------]. "Beckford the Caliph: A Traveller of Two Worlds, 13/69
Passion and Fantasy", TLS (May 6, 1944), p. 222.

Sees a "natural dichotomy" in WB's character. "His style
reflects the measured flow of the fading Augustans, his
matter the dawn of the Romantic Revival." Vathek was
written in two modes. "The first two-thirds are conceived
in boisterous spirits, with enormous relish for the buffooneries of the serio-comic Caliph and his grotesque
Giaour." Then, WB's views darken; the comic mood of his
earlier writings disappear and his own menaced existence
enters the pages. "It is permissible to believe that
during the period from his marriage in 1783 to the death
of his wife and the surreptitious publication by Henley
of Vathek in the summer of 1786, Beckford was living in
two worlds, one of reality, the other, pays des chimères,
and that his imagination made him take the dream for the
real world."

--------. "Memoir of William Beckford", in his The Travel- 13/70
Diaries of William Beckford of Fonthill. 2 vols. London:
Constable, 1928.

Proposing to clarify the Beckford-Courtenay affair, Chapman suggests WB was innocent of allegations, and "at the
worst to have been overreachingly silly". But he thinks
WB was extravagant and wasteful, lacked "spontaneous generosity", had a "deficient sense of humour" and lived, all
in all, "a wasted life". The letters of Dreams were probably not written to anyone in particular but were intended
for publication. If there were actual correspondence, GC
suggests Cozens, and not Courtenay as recipient. (In the
1930 introduction to The Vision and Liber Veritatis [13/

25], GC corrects some biographical errors which are presented here in TD. See also 13/40.)

Chapman, Guy. "The Story of Al Raoui", TLS (Nov. 25, 1960),   13/71
p. 759.

In an appendix to Gotlieb's Centenary Catalogue (13/42),
Alexander contests Chapman's views on the authorship of
Al Raoui. Here, Chapman clarifies his statement of 24
years ago. WB, he says, translated from Arabic into
French, Histoire d'Alroui and Suite de l'Histoire d'Alroui,
but this "does not confirm that the English publication of
The Story of Al Raoui, was published by Beckford or that
he had any hand in it".

Crallan, Hugh. "Beckford in Bath", Architectural Review,   13/72
CXLIII (1968), 204-208.

Contains thirteen photos, a map, and a very brief text
based on research done by Peter Summers (13/52). Interesting points: H.E. Goodridge was the architect; WB had
the staircase (at No. 19) tunnel-vaulted in timber; much
of the Lansdown Tower is cast iron; the grounds feature
"dramatic progressions and contrasts between openness and
enclosure, small and large scale -- ruggedness and suavity
-- the works of man and nature"; a miniature Moslem summer
house was built behind the main house.

"The Episodes of Vathek", Blackwood's, CXCII (1912), 699-701.   13/73

A general introduction to the recently published episodes. Speculates on a source for Vathek in Wortley Montague's MSS.

Folsom, James K. "Beckford's Vathek and the Tradition of   13/74
Oriental Satire", Criticism, VI (1964), 53-69.

Sees Vathek as satire on the Oriental tale just as Modern
Novel Writing is satire on Gothic and sentimental novel,
and Biographical Memoirs is of the biographical method of
artistic criticism. WB's usual method of satire is "the
reductio ad absurdum of the artificialities within a literary tradition". Thus, the extravagances of Vathek "are
signs of a literary extravagance within this tradition
rather than of psychological infirmities on the part of
the author".

281

Furst, Herbert. "Two Famous Connoisseurs and Collectors --   13/75
Beaumont and Beckford", Apollo, XXXV (1942), 59-61,
75, 81-84.

Compares Sir George Beaumont (1753-1827) with Beckford
(1760-1844). Concludes that "Beaumont's 'taste' was correct, that is to say intellectual; Beckford was both more
emotional and more intelligent. He relied, that is to say,
on his own judgment, and not on supposedly abstract laws.
Beaumont was more public spirited and altruistic; Beckford
was entirely self-centered; his altruism took the form of
responsibility for his employees and the poor."

G., W. "Candid Critique on the Architecture of Fonthill   13/76
Abbey", Gentleman's Magazine, NS, XCII, pt. 2 (1822),
491-494.

A highly technical look at the abbey. Points out deviations from true Gothic but notes that there are strong
reasons to believe that definite rules for this style
never existed, and in any case, modern conveniences dictated certain structural alterations.

Garnett, Dr. [Richard]. Introduction to Vathek [1893].   13/77
London: William Glaisher, 1924. (Reprinted in his
Essays of an Ex-Librarian [1901]. Essay Index Reprint
Series. Freeport: Books for Libraries, 1970.)

Debunks the one-sitting story; offers extracts of letters
between Henley and WB; speculates upon reasons for the
unauthorized edition; compares extracts of the Paris and
Lausanne editions; sees Vathek as mixture of the "lucidity"
and "sarcastic persiflage" of the 18th century with the
"spirit of vague unrest and yearning melancholy" of the
Romantics.

--------. "William Beckford", in Leslie Stephen and Sidney   13/78
Lee, eds., Dictionary of National Biography. 63 vols.
London: Smith, Elder, 1885 --.

Vathek "combines two things most difficult of alliance --
the fantastic and the sublime". WB "paints nature like
Salvator, and courts like Watteau. His other works make
us bitterly regret the curse of wealth and idleness which
converted a true son of the muses into an eccentric dilettante."

Gemmett, Robert J. "The Beckford Book Sale of 1808", PBSA,   13/79
LXIV (1970), 127-164.

In addition to the 1882 Hamilton Place sale and the 1823
Fonthill sale, there were earlier disposals in 1804, 1808,
and 1817. Gemmett, in this the first of three articles
devoted to these sales, reprints the complete 1808 catalogue of 321 items.

--------. "Beckford in the Saleroom", TLS (Nov. 17, 1966),   13/80
p. 1056.

Not only did Hodgkin leave his Beckford book collection to
Bodleian, he gave also his own personal notes, essays, and
transcripts relating to bibliographical studies and other
work on WB. Offers a summary of these items.

--------. "The Beckford Library Sale of 1817", LC, XXXVII   13/81
(1971), 37-69.

The sale of 1817 was owing to WB's financial decline and
the economic depression of 1815-16. Unlike the 1804 and
1808 sales, the one of 1817 was made in B's name.

--------. "The Behnes' Portrait of William Beckford", EA   13/82
XIX (1966), 261-262.

Contests Boyd Alexander's statement (13/27) that the
Behnes' drawing of WB represents "what Beckford really
looked like". Says "at best", it is "a fanciful exaggeration and not a faithful portrait of the author of Vathek
at 56". Contends that Chapman's idea (13/30) that the
spectacles and baldness were a disguise should   stand.

--------. "The Birth Date of William Beckford", AN&Q, VI   13/83
(1968), 149-150.

When was WB born? Redding said 1759; Garnett claimed 1
October, 1760; Melville also argued 1 October, 1760;
Chapman asserted 29 September, 1760. Oliver and Parreaux
back away from the argument. Now, Gemmett sides with
Chapman and claims 29 September, 1760. He bases this date
on Mrs. Beckford's obituary and on a letter she wrote
mentioning her son's twelfth birthday -- on Michaelmas
day -- 29 September.

Gemmett, Robert J. "The Caliph Vathek From England and the   13/84
     Continent to America", ABC, XVIII (1968), 12-19.

     Concentrates mainly on problems of editions and sorts out
     scholarship. Marcel May (A/44) argued that WB had Henley's
     English version retranslated to French since he possessed
     no copy of the MS. Carter (13/65) bolstered this error,
     but Parreaux (A/59) shows that WB did indeed possess a
     French copy of the MS; moreover, the anglicisms are not
     flaws of the translator, but traces of B's imperfect
     French. Thus, the Lausanne edition is B's earliest draft
     of V. Vathek was well received in England, denounced in
     the USA, but its influence is seen in Hawthorne and Mel-
     ville. Even Harriet Beecher Stowe cited it as a master-
     piece of imaginative literature.

--------. "The Composition of William Beckford's Biographical 13/85
     Memoirs of Extraordinary Painters", PQ, XLVII (1968),
     139-141.

     Memoirs, published in 1780, was composed, says Chapman
     (13/30), between autumn, 1779 and spring, 1780 when B was
     seventeen. Not so says Alexander (13/38); B wrote it when
     he was sixteen, sometime before June of 1777. Gemmett
     draws on letters of 1779-80, asserts BM was started in
     1777 but remained unfinished till winter of 1780. "Thus,
     it is clear that although Beckford may have begun writing
     this satirical piece at sixteen years of age, he did not
     complete it until he was nineteen."

--------. "The Critical Reception of William Beckford's   13/86
     Fonthill", EM, XIX (1968), 133-151.

     "Fonthill was not only received in the early part of the
     19th century as one of the most enchanting landed estates
     in its day, but it was also recognized by many admirers as
     illustrative of a new style of informal landscape within
     which a striking neo-Gothic building was incorporated as
     the pièce de résistance of the design." Essentially, a
     distillation of Gemmett's Ph.D. dissertation (13/41).

--------. Introduction to Dreams, Waking Thoughts and In-   13/87
     cidents. Rutherford: Fairleigh Dickinson Univ. Press,
     1971.

     Calls Dreams "one of the best illustrations of 'literary
     picturesque' that was produced in the declining years of

284

the 18th century". Notes influence of Gilpin; says that
in both Dreams and Vathek, WB "aimed for pictorial effects".

Gemmett, Robert J.   Introduction to Vathek.   Delmar: Scho-   13/88
lar's Facsimiles & Reprints, 1972.

A general overview. Biography with some incisive comments;
genesis and publication of Vathek; notes on editions
omitted from standard bibliographies; extracts from contemporary reviews; influence on Byron, Keats, Southey,
Moore, Disraeli, and Melville. Takes note of existant
scholarship and probes problem areas. Does not seem satisfied with the standard version of the Henley publication.

Gifford, Stephanie.   "Genesis of a Caliph", John O'London's   13/89
V (Aug. 24, 1961), 221.

"Like the majority of first novels, Vathek is mainly autobiographical, fantastic as such a claim may be for this
brew of splendour, magic, mystery and horror, with its
welcome lacing of wit." Sees: (1) the Caliph as WB,
(2) Princess Carathis as WB's mother, (3) Nouronihar as
Louisa Beckford, (4) Gulchenrouz as William Courtenay,
(5) the inspiring Indian stranger as Alexander Cozens,
(6) the concubines as servants.

Green, Andrew J.   "Essays in Miniature: Vathek", CE, III   13/90
(1942), 723-724.

Calls V "a potpourri of the absurd and the unforgettable".
Says it is "without real art, without form, without sub-
stance, spun from a spider's thread from an idle pate, a
book without utility, whose humor is without point. . . ,
[and] worst of all, a book without truth, either of
reality or of imagination". Calls Beckford "the most competent of literary impostors".

Grimsditch, Herbert B.   Introduction to Vathek.   Bloomsbury: 13/91
Nonesuch, 1929.

Argues for primacy of the Lausanne edition. Presents
seven points: (1) Lausanne preface, (2) Chavannes' note,
(3) rushed appearance of Lausanne edition, (4) Paris text
appears a revision, (5) WB was close to Lausanne when he
heard of Henley's issue, (6) Lausanne edition was to have

285

four episodes, Paris, three, (7)names of princes and
princesses are nearer final form in Paris edition.

Grimsditch, Herbert B.   Introduction to Vathek. London: 13/92
Folio, 1958.

A new introduction written for the 1958 reissue. Offers
a brief biographical sketch; suggests two possible reasons why WB wrote V in French: (1)Because the Oriental
romances he read were in French, and (2)to épater le bourgeois. Says "Henley's version has certain definite virtues, but is somewhat elephantine and in no wise catches
the glitter and epigrammatic force of the original."

Hodgkin, John.   "The Nonesuch Vathek", TLS (Dec. 26, 1929),   13/93
p. 1097.

Grimsditch (13/91) had said there was no English translation of the definitive edition of 1815 and he offers
a translation of an undated edition published by Clarke
with a preface dated 1815. Hodgkin says the preface may
have been written in 1815, but the edition was of 1816,
1817, or later. In any case, there exists a translation
of the 1815 edition. Also, he contends that the Paris
edition is earlier than the Lausanne edition, and the
latter is "a more or less unauthorized edition of a text
which was never intended to have been published in this
form".

Chapman, Guy.   "The Nonesuch Vathek", TLS (Jan. 2, 1930),   13/94
p. 12.

Defends Grimsditch. Says he was not in error claiming
his translation to be the first from the 1815 edition,
but errs in calling the issue of 1815 an edition.   Says
Hodgkin (13/93) wrong on the 1816 translation -- it is
not of the 1815 edition but rather "a revised and corrected edition of Henley's 1786 translation". Doesn't
agree with Hodgkin that Lausanne edition was unauthorized; refers him to the Chavannes note.

Grimsditch, Herbert B.   "The Nonesuch Vathek", TLS (Jan. 9,   13/95
   1930), p. 28.

   Defends himself against Hodgkin's letter of 26 December
   (13/93). Hodgkin argues that the Mount St. French edition
   was issued later than the New Bond St. French edition
   dated 1815, but G asserts that these two editions are from
   the same plates, and the Bond St. edition has an errata
   slip, thus providing evidence that it is a later issue.

Hodgkin, John.   "The Nonesuch Vathek", TLS (Jan. 9, 1930),   13/96
   p. 28.

   Claims Chapman (13/94) misquoted him. Sticks to his story.

Chapman, Guy.   "The Nonesuch Vathek", TLS (Jan. 16, 1930),   13/97
   p. 44.

   Repeats his arguments against Hodgkin.

Hodgkin, John.   "The Nonesuch Vathek", TLS (Jan. 23, 1930),   13/98
   p. 60.

   Refutes, one at a time, Grimsditch's seven reasons for
   the primacy of the Lausanne edition (13/91).

Grimsditch, Herbert B.   "The Nonesuch Vathek", TLS (Feb. 20,   13/99
   1930), p. 142.

   Refutation of Hodgkin's refutation of the seven points.

--------. "William Beckford's Minor Works", London Mercury,   13/100
   XIV (1926), 599-605.

   Praises WB's literary efforts and laments that his minor
   works -- Extraordinary Painters, Modern Novel Writing,
   Azemia, Italy, Alcobaca, are not better known. Provides
   sketches of their content and urges reprinting. Contends
   that if Dreams and Alcobaca had been published "when
   they were conceived instead of delaying their publication
   for 51 and 41 years respectively, they might now be
   counted among the early and important manifestations of
   the romantic revival".

H. "Conversations With the Late W. Beckford, Esq." New   13/10
Monthly Magazine, LXII (1844), 18-24, 212-221, 418-427.

A three-part article recounting how WB took an interest in
the author's youthful drawings and invited him to Lansdown Crescent. Presents a flattering picture of WB as
host, gentleman, art critic, conversationalist, and gar-
dener. Says that "his countenance struck me to be a mixture of the divine Dante, Lorenzo de Medici, and the Me-
phistophiles of Faust."

H., W.H. "Conversations of the Late W. Beckford, Esq. with   13/10
Various Friends", New Monthly Magazine, LXXII (1844),
516-522.

Includes a few notable remarks: (1)Fonthill was built not
on B's plan, but on that of Wyatt; (2)much of the interior
decoration was of B's own design; (3)Hayter, the clerk of
the works, on his death bed, told WB that he (Hayter) "had
recommended the turning of an arch under the tower, but
his suggestion was over-ruled, and treated with contempt
by the architect". Hayter added that "the tower will make
a curtsey one of these days." (4)WB called Lansdown Tower
"a famous landmark for the drunken farmers on their return from market".

Hazlitt, William. "Fonthill Abbey", in P.P. Howe, ed., The   13/10
Complete Works of William Hazlitt. 21 vols. Toronto:
Dent, 1933.

Fonthill Abbey "is, in a word, a desart of magnificence,
a glittering waste of laborious idleness, a cathedral
turned into a toy-shop, an immense Museum of all that is
most curious and costly, and , at the same time, most
worthless in the productions of art and nature". Writing
in 1822 when Fonthill had been offered for sale, Hazlitt
inspected the premises and concluded that there was "scarce
one genuine work of art, one solid proof of taste, one
lasting relic of sentiment or imagination". The paintings
he calls "mere furniture-pictures, remarkable chiefly for
their antiquity or painful finishing" and says there was
"not one great work by one great name".

Herrick, George H. 'Fabulous Fonthill", College Art Journal, 13/104
XII (1953), 128-131.

A general introductory article drawn from standard sources.
Defends WB against Hazlitt's charges (13/103); describes
and/or catalogues some possessions at Fonthill and Lansdown.

Hollingsworth, Keith. "Vathek and the 'Ode to a Nightin- 13/105
gale'", TLS, (Oct. 27, 1961), p. 771.

Keats read Vathek. Borrowings have been found in "Endy-
mion", "Hyperion", and "The Fall of Hyperion", and now
it is suggested that "Ode to a Nightingale" may owe to
"The Flower and the Leaf" , but "when he wrote the Ode,
Beckford's luxuriant arbor seems to have been there too".

Hussain, Imdad. "Beckford, Wainewright, De Quincey, and 13/106
Oriental Exoticism", Venture, I (1960), 234-248.

The bulk of the article deals with Beckford, treats him
as "the first real exoticist in English literature" and
sees him as the originator of a "new type of Orientalism
which is at once visionary and concrete" and much different
from the neo-classical Oriental tale. Denies WB the title
"Romantic" and asserts "his emotional expansiveness was
always held in check by Reason". But the proof positive
lies in WB's prose: "We have the characteristic moods of
romanticism set forth in a prose that has not yet yielded
its classical restraint to the turgidity that followed the
Romantic triumph. Nowhere is this contrast of classical
style and romantic subject matter more obvious than in
Vathek."

Johnson, R[eginald] Brimley. Introduction to Vathek. Abbey 13/107
Classics. Boston: Small, Maynard, [1922].

Mainly plot summary and comments on the fictional characters. Thinks that WB saw Vathek as "a real and living
man" and wrote "as one who knew him well". Says WB
created attractive royal criminals and fulfilled his obligation with "the accepted, and purely conventional,
moral tag of just nine lines on the last page".

Keegan, P.Q. "Gleanings From Anglo-Oriental Literature: 13/1
Vathek -- Anastatius -- Hajji Baba", New Monthly Magazine, NS, XI (1877), 674-687.

A tract asserting the superiority of Europeans, especially
"the Teutonic races", over the "lying, dissembling pro-
clivities of the typical Persian, Arabian, or Hindoo".
As proof, the author draws on Vathek, Anastatius, and
Hajji Baba. "With respect to imagination", Vathek stands
"unrivalled, while as a picture of eastern selfish ethics
and the consequences thereof, it is entitled to much consideration". Offers plot summary, dissects the Caliph as
if he were an actual, typical Eastern prince, and draws
attention to his atheism, his licentiousness, and his
dissolute life.

L.   "Armorial Decorations at Fonthill Abbey", Gentleman's   13/1
Magazine, XCII, pt. 2 (1822), 201-204, 317-320, 409-414.

Describes the armorial decorations displayed by WB and
offers a genealogical table showing his descent from
King Edward I.

Lane-Poole, Stanley. "The Author of Vathek", Quarterly Re-   13/1
view, CCXIII (1910), 377-401.

Draws upon Conant (13/157), defends Redding (13/50), criticizes Melville's Life & Letters (13/48) as "wanting in
courage" and avoiding the "mysterious incidents and hinted
scandals". Points out errors in the letters.

Levy, Herman Mittle, Jr. Introduction to Modern Novel   13/1
Writing (1796) and Azemia (1797). Gainesville: Scholar's
Facsimiles & Reprints, 1970.

In MNW, Beckford "is pointing to the decline of the [novel]
genre and warning the then moderns away from the school of
sentiment, as well as the Gothic, because of its extensive
use of overblown emotions". Azemia "adds the plot of the
damsel in distress to show the lack of originality at
every level of sentimental fiction".

[ockhart], J[ohn] G[ibson].   Introduction to Vathek [n.d.].   13/112
[London]:   Philip Allan, [1923].

Lockhart (d. 1854), the "Scorpion" of Blackwood's and
Quarterly Review, presents a general, but favourable picture. Sees possible influence of Voltaire in the cyni-
cism,and of Gibbon in the style. Calls WB "an oriental,
born out of due time and place, a Caliph condemned not
to the tortures of Eblis but to the dull limitations of
the English country-side".

onsdale, Roger.   Introduction to Vathek. Oxford English   13/113
Novels. New York: Oxford Univ. Press, 1970.

Deals mainly with the genesis, the translations, and the
editions. Paraphrases contemporary reviews and offers
some biography. Asserts that Vathek is not Gothic as
Beckford does not set out to exploit terror, and in fact,
often undermines this emotion with a comic tone. Contains
a very extensive bibliography and an explanation of the
various editions.

--------].   "The Mask of Beckford", TLS (Feb. 10, 1961),   13/114
pp. 1-2.

A very long, very full treatment of Parreaux's William
Beckford (A/59).

ahmoud, Fatma Moussa.   "Beckford, Vathek and the Oriental   13/115
Tale", in his William Beckford of Fonthill, 1760-1844.
Bicentenary Essays [1960]. Port Washington: Kennikat,
1972.

Asserts that Vathek had very little effect upon the course
of the oriental prose tale since, contrary to what some
have claimed, this book was practically unknown. WB himself suppressed V and ordered the books "wrested" from
the publisher. A few copies circulated, but Byron, in
drawing upon the work, brought fame to the novel and himself. Vathek, of little influence on the prose tale,
was "of great impact on the verse tales of the Romantics".

Mahmoud, Fatma Moussa. "A Monument to the Author of Vathek",   13/1
EA, XV (1962), 138-147.

A long review of Parreaux's William Beckford (A/59) which
summarizes and presents the major findings.

Manzalaoui, Mahmoud. "Pseudo-Orientalism in Transition: The   13/1
Age of Vathek", in Fatma Moussa Mahmoud, ed., William
Beckford of Fonthill, 1760-1844. Bicentenary Essays [1960].
Port Washington: Kennikat, 1972.

Sees V as pivotal in transition from the 18th-century
pseudo-oriental moralizing tale to the 19th-century Romantic's oriental verse. Points out pseudo-orientalism's
appeal: exotic, erotic, fresh theme, background for satire,
useful for self-projection, linked with medievalism. Vathek
displays not the didactic tendency of classicism, but the
anti-moralism, egotism, and satanism which classes it with
the verse tales of the Romantics.

Marshall, Julian. "Beckford's Vathek", N&Q, 7th ser., I   13/1
(1886), 69.

In the preface to the French edition of 1815, WB stated
that the English translation of 1786 was brought about by
"circumstances of little interest to the public". Marshall asks what might be these "circumstances" and in-
quires also, what are the differences, if any, in the
Lausanne and Paris editions. Two replies follow:

Buckley, W.E. "Beckford's Vathek", N&Q, 7th ser., I (1886),   13/1
154.

This reader has copies of both the Paris and Lausanne
editions of 1787 and offers descriptions of both. "The
English translation follows the Lausanne where it differs
from the Paris edition. The reprint of the French text
in 1815 varies in some instances from the Paris of 1787."

B., G.F.R. "Beckford's Vathek", N&Q, 7th ser., I (1886),   13/12
154.

Attributes the translation to the Rev. S. Henley, Rector
of Rendlesham.

Marshall, Julian. "Beckford's Vathek", N&Q, 7th ser., VII   13/121
(1889), 312-313.

Marshall has discovered a copy of Vathek, "Lausanne, chez
Isaac Hignon and Comp, 1787" which contains a note by M.
Chavannes, claiming that on orders from WB, he personally
worked on the first edition, the Lausanne edition. Also,
he accuses WB of a fraud but Marshall remarks that "there
seems here a strange want of motive and likelihood in the
fraud".

[Mayer, Mrs. G. Townshend]. "The Sultan of Lansdown Tower",   13/122
Temple Bar, CXX (1900), 182-212.

Offers extracts from previously unpublished letters between
WB and "his literary agent in London, the bookseller Clark"
written between August, 1830 and October, 1834. Views WB
as a difficult, spiteful, pompous, impetuous man; believes
"there was probably a latent strain of insanity in the
family".

"Beckford's Letters to George Clark", TLS (Feb. 16, 1962),   13/123
p. 112.

The Beckford-Clark letters (13/122) were rediscovered in
1961 and sold to a private collector. Present location
unknown.

Melville, Lewis. "William Beckford, of Fonthill Abbey",   13/124
Fortnightly Review, NS, LXXXVI (1909), 1011-1023. (Re-
printed in his Some Eccentrics and a Woman. London:
Martin Secker, 1911.)

An introductory, biographical account which raises and dismisses adverse charges, sees enthusiasm as "the keynote"
of WB's character and regards him as a serious writer and
a much maligned man.

--------. "William Beckford's Adventure in Diplomacy: An   13/125
Unpublished Correspondence", Nineteenth Century, LXV
(1909) , 783-799.

Shows WB's effort to bring about peace between England and
France in 1797. Offers twelve letters, two by WB, the remainder either to him, or in regard to his proposals. Includes some editorial comments. "The correspondence is

now printed with the object to make public Beckford's interesting adventure in diplomacy, but it also throws some
light upon Beckford's activity and thoroughness as a
collector."

Melville, Lewis. "'Vathek'", Athenaeum, No. 4283 (Nov. 27,   13/12
1909), p. 696.

Melville has unearthed "among other unpublished correspondence bearing on the subject, the letter in which Henley defends himself". Offered here is a letter from WB
to Henley dated January 21, 1782, and five from Henley
to WB dated April 12, 1785; April 26, 1785; June 15, 1785;
July 19, 1785; October 23, 1786.

Hodgkin, John. "'Vathek': The Henley Letters", Athenaeum,   13/12
No. 4287 (Dec. 25, 1909), pp. 789-790.

Collates letters offered by Melville (13/126) with published letters and suggests changes in dates for two of
the latter. Says Melville errs in asserting WB worked on
episodes for five years -- it was only three. Says Melville errs in placing the Lausanne earlier than the Paris
edition, and asserts there were three, not four episodes
-- "three stories of four princes".

Nerke. "The Tower of the Caliph", New Monthly Magazine,   13/12
LXXI (1844), 457-466.

A description of the Lansdown tower and gardens, related
as the true account of a gentleman who, uninvited, wan-
dered unmolested across grounds and through apartments.
The result is an effort which seems more concerned with
beautiful prose than actual description.

Oldman, C.B. "Beckford and Mozart", M&L, XLVII (1966),   13/12
110-115.

Did Beckford study under Mozart? Did Mozart use an air
which B composed? Did these two men meet again in Vienna?
Oldman discusses these questions, but unfortunately,
comes to no conclusion. He seems to doubt the existence
of any connection and notes that we have only B's word.
Mozart did meet a Mr. Beckford in London and later in
Italy, but Oldman suggests this was not the author of
Vathek but his cousin, William Beckford of Somerly, and

294

the Caliph, "who hated to be outdone . . . , exaggerate[d] the part that Mozart, whose music he so passionately admired, had played in his life".

Parreaux, André. "Beckford's Vathek, 'Londres 1791'", BC, 13/130
VII (1958), 297-299.

The mysterious 1791 London edition of Vathek becomes identified as the Lausanne edition in a new guise. When French customs officials seized 300 copies of the Lausanne Vathek, the publisher resorted to a trick and entitled his unsold copies Les caprises et les malheurs du calife Vathek, Traduit de l'Arabe , Londres, 1791. "The change of title, the misleading mention of London and the omission of a publisher's name indicate the intention of throwing the French Customs off the scent." Suggests also that this edition may have been shipped to Germany and Austria for the new French emigres of 1791.

Marlow, Harriet. "Beckford's Vathek, 'Londres 1791'", BC, 13/131
XI (1962), 211.

Parreaux (13/130) located two copies of the Londres 1791 edition, one in Gottingen, the other in Vienna. A third copy has turned up, (place unidentified) which "conforms precisely to Professor Parreaux's description" and the binding is "undoubtedly continental, probably German".

Parreaux, André. "The Caliph and the Swinish Multitude", in 13/132
Fatma Moussa Mahmoud, ed., William Beckford of Fonthill, 1760-1844. Bicentenary Essays [1960]. Port Washington: Kennikat, 1972.

Challenges the usual view that Modern Novel Writing and Azemia are anti-romantic satires, parodies of WB's half-sister's work, barbs against Mrs. Radcliffe and her fellows. Instead, Parreaux asserts they are political satires, tracts against the war with France and on the democratic side with "the swinish multitude".

Pritchett, V.S. "Vile Body", New Statesman, LXIII (Feb. 22, 13/133
1962), 265-266.

Views Vathek as "an astonishing but merely curious book" which nowadays "can be read with interest only by the biographical detective". Calls the Journals of Spain and

295

Portugal the only work of "uncommon interest". Sees WB
as a great actor, a poser, a pseudo-monster. "For the
psychologist he is, as all the extreme Romantics were, a
creature of great importance, simply because he is expert
in mystification, inventing and re-inventing his life with
the instinct of the artist and the skill of certain neu-
rotics and criminals."

"Projected Union between Comte D'Egmont and Miss Beckford",   13/13
Lady's Monthly Museum, XIV (1805), 167-168.

Reports that WB's second daughter, "one of the most beautiful women our country can boast", declined a marriage
proposal from the Comte D'Egmont, "the richest subject in
Europe". The father had invited the grandee to England
with a marriage in mind and became "extremely mortified at
the disappointment".

Pryce-Jones, Alan. "William Beckford, Dilettante", New York   13/13
Times Book Review, (Feb. 16, 1969), pp. 2, 40.

Views WB as a dilettante, a rich man who wrote a famous
but "almost universally unread" novel, but who excelled
because of his wealth, "as a taste-maker" and devotee of
the arts.

Redding, Cyrus. "Recollections of the Author of Vathek",   13/13
New Monthly Magazine, LXXI (1844), 143-158, 302-319.

Describes Lansdown House, the library, paintings, grounds,
and tower. Praises the writer's accomplishments, his pro-
digious reading, his generosity, his kindness to animals.
Claims he was misunderstood and maligned. Gives the "one
sitting" story of V; says WB did not know the translator.
Says WB read him two of the episodes; the third had been
destroyed as "too wild".

Rieger, James Henry. "Au Pied de la Lettre: Stylistic Un-   13/13
certainty in Vathek", Criticism, IV (1962), 302-312.

Probes the oft-mentioned stylistic uncertainties, the
rapid changes of direction, the undermining of the author's
own best effects. Sees V as neither realistic nor as a
fantastical piece of irony, but rather as a forerunner of
"Kubla Khan", a piece of dream literature. Beckford displays a "split sensibility" and his revisions of V repre-

sent the conscious artist treating the work of a blind
expressionist. Thus, the irony should be regarded "as
deprecation, as nervous, self-conscious shoulder-shrug-
ging". "The author seems anxious to pass off his creation
as the well-bred jest of a light-hearted litterateur, as
the frivolous product of a country gentleman's leisure
hours. But the embarrassment shows through the facade
and giggles like a guilty thing surprised."

Rosebery, Eva. "Books from Beckford's Library Now at Barn-   13/138
bougle", BC, XIV (1965), 324-334.

The Earl of Rosebery built a Beckford collection, and after
his death in 1929, his daughter sold 86 books from the
family home at Epsom. In addition, ninety were bequeathed
to the National Library of Scotland and many disposed of
privately. This was thought to have been the entire Rosebery collection, but it was discovered that two additional
libraries, in Scotland and Buckinghamshire, contained some
600 WB books. The works (identified in this article), are
now assembled at Barnbougle Castle in Scotland.

Sizer, Theodore. "William Beckford and his American Prop-   13/139
erty", YULG, XXXIX (1964), 42-45.

In 1798, WB purchased 23,340 acres of land in the Genesee
River district of northwestern New York state. Colonel
John Trumbull or his master Benjamin West probably intro-
duced WB to the agent, James Wadsworth of Connecticut, and
Trumbull thought that the Caliph might move to the U.S.

Steeves, Harrison R. Introduction to Vathek, in Three Eight-   13/140
eenth Century Romances [1931]. New York: Scribner's,
1971.

Steeves seems to like Vathek, says it has "lasting and
intrinsic merit", but dismisses the rest of WB's works as
"without interest". He calls V "one of the great literary
burlesques" and asserts that it "ridicules the romantic
vogue by accentuating the romantic styles".

Thompson, Karl F. "Beckford, Byron, and Henley", EA, XIV   13/141
(1961), 225-228.

Basically a defense of Henley. Thompson sees H as a collaborator in V and asserts "just as Beckford's hand is

297

apparent from time to time in the notes, so Henley's
judgment intrudes occasionally into the text of the novel
itself". Contends that WB would probably not have published V, and thus to regain his investment, Henley was
forced to publish it himself. Asserts also that Byron was
influenced by Henley since he drew on H's notes.
    Appended to this article is André Parreaux's "A Note
on Mr. K.F. Thompson's Note" (228-229), which very briefly
refutes the argument.

Thompson, Karl F. "Henley's Share in Beckford's Vathek",   13/142
PQ, XXXI (1952), 75-80.

An earlier version of the above article (13/141). Views
Henley as a "literary collaborator" who suggested, shaped,
revised and conceived the idea of annotating V. Notes WB's
tardiness with the episodes, his previous suppression of
Dreams, and asserts that Vathek might never have been published by WB himself. Says undoubtedly Henley betrayed a
trust, but he was pressured into publication by pressing
family finances, and with WB's alleged homosexuality, he,
a clergyman, "could scarcely lend his name as editor or
translator of a book by Beckford". Suggests also that Henley did not think that the addition of the episodes would
be beneficial to the structure of the book.

[Tiffany, O.]. A review of Memoirs of William Beckford,   13/143
[by Cyrus Redding]. North American Review, XC (1860),
297-321.

A titleless, anonymous article, heavy on summary of
Memoir and Vathek. The former, he calls "in some respects
a readable work, but the greater part of it is silly,
mawkish trash". Praises the "wondrous invention and
splendour of language" in V. Says "its magic incantations
and stupendous horrors have no parallel in the Arabian
Nights, nor indeed in the whole compass of fiction."
Speculates upon sources of WB's "supernatural machinery,
as his demons, gnomes, and sprites differ from those of
Arabian imagery, and partake in some degree of those of
India".

[Tresham, Henry]. "Letter from a Gentleman, Present at the   13/144
Festivities at Fonthill, to a Correspondent in Town",
Gentleman's Magazine, LXXI , pt. 1 (1801), 206-208,
297-298.

Lord Nelson, accompanied by a cavalry escort, arrived at
Fonthill where the awaiting musicians struck up "Rule
Britannia", the Fonthill Volunteers fired salutes and
marched about, and the Caliph offered his home. The correspondent describes the edifice, notes the "monastic or-
nament", the "solemn music" and the staircase which was
"lighted by certain mysterious living figures at different
intervals, dressed in hooded gowns, and standing with large
wax-torches in their hands".

Tuckerman, H.T. "William Beckford and the Literature of   13/145
Travel", Southern Literary Messenger, XVI (1850), 7-14.

Deals more with travel literature than with Beckford.
Rambles through history, philosophy and literature from
Lewis and Clark to Marco Polo, from De Tocqueville to
Dickens. Praises WB's travel accounts: "His facts are
enlivened by fancy, and his descriptions not only convey
a series of images, but they have the unity of impression
which is derived from sensation. In a word, he not only
tells us how things appear to him and how their phenomena
may be explained, but how they make him feel."

Viator. "Fonthill Abbey. On Its Close", Gentleman's Maga-   13/146
zine, XCII, pt. 2 (1822), 291-292.

Viator [WB?] notes that 7,200 admission tickets were sold
to Fonthill Abbey visitors; that Farquhar, the India mer-
chant and principal partner in Whitbread's Brewery paid
₤330,000 or ₤350,000 for the estate; that WB retained
"only his family pictures and a few books". In offering
his criticism of Fonthill, Viator seems greatly concerned
with variety, novelty, and surprise and seems more pleased
with the grounds than the buildings. In landscaping, nature did not offer a variety of ground, "but art has accomplished wonders, by a happy mixture of lawn and wood".

Villiers, G.H. "Mr. Beckford in Portugal", National Review,   13/147
LXXIV (1920), 808-816.

Consists mainly of a brief paraphrase of Alcobaca interspersed with brief comments on Portuguese history. As-

serts that "Beckford goes too far in his descriptions of
the wealth and prosperity of Portugal".

Wahba, Magdi. "Beckford, Portugal and 'Childish Error'", in   13/14
    Fatma Moussa Mahmoud, ed., William Beckford of Fonthill,
    1760-1844. Bicentenary Essays [1960]. Port Washington:
    Kennikat, 1972.

    Contends that WB, after his stay in Portugal, "became ex-
    clusively paederastic". Views this aberration as "part of
    a general obsession with 'childishness' which pervades
    most of Beckford's personal reveries". Asserts that the
    Caliph used this childishness as an ego defense mechanism
    since, at worst, he could be guilty of but "childish
    error".

Weitzman, Arthur J. "The Oriental Tale in the Eighteenth   13/14
    Century: A Reconsideration", SVEC, LVIII (1967), 1839-
    1855.

    Rejects Conant's (13/157) explanation that the popularity
    of the oriental tale was due to exotic properties and re-
    action against strict artistic rules. The bulk of the
    18th-century oriental tales are neo-classical, satirical,
    and not romantic escape tales. Says Galland's version of
    Arabian Nights is an extremely free paraphrase with exotic
    and erotic elements suppressed, and stories exist as
    bourgeois exemplums and tales showing importance of pru-
    dence and reason. Vathek, he places in an era past clas-
    sicism, and the product of "an eccentric and disturbed
    man".

W[eston], S[tephen]. "Conjectural Criticism of a Famous   13/15
    Passage in Virgil", Gentleman's Magazine, LVII, pt. 1
    (1787), 55-56.

    Deals with a passage of Virgil quoted in Vathek, a work
    "which, it should seem has been composed as a text, for
    the purpose of giving to the publick the information con-
    tained in the notes".

[enley], S[amuel]. "Conjectures Concerning the History of   13/151
Vathek Obviated", Gentleman's Magazine, LVII, pt. 1
(1787), 120.

Replies that it is "certain that the said History is, as
the preface declares, a translation of an unpublished
manuscript, which Mr. W. himself will be welcome to
examine".

William Beckford". Obituary notice in Gentleman's Magazine,   13/152
NS, XXII (1844), 209-213.

Offers a long biographical account and devotes some attention to Fonthill and its contents.

William Beckford in the Saleroom", TLS (Oct. 20, 1966),   13/153
p. 968.

Covers the July, 1966, sale at Southeby's of the Henry J.
B. Clement's Beckford Collection of 330 lots. Comments
on other collections and their present whereabouts.

                          e.

        Notices in General Works, Diaries, Etc.

yron, George Gordon, Lord. Childe Harold's Pilgrimage,   13/154
I [1812], in Thomas Moore, ed., The Works of Lord Byron:
With His Letters and Journals, and His Life. 17 vols.
London: John Murray, 1833.

In Canto I, verses xxii-xxiii, Byron, writing on Portugal,
alludes to Beckford:

"There thou too, Vathek! England's wealthiest son,
Once found thy Paradise, as not aware
When wanton Wealth her mightiest deeds hath done,
Meek Peace voluptuous Lures was ever wont to shun.

Here didst thou dwell, here schemes of pleasure plan,
Beneath yon mountain's ever beauteous brow:
But now, as if a thing unblest by Man,
Thy fairy dwelling is as lone as thou!"

                          301

Byron, George Gordon, Lord, in Thomas Moore, ed., The Works   13/15
of Lord Byron.

"Vathek was one of the tales I had a very early admiration
of. For correctness of costume, beauty of description,
and power of imagination, it far surpasses all European
imitations, and bears such marks of originality, that
those who have visited the Fast will find some difficulty
in believing it to be more than a translation. As an
eastern tale, even Rasselas must bow before it: his
'happy valley' will not bear comparison with the 'Hall of
Eblis'".

--------, in Moore, Works.   13/15

Byron, in a letter to Mr. Rogers, dated May 3, 1828,
writes: "Your account of your visit to Fonthill is very
striking: could you beg of him for me a copy in MS. of
the remaining Tales? [the episodes] I think I deserve
them, as a strenuous and public admirer of the first one
. . . . If ever I return to England, I should like very
much to see the author, with his permission. . . . I
have a French copy of Vathek which I bought at Lausanne.
I can read French with great pleasure and facility, though
I neither speak nor write it."

Conant, Martha Pike. The Oriental Tale in English in the   13/15
Eighteenth Century. Columbia Univ. Studies in Comparative Literature. New York: Columbia Univ. Press, 1908.

Traces the rise and popularity of the oriental tale; emphasizes the idea of weary Classicism and welcomed Romanticism. Isolates and discusses four species: (1)"imaginative", (2)"moralistic", (3)"philosophic", and (4)"satiric". Heavy on plot summary, sources, analogies, influences. Calls Vathek "a thoroughly oriental tale of
terror"; criticizes its "repulsive mockery and sensuality"
and sees as the most serious defect, a lack of characterization. Traces WB's sources; lessens the "imaginative"
aspect of V.

Moore, Thomas. Memoirs, Journals, and Correspondence. Edited   13/15
by John Russell. 2 vols. New York: Appleton, 1858.

Moore records in his diary for Oct. 18, 1818, that Beckford wanted him to go to Fonthill and prepare the suppressed
"Travels" for publication. But even for ₤100,000, were

it offered, "I would not have my name coupled with his.
To be Beckford's sub, not very desirable."

Robinson, Henry Crabb. Henry Crabb Robinson on Books and   13/159
their Writers. Edited by Edith J. Morley. 3 vols.
London: Dent, 1938.

In his diary for March, 1816, HCR records reading Vathek.
At first he was amused and thought the book "marvellous",
then as he progressed and the horrors increased, he thought
it "powerful" but "disgusting". He objects to a "John-
sonian parade being blended with colloquial familiarities,
and an unsuccessful attempt to unite the descriptions of
horrid situations and incidents with strokes of humour".
Eighteen years later, in 1834, he calls V "one of the
most odious books I ever laid eyes on". Finally, in
1837, HCR reread V "with renewed disgust".

Rogers, Samuel. Recollections of the Table Talk of Samuel   13/160
Rogers. Edited by Rev. Alexander Dyce. New Southgate:
Rogers, 1887.

Devotes four pages to a three-day stay at Fonthill. Recounts that WB "would extemporise on the pianoforte producing the most novel and charming melodies" and would
read from his unpublished works. Claims to have heard
WB read two of the episodes of V and says "they are extremely fine, but very objectionable on account of their
subjects. Indeed, they show that the mind of the author
was to a certain degree diseased."

Scott, Sir Walter, in J[ohn] G. Lockhart, The Life of Sir   13/161
Walter Scott, Bart. 1771-1832. London: Adam & Charles
Black, 1893.

Scott, in an 1815 letter to Byron, writes: "Vathek,
bating some passages, would have made a charming subject
for a tale. The conclusion is truly grand. I would give
a great deal to know the originals from which it was
drawn."

Thrale, Mrs. Hester Lynch. Thraliana: The Diary of Mrs.   13/162
   Hester Lynch Thrale (Later Mrs. Piozzi) 1776-1809 [1942].
   Edited by Katharine C. Balderston. 2 vols. 2nd ed.
   Oxford: Clarendon, 1951.

   January 27, 1791: "I have been reading Vathek, 'tis a
   mad Book to be sure, and written by a mad Author, yet
   there is a sublimity about it -- particularly towards the
   Conclusion. Mr. Beckford's favourite Propensity is all
   along visible I think; particularly in the luscious Descriptions given of Gulchenrouz; but his Quarantine seems
   to be performed, & I am told he is return'd quietly to
   Fonthill. When we were at Milan Mr. Bisset brought over
   the news how he was hooted from Society by my Lord Loughborough, who threatened corporal or legal Punishment for
   Mr. Beckford's Violation of young Courtenay -- Brother to
   Lady Loughborough. At Lausanne no Englishman would ex-
   change a Word with the Creature. . . ."

                            f.

                      Early Reviews

                    1. Vathek (1786)

Critical Review, LXII (1786), 32-42.   13/163

   "The authors who employ spirits of the air, or of the
   earth", says the reviewer, "are the favourites of every
   age and every climate." Notes Shakespeare's use of spirits; cites popularity of Arabian Night's Entertainments.
   Suspects that V is not a translation; observes its "intimate knowledge of oriental customs, the extensive reading in the magic poets". Laments that "the notes, though
   extensive, we found too short. They contain a great fund
   of ancient learning, much elegant and judicious criticism."

English Review, VIII (1786), 180-184.   13/164

   "As an imitation of Arabian tales, this work possesses no
   inconsiderable merit. The characters are strongly marked,
   though carried beyond nature; the incidents are suffi-
   ciently wild and improbable; the magic is solemn and awful, though sometimes horrid; anachronisms and inconsis-

tencies frequently appear; and the catastrophe is bold
and shocking." But "the moral which is here conveyed,
that ignorance, childishness, and the want of ambition,
are the sources of human happiness, though agreeable to
the strain of eastern fiction, is inconsistent with true
philosophy, and with the nature of man." The notes "contain much oriental learning, and merit the attention of
the curious reader".

European Magazine, X (1786), 102-104.   13/165

Wonders if the tale is "the produce of Arabia, or of the
fertile banks of the Seine, (which a variety of circumstances induces us to believe it is)". If it is original,
"the author has . . . shown himself, generally speaking,
well acquainted with the customs of the East, and has introduced a sufficient quantity of the marvellous, an absolutely necessary ingredient to enable the work to pass
muster as an Arabian Tale. It however differs from the
generality of them, in this, that it inculcates a moral of
the greatest importance." The reviewer also points out
that the notes 'display a considerable share of learning,
and critical knowledge and acumen."

Gentleman's Magazine, LVI, pt. 2 (1786), 593-594.   13/166

"We earnestly recommend Vathek to every class of our
readers; for the morality of the design, and the excellence
of the execution, entitle it to universal attention: and
the labours of the edition demand our particular acknowledgement, for the notes adjoined to the work abound with
various examples of the most refined taste, and the most
extensive erudition."

Monthly Review, LXXVI (1787), 450.   13/167

"Though there are in this work too many ideas and sentiments of European growth, to admit of its passing for a
translation of an Eastern manuscript, the piece has all
the wildness of Eastern fable; we will add, too, that it
preserves the peculiar character of the Arabian Tale,
which is not only to overstep nature and probability, but
even to pass beyond the verge of possibility, and suppose
things, which cannot be for a moment conceived." "It is
accompanied with notes, which are of a character entirely
different from that of the work, containing many learned
quotations, elegant criticisms and judicious remarks."

Review of the 1815 edition. "This is in every respect an
extraordinary work. The circumstances of its having been
written by an Englishman in <u>pure</u> <u>French</u>, is nearly <u>unique</u>,
and the wildness of imagination displayed in it, and that
property of genius which elicits from a reader a corres-
ponding train of thought, and distinguishes character or
describes passion by a few striking traits, claim for the
author of <u>Vathek</u> not only our praise, which we are always
unwilling to deny to laudable exertion, but that admiration
which is due to distinguished merit. The manners of the
piece and some historical allusions evince a familiar acquaintance with the customs and literature of the east;
and the story is conducted with the rapid march, and
adorned with the vivid coloring of Voltaire, whose style,
termed by his contemporary admirers, '<u>l'imprimatur</u> de
<u>Voltaire</u>', Mr. Beckford seems to have combined with his
own perceptions of human and supernatural agency, and of
moral causes and effects."

The 1834, Carey, Lea & Blanchard edition has been issued
from Philadelphia, and "by way of smoothing its path to
general reception and favor", favourable reviews have
been attached. But <u>SLM</u> asserts "that a more impure, disgusting, and execrable production . . . never issued from
the English or American press. That the author was a
youth of extraordinary genius, is acknowledged . . . but
it was genius totally perverted and poisoned at its source.
The work could have been written by no one whose heart
was not polluted at its very core. Obscene and blasphemous
in the highest degree, its shocking pictures are in no
wise redeemed by the beauty and simplicity of oriental
fiction. We should pronounce it, without knowing any
thing of Mr. B's character, to be the production of a sen-
sualist and an infidel -- one who could riot in the most
abhorred and depraved conceptions -- and whose prolific
fancy preferred as its repast all that was diabolical and
monstrous, rather than what was beautiful and good."
(Robert D. Jacobs in his <u>Poe: Journalist and Critic</u>,
Baton Rouge: LSU, 1969, attributes this review to James
E. Heath.)

Southern Literary Messenger, I (1835), 270.   13/170

Complete item: "The Western Monthly Magazine concurs
with us in our opinions of Vathek. The editor says,
'Vathek is the production of a sensual and perverted
mind. The events are extravagant, the sentiments pernicious, and the moral bad. It has nothing to recommend it
but ease of style and copiousness of language.'"

--------, I (1835), 386.   13/171

The editor says that "it would argue a great decline in
the moral feeling of our country, and a most adulterated
literary taste, if such works as Vathek could be generally
admired" and prints a letter from an unnamed critic in
which V becomes condemned as "revolting, disgusting, impure, etc".

        2. Popular Tales of the Germans (1791)

        (Montague Summers [1/39] attributes this
         anonymous work to Beckford.)

European Magazine, XIX (1791), 350-352.   13/172

The reviewer finds that this work conveys "much shrewd
humour, laughing satire, and extensive learning". PT is
a "very singular display of the most risible absurdities
of the Gothic Romance, a bizarre mixture of ancient with
modern manners, frequently of lively sallies of wit, of a
prevailing humour highly facetious. . . ." Objects to a
mixed style, humourous and pathetic.

Monthly Review, 2nd ser., V (1791), 467.   13/173

"The Tales, whether domestic or foreign, are in our judgment, extravagant in the extreme, without a sufficient
portion of humour, satire, or sentiment, to repay the
reader for the pain of putting his imagination on the rack.
Powers of invention, directed to no good end, might as
well be suffered to sleep; and at monsters of fiction,
which only excite a momentary wonder, we gaze for a day,
and forget them."

3. Modern Novel Writing (1796)

Critical Review, 2nd ser., XVIII (1796), 472-474.   13/174

"In flights of wild and digressive humour, Tristram
Shandy, compared with the present performance, is a regular and methodical work. Our author seems, by his rambling, unconnected style, to intend a satire on the obscure, desultory, incorrect manner of the inferior modern
novelists. . . ." Believes the author to be "a gentleman
well known for his poetical compositions".

Monthly Mirror, II (1796), 286.   13/175

Calls MNW "a very ingenious and successful satire on the
lumber of circulating libraries" but asserts that it "is
not the first work of the kind we have met with, nor do
we think it is the best."

Monthly Review, XX (1796), 477.   13/176

"Swift's celebrated 'Love-Song in the modern taste' surely
suggested this truly comic, diverting, and satiric performance; the design of which is to burlesque the ordinary
run of our circulating-library -novels." Adds that "we
have, in our language, few instances in which literary
mimicry, or imitative ridicule, has so happily produced
its full effect, without the formality of censure, or the
trouble of criticism." Believes the author to be, not
the Lady Harriet Marlow, but a man.

British Critic, IX (1797), 75-76.   13/177

Complete item: "This is a very humorous and successful,
though sometimes overcharged, attack upon modern novel-
writing, which certainly gives too frequent occasion for
the exercise of such weapons as the author here uses.
There is a great deal of good food for laughter in these
volumes in which we have heartily joined, though we ourselves are occasionally the subject of the writer's
humour. Lady H. Marlow is a fictitious personage; the
book has been attributed to Mr. Merry."

4. Azemia (1797)

British Critic, X (1797), 433.   13/178

    Suggests it is by author of MNW. "But the idea was ex-
hausted in the first attempt; and there is little of peculiar wit and humour in Azemia, to give a new point to
the satire. Some of the poetry, however, is an exception
. . . . "

Critical Review, 2nd ser., XX (1797), 470.   13/179

    Attributes MNW to Robert Merry; says Azemia is a "servile
imitation" and "far inferior in point of execution."

Monthly Mirror, IV (1797), 95-97.   13/180

    Notes affinity to MNW. Says "the author has displayed a
tolerable portion of humour in his ridicule of the modern
romance, and of the hackneyed sensibility which is so
abundantly distributed to the heroes and heroines of all
our novels. The particular objects of attack . . . appear to be Mr. Cumberland, Madame D'Arblay, Mrs. Radcliffe,
Mrs. Robinson, the Gunnings, Mrs. Piozzi, etc." "Azemia,
upon the whole, seems to the the hasty production of a
person of talent."

Monthly Review, XXIV (1797), 338.   13/181

    Says this seems "an imitation" of MNW and calls it "an
entertaining compound of good taste and good writing".

5. Recollections of an Excursion to the Monasteries of Alcobaça and Batalha (1835)

Southern Literary Messenger, I (1835), 714.   13/182

    Reviewer has not seen Recollections but predicts that it
"will be read with eagerness; and this for no better reason
which we can discover, than that the world have habituated

themselves to mix up in their fancy the mind and writings with the former fine house and furniture of Mr. Beckford -- the gorgeous nonsense of Vathek, with the vast and absolute magnificence of the Abbey of Fonthill. We predict for the book a rapid sale in this country." Adds a postscript that "Recollections consists of little more than a glowing description of monastic epicurism and gourmandise."

6. Miscellaneous

Story of Al Raoui. Reviewed in British Critic, XV (1800),   13/183
78.

Complete item: "This beautiful specimen of English typography, calculated to extend the fame of our press on the continent (being sold at Hamburg, Leipsig, etc.) is a production of the learned amusements of Mr. Henley, whose notes on the tale of Vathek have stamped so much value on that production. It is taken from a collection of tales, mentioned formerly in the Preface to Vathek. The story is plain and simple, but very characteristic of Oriental notions and manners; and subjoined are some original verses, by the translator, of much elegance and merit. The tale is given in English and German."

APPENDIX

Selected Foreign Language Items

a.

General

Brauchli, Jakob. Der Englische Schauerroman um 1800, unter   A/1
Berücksichtigung der Unbekannten Bücher. Ein Beitrag
zur Geschichte der Volksliteratur. Weida: Thomas &
Hubert, 1928.

Haferkorn, Reinhard. Gotik und Ruine in der Englischen Dich-   A/2
tung des Achtzehnten Jahrhunderts. Leipzig: Tauchnits,
1924.

Killen, Alice Mary. Le Roman Terrifiant ou Roman Noir de   A/3
Walpole à Anne Radcliffe et son Influence sur la Littérature Française Jusqu' en 1840. Paris: E. Champion, 1923.

Lévy, Maurice. Images du Roman Noir. Paris: Eric Losfeld,   A/4
1973.

--------. Le Roman "Gothique" Anglais, 1764-1824. Toulouse: A/5
Association des Publications de la Faculté des Lettres
et Sciences Humaines de Toulouse, 1968.

--------. "Shakespeare et le Roman Gothique", Caliban, II   A/6
(1965), 47-63.

Poenicke, Klaus. "'Schönheit im Schosse des Schreckens':   A/7
Raumgefüge und Menchenbild im Englischen Schauerroman",
Archiv, CCVII (1970), 1-19.

Roudaut, Jean. "Les Demeures dans le Roman Noir", Critique   A/8
(Paris), XV (1959), 147-148.

Yvon, Paul. Le Gothique et la Renaissance Gothique en Angle-   A/9
terre (1750-1880), Essai de Psychologie Littéraire, Ar-
tistique et Sociale. Caen: Jouan & Bigot, 1931.

b.

Horace Walpole

Yvon, Paul. La Vie d'un Dilettante. Horace Walpole (1717-   A/10
1797), essai de Biographie Psychologique et Litteraire.
Paris: Les Presses Universitaires de France, 1924.

c.

Ann Radcliffe

Arnaud, Pierre. "Un Document Inédit: Le Contrat des Mys-   A/11
teries of Udolpho", Etudes Anglaises, XX (1967),
55-57.

Brey, Joseph. Die Naturschilderungen in den Romanen und   A/12
Gedichten der Mrs. Ann Radcliffe, nebst einem Rück-
blick auf die Entwicklung der Naturschilderung in
Englischen Romane des 18. Jahrhunderts. Nurnberg:
F. Korn, 1911.

Decottignies, Jean. "A l'Occasion Centenaire de la Nais-   A/13
sance d'Anne Radcliffe: Un Domaine 'Maudit' dans les
Lettres Françaises Aux Environs de 1800", Revue des
Sciences Humaines, CXVI (1964), 447-475.

Humphrey, George. "'Victor: ou l'Enfant de le Forèt' et   A/14
le Roman Terrifiant", French Review, XXXIII (1959),
137-145.

Levy, Maurice. "Une Nouvelle Source d'Anne Radcliffe: Les   A/15
Mémoires du Comte de Comminge", Caliban, I (1964),
149-156.

Meyer, Georges. "Les Romans de Mrs. Radcliffe", Revue Ger-   A/16
manique, V (1909), 509-550.

Moesch, Vasil. Naturschau und Naturgefühl in den Romanen   A/17
der Mrs. Radcliffe und in der Zeitgenössischen Englischen Reiseliteratur. Freiburg: Caritas-Druckerei,
1924.

312

Spina, Giorgio. L'Epoca D'Oro Dei "Tales of Terror": Ann   A/18
    Radcliffe. Genova: Fratelli Bozzi, [1970].

                        d.

                  M.G. Lewis

Baldensperger, F. "Le Moine de Lewis dans le Litterature   A/19
    Française", Journal of Comparative Literature, I
    (1903), 201-219.

Guthke, Karl Siegfried. Englische Vorromantik und Deutscher A/20
    Sturm und Drang: M.G. Lewis' Stellung in der Geschichte
    des Deutsch-Englischen Literaturbeziehungen. Göttingen:
    Vandenhoek & Ruprecht, 1958.

Herzfeld, Georg. "Eine Neue Quelle für Lewis' Monk", Archiv, A/21
    NS, IV (1900), 310-312.

--------. "Die Eigentliche Quelle von Lewis'Monk", Archiv,   A/22
    NS, XI (1903), 316-323.

--------. "Noch Einmal die Quelle des Monk", Archiv, NS,   A/23
    XV (1905), 70-73.

Lévy, Maurice. "Le Manuscrit du Moine", Caliban, III (1966), A/24
    129-131.

Pichois, Claude. "Actualités du Moine", Mercure de France,   A/25
    CCCXXXIV (1958), 512-516.

Rentsch, Max. Matthew Gregory Lewis. Mit Besonderer Berück- A/26
    sichtigung Seines Romans "Ambrosio, or the Monk". Leip-
    zig: Druck von Pöschel Trepte, 1902.

Ritter, Otto. "Studien zu M.G. Lewis' Roman Ambrosio, or   A/27
    the Monk", Archiv, NS, XI (1903), 106-121.

Schneider, Rudolph Konrad. Der Mönch in der Englischen Dich- A/28
    tung bis auf Lewis's "Monk", 1795. Leipzig: Mayer &
    Müller, 1928.

                        313

e.

William Beckford

Brion, Marcel. "Le Secret du Calife Beckford", Revue des   A/29
Deux Mondes, (July 1, 1949), pp. 156-165.

Brulé, A. "Une Visite à Fonthill en 1792", Revue Anglo-   A/30
Americaine, X (1933), 33-42.

Carnero, Guillermo. "William Beckford (1760-1844) o el   A/31
Erotismo de Fina Estampa", Insula, XXIV (Oct.-Nov.,
1969), 18-19.

Chadourne, Marc. Eblis, ou L'Enfer de William Beckford.   A/32
Suivi d'une Anthologie de l'Oeuvre [de W. Beckford] en
ses Meilleures Pages. Paris: J.J. Pauvert, 1967.

--------. "L'Incroyable William Beckford", Revue de Paris,   A/33
LXIX (1962), 43-58.

Chapman, Guy. "Un Portrait Inconnu de William Beckford",   A/34
Revue de Littérature Comparée, XXVII (1953), 113-114.

De Graaf, D.A. "Potgieter en Vathek", Revue des Languages   A/35
Vivantes, XXIV (1958), 469-475.

De Magny, Olivier. "L'Esthétique de l'Ennui", Les Lettres   A/36
Nouvelles, V (March, 1957), 403-411.

Gide, André, Lucien Lavault, Lewis Melville, and Valéry Lar-   A/37
baud. "Le Dossier Vathek", Nouvelle Revue Francaise,
LIV (1913), 1044-1050.

Grimm, Reinhold. "Vathek in Deutschland: Zwei Zwischen   A/38
fälle ohne Folgen?", Revue de Littérature Comparée,
XXXVIII (1964), 42-45.

Guerra, Oliva. "Sintra e Lord Beckford", Cóloquio, XLVI   A/39
(1967), 14-16.

Hunter, A.O. "Le Vathek de William Beckford: Historique des   A/40
Editions Francaises", Revue de Littérature Comparée,
XV (1935), 119-126.

Jean-Aubry, G. "Autour de Vathek de William Beckford",   A/41
Revue de Littérature Comparée, XVI (1936), 549-562.

Jean-Aubry, G. "Beckford et la Musique", Revue Musicale,   A/42
XIV (Feb., 1934), 103-122.

Mallarmé, Stéphane. Préface a Vathek. Paris: Adolphe   A/43
Labitte, 1876.

May, Marcel. La Jeunesse de William Beckford et la Genèse   A/44
de son "Vathek". Paris: Les Presses Universitaires
de France, 1928.

Mayoux, Jean-Jacques. "La Damnation de Beckford", English   A/45
Miscellany, XII (1961), 41-77.

--------. "Note sur l'Excursion a Alcobaça et Batalha",   A/46
Critique, XIII (1957), 905-907.

Morgulis, Gregoire. "Un Episode de la Vie de Beckford",   A/47
Revue de Littérature Comparée, XIV (1934), 690-694.

Mouret, François J. "Le Vathek de William Beckford et le   A/48
'Voyage d'Urien' d'André Gide", MLR, LXIV (1969),
774-776.

Parreaux, André. "Beckford en Italie: Rêve et Voyage, au   A/49
XVIII Siècle", Revue de Littérature Comparée, XXXIII
(1959), 321-347.

--------. "Beckford et Byron", Etudes Anglaises, VII (1955),   A/50
11-31, 113-132.

--------. "Beckford et la Portugal, ou Une Patrie pour   A/51
l'Imagination et la Sensibilité", Bulletin des Etudes
Portugaises, NS, XXI (1959 for 1958), 97-115.

--------. "Etudes Portugaises sur William Beckford",   A/52
Bulletin des Etudes Portugaises, II (1932), 3-4.

--------. "Le Journal de Beckford", Etudes Anglaises, VII   A/53
(1954), 4.

--------. "Note sur la Partie Portugaise de la Biblio-   A/54
theque de William Beckford", Bulletin des Etudes Portugaises, II (1932), 1-2.

--------. Le Portugal dans l'Oeuvre de William Beckford.   A/55
Paris: Les Belles Lettres, 1935.

Parreaux, Andre. "Précisions sur les Séjours de William   A/56
    Beckford au Portugal", Bulletin des Etudes Portugaises,
    VI (1939), 2.

--------. "Le Tombeau de Beckford par Stéphane Mallarmé",   A/57
    Revue d'Histoire Littéraire de la France, LV (1955),
    327-338.

--------. "Un Vathek Ignoré", Bulletin du Bibliophile et   A/58
    du Bibliothecaire, No. 5 (1957), pp. 176-179.

--------. William Beckford Auteur de "Vathek" (1760-1844):   A/59
    Etude de la Création Littéraire. Paris: Nizet, 1960.

--------. "William Beckford: Principaux Problèmes Chrono-   A/60
    logiques", Bulletin des Etudes Portugaises, II (1931),
    1-2.

Praz, Mario. "Il Califfo Beckford", in his Studi e Svaghi   A/61
    Inglesi. Firenze: Sansoni, 1937.

Soares, J.E.F. "Recordando o Segundo Centánario de William   A/62
    Beckford", Boletim da Academia Portuguesa de Ex-Libris,
    XVIII (1961), 25-29.

Thiebaut, Marcel. "De Romain Gary a William Beckford", Re-   A/63
    vue de Paris, LXIII (Dec., 1956), 159-163.

Vortirede, Werner. "Die Masken des Vladimir Nabokov", Mer-   A/64
    kur, XX (Feb., 1966), 138-151.

318

De La Torre, L., 4/10

De Magny, O., A/36

Dennis, J., 3/9

Dobrée, B., 8/57, 11/12,
    11/44

Dobson, A., 8/32, 8/58,
    8/59

Dolan, J.A., 8/13

D'Oliveira, M., 4/40

Doughty, O., 4/2, 8/3, 8/60

Douglas, D., 7/55

Drake, N., 3/10, 3/11

Draper, J.W., 1/12, 3/29

Dryden, J., 3/12

Duff, W., 3/13

Dutt, S., 7/2

Dyce, A., 7/3

Eagle, D., 1/47

Eastlake, C.L., 2/25

Eenhoorn, M., 11/10

Ehrenpreis, A.H., 10/1,
    10/2

Ellis, S.M., 11/45

Elton, O., 5/12

Elwood, A., 10/26

Emden, C.S., 7/36

Emerson, O.F., 12/36

Epstein, L., 11/46

Esdaile, Mrs., 8/61

Evans, B., 6/15, 6/16

Everson, W.K., 7/56

Fairchild, H.N., 12/37

Fairclough, P., 8/11, 13/15

Fairfax, J.G., 8/62

Farrand, M.L., 11/48

Fehr, B., 2/4

Fiedler, L.A., 5/31

Fiske, C.F., 6/40

Fletcher, A., 5/32

Florescu, R., 4/39

Folsom, J.K., 13/74

Foster, J.R., 5/13, 10/17,
    11/49

Frankl, P., 2/26, 2/27

Freeman, R.A., 11/9, 11/50

Freud, S., 4/3

Freye, W., 7/42

Friend of Accuracy, 12/44

Friend to Genius, 12/38

Frye, N., 5/33

Furst, H., 13/75

320

321

Hazen, A.T., 8/24, 8/37,
   8/64

Hazlitt, W., 6/10, 8/105,
   11/87, 12/76, 13/103

Heath, J.E., 13/169

Heilman, R.B., 2/29, 7/5,
   10/27

Henderson, G., 2/30

Henderson, J., 6/42

Henderson, P., 8/4, 8/65,
   13/11

Henley, S., 13/151

Herrick, G.H., 13/104

Herzfeld, G., A/21, A/22,
   A/23

Hibbert, C., 2/46, 4/11

Hilbish, F.M.A., 10/11

Hipple, W.J., 2/5, 3/14

Hodgkin, J., 13/30, 13/93,
   13/96, 13/98, 13/127

Hogan, C.B., 8/46

Hogg, J., 11/88

Hohlfeld, A.R., 3/50

Holbrook, W.C., 6/1

Hole, C., 4/23

Hollingsworth, K., 7/6,
   13/105

Holzkneckt, K.J., 8/66

Honor, H., 8/38

Horner, J.M., 5/21

Howard, E.G., 10/18

Howells, W.D., 11/89

Howland, A.C., 4/26

Howson, G., 4/12

Hudson, R.H., 6/23

Hume, D., 3/15

Hume, R.D., 3/39, 6/44

Humphrey, G., A/14

Hunt, B.C., 10/19

Hunt, L., 11/90

Hunter, A.O., A/40

Hurd, R., 3/16, 3/17

Huss, R., 7/57

Hussain, I., 13/106

Hussey, C., 2/6, 2/31, 2/47

Jacobin Novelist, 6/134

Jean-Aubry, G., A/41, A/42

Johnson, A.F., 1/45

Johnson, J.W., 8/68

Johnson, R.B., 13/6, 13/107

Johnston, G., 12/45, 12/46

Jones, E., 4/4

Jones, H.M., 11/5

322

323

324

325

Pirie, D., 7/58

Platzner, R.L., 6/44

Poenicke, K., A/7

Pollin, B.R., 10/22

Pope, A., 2/35

Pound, E.F., 11/30

Pound, L., 12/60

Praz, M., 4/6, 8/11, 13/15, A/61

Preu, J.A., 6/56

Prior, M.E., 4/29

Pritchett, V.S., 13/133

Prothero, R.E., 8/86

Pryce-Jones, A., 13/135

Quennell, P., 2/17, 6/57

R., E., 6/137

Radcliffe, A., 11/63

Railo, E., 6/26

Raleigh, W., 5/6

Rank, O., 4/7

Redden, M.M., 7/23

Redding, C., 13/50, 13/136

Redman, B.R., 13/8

Reed, A.L., 3/32

Reed, J.W., 8/9

Reeves, J.K., 9/16

Rentsch, M., A/26

Reynolds, M., 2/53

Rhodes, D.E., 1/46

Richardson, A.E., 2/36

Rieger, J.H., 13/137

Rimelli, 6/139

Ritter, O., A/27

Robbins, R.H., 4/30

Roberts, R.E., 6/58

Roberts, W., 9/17, 12/61

Robinson, H.C., 11/95, 13/159

Rogers, S., 13/160

Rogers, W.H., 6/59

Ronald, M.A., 11/31

Rose, E.J., 8/87

Rosebery, E., 13/138

Ross, T.J., 7/57

Roudaut, J., A/8

Rudwin, M., 4/31, 7/9

Ruff, W., 11/66

Ruland, R.E., 11/67

329

Wright, W.T., 5/20

Y., A., 11/109

Yardley, E., 6/33

Yardley, M., 4/38

Young, A.B., 7/11, 12/71

Yvon, P., A/9, A/10

Zucker, P., 2/57